KW-325-304

LIBRARY INFORMATION
AND
STUDENT SERVICES
UNIVERSITY OF CUMBRIA

6140114172

341. 24.22

(Dre)

France and EC Membership Evaluated

LIBRARY INFORMATIO
AND
STUDENT SERVICE'
UNIVERSITY OF CUM⁻

France and EC Membership Evaluated

Edited by François-Georges Dreyfus,
Jacques Morizet and Max Peyrard

Pinter Publishers
London
St. Martin's Press
New York

Pinter Publishers Ltd.
25 Floral Street, London, WC2E 9DS, United Kingdom
and **St. Martin's Press**
175 Fifth Avenue, New York, NY 10010, USA

First published in 1993

© The editors and contributors, 1993

Apart from any fair dealing for the purposes of research or private study, or criticism or review, as permitted under the Copyright, Designs and Patents Act, 1988, this publication may not be reproduced, stored or transmitted in any form or by any means or process without the prior permission in writing of the copyright holders or their agents. Except for reproduction in accordance with the terms of licences issued by the Copyright Licensing Agency, photocopying of whole or part of this publication without the prior written permission of the copyright holders or their agents in single or multiple copies whether for gain or not is illegal and expressly forbidden. Please direct all enquiries concerning copyright to the Publishers at the address above.

British Library Cataloguing in Publication Data

A CIP catalogue record for this book is available from the British Library.

ISBN 0 86187 107 3 (Pinter)

ISBN 0–312–09977–0 (St. Martin's)

Library of Congress Cataloging in Publication Data

France and EC membership evaluated / edited by François-Georges Dreyfus and
Jacques Morizet.
    p. cm. — (EC membership evaluated series)
    Includes index.
    ISBN 0–312–09977–0
    1. European Economic Community — France. 2. France — Economic policy —
1981–   I. Dreyfus, François G. II. Morizet, Jacques.
III. Series.
HC241.25.F8F69 1993
341.24'22—dc20   93–15199
                                                             CIP

Typeset by Mayhew Typesetting, Rhayader, Powys
Printed and bound in Great Britain by Biddles Ltd., Guildford and King's Lynn

Contents

List of contributors

Jean A. Belotti, Doctor of Economics (Paris), graduated from the French Center for Management, and from Ecole Nationale de l'Aviation (ENAC). He is the General Manager of CRETEL (Research Center for Logistics Studies and the Economics of Transportation), and is a former airline chief pilot and instructor with Air France. He has published several articles and reports and his main publications are *L'Economie du transport Aérien* (1975), *La Sécurité du Transport Aérien* (1968), and *Bon Vol* (1980).

Danielle Bahu-Leyser, Doctor of Political Sciences, is Professor at the University of Nancy II and lecturer at the Institut Français de Presse at the University of Paris II. She has published many articles and two books on European affairs: the first *De Gaulle, les Français et l'Europe* (1981) won an award from the EC Commission; the second, *Media Audiences – Guide France Europe* was published in 1990 in co-operation with Hughes Chavenon and Jacques Durand.

François Bilger, Doctor of Economics, Professor at the University Louis Pasteur in Strasbourg, Director of the Research Centre in Economics, won an Award of the Académie des Sciences Morales et Politiques (1985). Formerly Deputy Mayor of Strasbourg and Member of the National Committee for National Accounts, he is Chairman of the Strasbourg Port Authority. He has published several articles and reports and his main publications are *La pensée économique libérale dans l'Allemagne contemporaine* (1964) and *L'Expansion dans la stabilité* (1985).

Jeans-Louis Burban, Doctor of Economics and Political Science, Professor at Institut d'Etudes Politiques in Paris. Counsellor in the European Parliament staff, he has been in Paris since 1982 as Deputy Director of the Information Office of the European Parliament for France. His principal publications are *Le Parlement Européen et son élection* (1979), *Le Conseil de l'Europe* (1985) and *Le Parlement Européen* (1991).

Alain Buzelay, Doctor of Economics, Professor at the University of Nancy II, Jean Monnet Chair in European Economics, Chairman of the Department of Economics and Management, Director of the University

European Centre. He has published more than 40 articles and reports on the analysis of the processes of European integration and his main publication is *L'Europe industrielle entre la Puissance Américaine et le défi asiatique* (1986).

Guy de Carmoy, Postgraduate in Political Economy and Public Law, graduate from the Ecole Libre des Sciences Politiques. Emeritus Professor at the INSEAD, Professor at the Institut d'Etudes Politiques de Paris, he is honorary Inspecteur des Finances. He is also Deputy Administrator of the IBRD, and Director of the European Organization for Economic Co-operation. He has published several articles and books on French foreign policy and on Energy in Europe.

Patrick Cohendet, Doctor of Economics, is Professor at the University Louis Pasteur in Strasbourg. He works for the Centre of Research in Economics (BETA) and has done numerous studies and research on innovation for the EC Commission and the European Space Agency. He has published several articles and books on the problems of assessing technological policies in the space industry and the diffusion of technology in chemistry and new materials.

François–Georges Dreyfus, Doctor of History, is Professor at the University of Paris IV Sorbonne. Formerly Dean of the Institute for European Studies in Strasbourg, he is a Member of the Executive Committee of the Research Committee on European Unification. He has published more than 40 articles and reports on political science on the European problems and 12 books, his main publications being *Le Syndicalisme allemand contemporain* (1968), *Les allemands entre l'Est et l'Ouest* (1987) and *L'Allemagne contemporaine* (1991).

Pierre Gerbet, Doctor of History, is Professor Emeritus at Institut d'Etudes Politiques de Paris, visiting professor at the European University Institute of Firenze and at the Insitute for European Studies of the Université Libre in Brussels. He has written various articles and books on European integration and French foreign policy. His main publications are *La construction de l'Europe* (1983) and *Le Relèvement 1944–1949* (1991).

Corinne Larrue, Doctor of Geography, formerly instructor at the University of Lausanne, is Research Assistant at the University of Paris XIII-Créteil in the Centre of Research for Local Economy and Institutions. She works on the analysis of the environment policies and regional policies. She has done studies for French Departments of Environmental Affairs and Public Works, as well as for OECD and CNRS. She has published the results of her research as articles and reports in several publications such as *Politiques et Management Public* (1984—85), and *Social Science Information* (1987).

Raymond Legrand-Lane, graduate from Ecole Centrale des Arts et Manufactures de Paris (ECP), from Ecole des Mines de Paris, and from

Institut d'Etudes politiques de Paris. He is now honorary Director General for Public Relations of the European Parliament. He has published several articles on Europe and a book on *L'Europe Communautaire* (1966).

Patrick Llerena, Doctor of Economics, is Professor at the University Louis Pasteur in Strasbourg and works for the Centre of Research in Economics (BETA) in the field of international comparison of technology policies. He has done numerous studies and research for the EC Commission (chemistry, materials, co-operation agreements). He has published several articles and books on technological policies in land transportation and the diffusion of technology (new products).

Jacques Mallet, graduate from Institut d'Etudes politiques de Paris and from Ecole Nationale d'Administration, is a former top civil officer at the EC Commission, a previous Member of the European Parliament from 1984 to 1989 and Chairman of the Committee on External Economic Relations. He has written numerous articles on European integration and intra-Community trade.

Jacques Morizet, graduate in history and geography and from Ecole Nationale d'Administration, won an award from United Nations Organization and has spent most of his career working on European problems as a Foreign Affairs Secretary, then as an Ambassador of France in the FRG. He is Vice-President of the Committee of Studies for National Defence and, since 1988, has been General Secretary for the French—German Cultural Committee. He has written several articles on European development and French—German relations.

Josette Peyrard, Doctor of Economics (Paris), postgraduate in Arts and from Centre d'Etudes des Programmes Economiques, Professor at the Institute for Business Administration (IAE de Paris) and at the Institute for International Studies (ILERI), is Senior Lecturer at the University of Paris I Panthéon Sorbonne. She has been Visiting Professor at the Universities of Ottawa and Québec (UQUAM) since 1976, as well as consultant for private companies. She has done numerous studies and research in International Finance and has published more than 40 articles, in publications such as *The Accounting Review* and *Revue Banque*. Her main books are *Analyse Financière* (5th edn, 1991), *Gestion financière Internationale* (2nd edn, 1989), *Gestion Internationale de Trésorerie* (1988), *La Bourse* (2nd edn in progress for 1993), *Les Bourses Européenes* (1992).

Max Peyrard, Doctor of International Economics (Paris), Graduate in Law and in Political Science, is Professor of International Management and Marketing, at the University of Paris I Panthéon Sorbonne, where he is Director for the European and International Management Post Graduate Programme and Centre of Research. He has previously taught at the Universities of Paris XII — Créteil and Orléans, as well as at the Universities of Utah, Ottawa and Montréal and in Africa. He has written articles on economic policies in the EC and on international trade, and books on *Banques et Fonds internationaux de financement du développement* (1981), on *Investment financing by International Development Banks* (1987) and on *Principes de Management* (1990).

Catherine Pivot, Doctor of Economics, Professor at the University Louis Pasteur in Strasbourg, is Dean of the School of Economics and Management and works for the Centre of Research in Economics (BETA). She is a member of numerous scientific organizations such as the French Association of Economics and the French Association for Agricultural Economics. She has written numerous articles on the international agricultural trade, and the international agro-business as well as diffusion of innovations in the rural world, such as *Le blé français face à l'environnement international* (1983).

Rémy Prud'homme, Doctor of Economics, Professor at the University of Paris XII — Créteil in the Institute for Urban Studies (Institut d'Urbanisme de Paris), graduate from the Universities of Paris and Harvard and the Institut d'Etudes Politiques de Paris. He was formerly Professor at the Universities of Phnom-Penh and Lille, visiting professor at the MIT, Deputy Director for the Directorate for Environmental Affairs in OECD, and advisor for several governments and the World Bank. His main books are *Environmental Policies in Japan* (1977) and *Le ménagement de la Nature* (1980). He has written articles and books in the field of local public finance, transportation and regional policies.

Patrick Rambaud, Doctor of Public Law, is Professor at the University of Paris V and previously at Nancy II, and Lecturer at the Institute for Political Sciences in Paris. He teaches European Law and transnational relations Law and is Director of Studies at the International Law Academy of La Haye. His main publications are on international litigation between states and foreign companies and on the relations between the French legal order and the international legal order.

Jacques Rojot, Doctor of Management (Rennes) and Ph.D. in Business Administration (UCLA), is Professor of Industrial Relations at the University of Paris I Panthéon Sorbonne. He is advisor for OECD and private businesses and, formerly, for the EC. He has previously taught at the Institute for International Studies and Research in Fujinomiya (Japan) and at the Universities of Québec in Montréal (UQAM), and Louvain. He is a member of the Executive Board of the International Industrial Relations Association and foreign correspondent of the National Academy of Arbitrators. He has written several articles and books on Industrial Relations, the last being on *Comportement et organisation* (1989).

Philippe Rollet, Doctor of Economics, is Professor at the University of

Lille, School of Economic and Social Sciences. His main publications are *Intégration économique européenne: théorie et pratique* (1988) and *Spécialisation internationale et intégration économique européenne* (2nd edn, 1990).

Annie Sabourin-Ragnaud, Doctor of Law, is General Manager of the family cognac business and Lecturer in European Social Law at the University of Paris-Nord. She has written several articles and a book on *L'égalité professionelle dans les pays de la Communauté* (1986).

Series introduction

This volume is one in a series entitled *European Community Membership Evaluated*. The series examines the gains and losses of European Community (EC) membership for a number of the twelve states.

Over the entire period since the first steps in European integration were taken, with the formation of the European Coal and Steel Community, the impact of membership upon the individual states has been both a matter of importance to, and an issue for evaluation by, the political parties, interest groups, government elites, researchers and, increasingly, the public at large. The renewed dynamism of the EC in the period following the signing of the Single European Act in 1986, and the approach of the completed internal market by the end of 1992, have raised awareness of EC membership to new heights.

It is against this backdrop that the project leading to this series was undertaken. Policy-makers and the European electorate alike require the information to make informed judgements about national gains and losses (or costs and benefits) arising from EC membership.

— How far have the EC's economic policies brought gains?
— Does EC membership impose constraints on the powers of national and regional/local government, or on the legal system?
— What have been the effects of the hitherto somewhat disparate EC activities in the social, cultural and educational policy areas?
— What are the gains and losses of foreign policy co-operation among the member states?
— How pronounced are the specific national interests of the individual member states?

In order to answer questions such as these, each volume brings together a team of specialists from various disciplines. Although the national teams are composed predominantly of academics, the series is aimed at a readership beyond the confines of the education world. Thus each volume seeks to present its findings in a manner accessible to *all* those affected by, or interested in, the EC. Extensive footnoting of academic literature is avoided, although some guidance is offered on the legal bases of EC policies; a bibliography at the end of each study gives guidance on narrower sectoral impact studies and on further reading.

A distinctive feature of the series as a whole is that a common framework has been followed for all eleven studies. This is aimed at facilitating comparison between the national studies. No systematic international comparative study of this kind has been attempted before. Indeed, for some member states there exists no study of the impact of EC membership. The absence of such a series of studies initially seemed rather surprising. However, as the project progressed, the reasons for this became clearer. It is by no means easy to find a common framework acceptable to the academic traditions of all the member states *and* all the policy areas and academic disciplines involved.

The project co-ordinators experienced these tensions in a striking way. Their international 'summit meetings' meant reaching compromises acceptable to all the diverse academic traditions of the countries involved. Then the individual national contributors had to be convinced of the merits of the international compromises. These negotiations brought many insights into precisely the type of problem faced by EC policy-makers themselves. Hence academic perfectionism has been subordinated to some extent to pragmatism and the wish to address a wider readership.

In some countries, for instance the Netherlands, Great Britain, Portugal and Germany, up to thirty scholars of various disciplines make up the national team. In other countries, such as Ireland, a team numbers less than ten authors. In the latter, *one* author deals with several parts of a subject-group or even with the whole of a subject-group. In either case, however, authors have assured comparability by making cross-references to subsections of policies.

The basic principle of the project has been to assess the gains and losses of EC membership for the individual state, with the hypothetical alternative in mind of that state leaving the EC. This alternative may be deemed to be somewhat simplistic but it is far more manageable than making assumptions about where individual states would be, had they not joined the EC in the first place. Such speculation is virtually impossible scientifically and would undermine efforts to make the findings accessible to a wider readership. The terms 'benefits', 'gains' and 'positive effects', and 'costs', 'losses' and 'negative effects', respectively, are used synonymously.

The activities of the EC, together with the foreign policy co-operation process EPC (European Political Co-operation), are grouped under four broad headings in the project (see Table A at the end of this Introduction). *Economic policy* covers a range of EC policies: from the internal market to the Common Agricultural Policy but also including environmental policy. *Foreign relations* comprise not only European Political Co-operation but also the EC's external trade policy and security policy. *Social and educational policy* brings together the rather disparate measures taken in a range of areas, some of which are now coming to be regarded as forming the 'social dimension' of the EC. Finally, the subject area *political and legal system* refers not to EC policies but rather to the EC's impact upon the principles and practices of government.

Each of the EC policy headings is assessed following a common approach. The objectives of the EC policy, and the accomplishments thus far, are assessed against the equivalent set of national policy goals and legislation, many of them common to all countries, some of them obviously specific national ones. The idea, then, is to arrive at a 'balance sheet', both at the level of the individual policy area or sector and, at the macro level, for the member state as a whole. Drawing up the individual sectoral balance sheets has to involve a rather flexible approach. The 'mix' of quantitative and qualitative assessments varies according to the subject matter. There can be no quantitative data on how far foreign policy co-operation has brought gains to national foreign policy; figures may be available, however, on the impact of EC trade policy on national trade patterns. In the case of quantitative data it is important to note that very little, if any, primary statistical research was involved in the project. In consequence, quantitative assessments generally present available evidence from previous studies; they follow no consistent methodological approach while qualitative assessments are often arrived at for the first time. One further point must be made with regard to the common approach of the project: it is clear that the importance of individual EC policy areas varies from one member state to another.

It follows, therefore, that the weighting, and in some cases the categorization, of EC policy areas will vary between the national studies. To assign the same weight to fisheries policy in the British and Luxembourg cases, for instance, would be irrational. Some national policy goals and national interests are related to specific interests of some member countries; for instance, the German question and the problem of Northern Ireland are specific to Germany, Ireland and the United Kingdom respectively.

The whole project has been brought to fruition under the auspices of 'Europe-12 — Research and Action Committee on the EC'. Created in 1986, Europe-12 brings together academics of all disciplines and from all member states, as well as policy-makers and senior politicians. It aims to inform the policy debate through collaborative research and to raise public awareness of the important issues raised by European integration.

As with any such project, a large number of acknowledgements must be made. A number of the participants took on the additional task of horizontal co-ordination, i.e. seeking to ensure consistency of approach across the national studies. For *economic policy* this was undertaken by Detlev Karsten, Bonn, and Peter Coffey, Amsterdam; for *foreign relations* by Carl-Christoph Schweitzer, Bonn, and Rudolf Hrbek, Tübingen; for contributions on the *political and legal system* by Francesco Francioni, Siena, and K. Kellermann, The Hague; finally, for *social and educational policies* by Bernard Henningsen, Munich, and Brigitte Mohr, Bonn. Sadly, Guenther Kloss, a co-ordinator of the British volume, died during the preparation of the series.

Last but by no means least, we are indebted to the Commission of the EC and to those bodies supporting the project: the German foundations, Stifterverband für die Deutsche Wissenschaft, Essen; Bosch GmbH, Stuttgart; Ernst Poensgen-Stiftung, Düsseldorf; as well as the Government of the Saarland and the Federal Ministry for Science and Technology, Bonn. The British and German Studies were made possible by the support of the Anglo-German Foundation for the Study of Industrial Society, London.

Carl-Christoph Schweitzer
Bonn

Table A: Project's categorization of EC policies and structures

I	**Economic policy**	
	Internal market policy	Agricultural policy
	Competition policy	Environmental policy
	Industrial policy	Fiscal/taxation policy
	Technology policy	Monetary policy
	Transport and communications policy	Regional policy
	Energy policy	
II	**Foreign relations**	
	Foreign policy co-operation	Development policy
	Security policy	External trade policy
III	**Political and legal system**	
	Sovereignty	National legal system
	Parliamentary control of the executive	Judicial procedures
	Electoral system	Maintenance of public order
	Political parties	Protection of fundamental rights
	Regional and local government	State organization
	Policy-making process	
IV	**Social, educational and cultural policies**	
	Manpower (employment/ unemployment)	Consumer protection
	Movement of labour and migrant workers	Education and training
	Industrial relations	European identity and cultural policies
	Social security and health	
	Equal treatment of men and women	Media policy

Note: This list was a schematic guideline for the project; not every subsection will be dealt with individually and the sequence is purely illustrative.

Europe-12: Action and Research Committee on the EC

Hon. Presidents:
Lord Jenkins of Hillhead
Chancellor of the University of Oxford
H.E. Emilio Colombo,
Minister Rome

Board:
Chairman: Former Minister Dr Ottokar Hahn
Senior Advisor, EC Commission, Brussels
Vice-Chairmen:
Prof Dr Hélène Ahrweiler
Rector and Chancellor, University of Paris
Enrico Baron Crespo, MEP,
President European Parliament Brussels, Madrid
Piet Dankert
Undersecretary, Foreign Office, Den Haag
Dr Garret FitzGerald
former Prime Minister, Dublin
Niels Anker Kofoed, MP
former Minister, Copenhagen
Dr Hans Stercken, MP
Chairman Bundestag Foreign Affairs Committee, Bonn
Franz Ludwig Graf von Stauffenberg,
MEP
*Representative of the President of the European
Parliament*

Senior Economic Advisor:
Dr Otto Graf Lambsdorff, MP
*former Minister of Economics, National Chairman
FDP, Bundestag, Bonn*

Co-ordinator of Committees:
Prof Dr C. C. Schweitzer
University of Bonn, Political Science

Steering Committee:
Spokesman: Dr Renate Hellwig, MP
*Bundestag, Bonn, Chairman Sub-Committee on
Europe*
Dr Peter Baehr
Netherlands Scientific Council, The Hague
Prof Dr P. D. Dagtoglou
University of Athens, Law
W. Dondelinger, MP
Chairman Foreign Affairs Committee, Luxembourg
Prof. Dr Francesco Francioni
University of Siena, Law

Fernand Herman, MEP
Chairman Institutional Committee, EP, Brussels
Dr J. de Silva Lopes
Caixa General de Depositos, Lisbon, Economics
Anthony J. Nicholls
Senior Fellow, St Antony's College, Oxford
Dr Hans-J. Seeler
Chairman FVS Foundation, Hamburg
Georges Sutra de Germa, MEP
*former Vice-Chairman, Institutional Committee, EP,
Pezenas, France*
Prof Count L. Ferraris
Council of State, Rome
Jacques Maison Rouge
ex Vice President IBM, Paris
Dr Claude Treyer
Director, European Affairs, IGS, Paris

Research Committee:
Dr Simon Bulmer
University of Manchester, Dept of Government
Gerry Danaher
*Secretary, Irish National Economic and Social Council,
Dublin*
Prof Alfonso Ortega
Political Science, University Pontifica Salamanca, Spain
Prof Dr Grotanelli de Santi
University of Siena, Law and Political Science
Prof Dr R Hrbek
University of Tübingen, Political Science
Prof Dr Detlev Karsten
University of Bonn, Economics
Prof Dr M. A. G. van Meerhaeghe
University of Ghent, Economics
Prof Dr Stavros Theofanides
Panteios School of Pol. Science, Athens
Prof Dr Christian Tomuschat
University of Bonn, International Law

Media Advisers:
Rolf Goll
*Chairman, Communications and Marketing, Ansin-
Goll, Frankfurt*
Prof Dr E. G. Wedell
*Chairman, European Media Centre, University of
Manchester*
Hon. Secretary:
Dr Hartmut Schweitzer, Bonn

Introduction: France's contribution to European development

Jacques Morizet and François-Georges Dreyfus

Over the past 40 years France has made a substantial contribution to European development. As early as November 1941 in Oxford, and then again in Algiers in March 1944, General de Gaulle stressed the need for building Europe:

For the renewed European continent to come to a balance which is in keeping with the conditions of our times, we believe that certain groups must be formed. As far as France is concerned . . . some type of Western group, hinging basically on economic ties, could have considerable advantages . . . such a group, reaching into Africa and having close links with the East . . . and for which the English Channel, the Rhine, and the Mediterranean would form the main routes, could well become one of the major centres co-ordinating production, trade and security worldwide.

Then on 9 May 1950, the French Foreign Minister, Robert Schuman, stunned everyone by suggesting to Germany that a supranational authority be set up to manage coal and steel production for both countries.

This proposal was drawn up by Jean Monnet, then head of the French Commissariat Général au Plan, and became known as the Schuman plan. It met with Chancellor Konrad Adenauer's immediate approval and served as a basis for the European Coal and Steel Community (ECSC) Treaty, signed in Paris on 18 April 1951.

Times had changed indeed. The war was just beginning to fade into the past and 1948 marked the breakdown of the four-nation Allied Control Council and the end of the first post-war phase. The Federal Republic of Germany was born. Faced with the problems at hand, the idea emerged that Europe could not be built without there being close harmony between France and Germany. This was just one of the points

General de Gaulle made in his press conference in Bordeaux in September 1949.

Slowly, Europe was being built. The ECSC was accepted by both the trade unions and many of the employers, but the concept of supranational authority met with reservations in some French political circles. The EDC (European Defence Community) proposal was rejected by the National Assembly in September 1954. However, when Mendès-France's Cabinet set out to solve the Saar problem, they did away with one of the major obstacles keeping France and Germany from coming together on a sustainable basis.

A more complex economic system was being implemented throughout the 1950s which was being defended by politicians of all persuasions — ranging from Christian Pineau, a Socialist, to Antoine Pinay, a moderate, to Jacques Chaban-Delmas, a Gaullist, to popular Republicans such as Pierre Pflimlin and Henri Teitgen, to Maurice Faure, a radical. Meanwhile the ECSC's six partners were patiently weaving a web which was growing stronger while waiting to spread over a wider area.

After being revived at the Messina Conference in 1956, the process of building Europe took a decisive step with the signing of the Treaty of Rome on 25 March 1957, setting up the European Economic Community (EEC) and the European Atomic Energy Community (EURATOM). France made a key contribution to the drafting thereof. A lesson had been learned from the EDC experience and the new treaty included fewer supranational provisions than the EDC one had. Upon returning to power in 1958, General de Gaulle did not question it, but sought to consolidate it and add the finishing touches before making any attempts to enlarge it. De Gaulle was, however, against the ECSC and EURATOM being supranational in character.

The EEC was, basically, no more than a customs union rounded off by a 'Common Market', the effectiveness of which depended on the sector under consideration; through it, France obtained the common agricultural policy, while Germany was intent on developing a competitive policy. France proposed to her five partners the setting up of a common European political organization, known as the Fouchet Plan. Some of them were against this plan which no doubt threw a spanner into the works of political construction for a number of years.

The new European institutions were taking shape and already trying to broaden their scope. De Gaulle was against this and challenged the use of majority voting at the 1 January 1966 session of the Council of Ministers. This was the reason behind the 1965/66 Franco-European crisis between France and her five partners, the upshot of which was the Luxembourg Compromise of 1966.

Another setup favouring the development of agricultural production was thus being formed which, while not taking structural problems into account sufficiently, was gradually paving the way for the implementation of legislation on free movement of persons, goods, services and capital, with the reservations which were to be expected under the circumstances. Problems cropped up daily, but the European Court of Justice (ECJ), an institution which had been virtually unheard of at the time, was forging a new type of law — Community law (or 'European law' as the media often called it) which made gradual headway at state level. Even though it did not take very long for the Luxembourg Court of Justice to be accepted in matters involving commercial law and competitiveness, France's Cour de Cassation[1] did not recognize the supremacy of European law until the mid-1970s. The Conseil d'Etat only recognized it in 1989 with the Nicolo judgement, bypassing all provisions of French law incompatible with those of an international treaty. This was confirmed by the Boisdet judgement in 1990 broadening such supremacy to include first Community regulations and then their directives by 1992. The number of pro-European initiatives by France increased throughout the 1970s.

Enlarging the Community to include other states, which was President Pompidou's intent in 1972, echoed by Mitterand 10 years later, was more than likely the reason the consolidation of the Community system was temporarily set back, as could be expected. It was beneficial, however, in that it provided possibilities for further political, economic and cultural action from which France has profited greatly.

The French Government stressed the need for strengthening the Community by proposing an Economic and Monetary Union to be implemented by 1980, but the monetary and oil crises and the drop in the growth rate over the 1970s made it impossible to bring these plans to fruition.

The close relationship between President Giscard d'Estaing and Chancellor Helmut Schmidt made further progress possible. Thanks to them another body, the Council of Europe, (in its early days bringing together the Heads of State and of Government two or three times a year) was set up and only had legal recognition with the ratification of the Single Act. Its purpose was to solve problems outside the scope of the Treaty and to spur on the activities of the Council and the Commission. An action was undertaken with a view to setting up direct elections for the European Parliament.

In February 1977, moreover, the French and German Governments agreed on setting up the European Monetary Union to resuscitate their projects which were at a standstill at the time. A plan was developed on the basis of their initiatives, aiming to set up a stable European monetary zone, replacing the monetary 'snake' which only involved some of the Community member countries. The ECU came out of this system, which the recent Maastricht agreements may adopt as the Community's future European currency. The project was based on the proposals that Helmut Schmidt and Valéry Giscard d'Estaing submitted which were adopted at the Bremen Conference held on 6 and 7 July 1978.

A determination to contribute further to the development of Europe, which Chancellor Kohl and President Mitterand had in common, led them to maintain close Franco-German ties, evidenced by the new initiatives taken and the new projects that were submitted. They both made a decisive contribution to the drafting of the 'reform package' at Stuttgart in June 1983, aiming to settle the pending European dispute (budget, reform of the agricultural policy) and to draw up guidelines for new Community policy.

The French Government submitted a memorandum in favour of a common industrial and research policy and suggested broadening the EEC partners' scientific and industrial collaboration so as to take up the challenges of the third technological revolutions together. This project led to the launching of Eureka (European Research Co-operation Agency) in 1985. The agreement reached on all scores on 25 and 26 June 1984 in Fontainebleau paved the way for another overall European revival.

In addressing the European Parliament on 24 May 1984, Mitterand made a plea for developing political integration. He stated that the authority of the Commission had to be intensified and that the Council had to focus on major guidelines. The French President also argued in favour of taking decisions on a majority basis at the Council of Ministers' meetings.

At the European conference which met in Luxembourg on 4 December 1985, it was decided to revise the Treaty of Rome and set up a fron-tierless economic zone by 1992, doing away with the barriers limiting the movement of persons, goods, services and capital within seven years. The agreement was ratified on 4 December and became known as the Single European Act. Despite reservations on the part of the RPR (one of the Gaullist parties) regarding the methods which were set out, the Single Act was ratified by Chirac's Cabinet.

This was the first of a long line of negotiations, culminating in the recent Maastricht Agreements (December 1991—February 1992) which, in very precise terms, provide for both the setting up of the Economic and Monetary Union, so important to France, and the groundwork for a common foreign policy.

The major concern of Europeans, many of the French included, is still the setting up of a European political authority to fill the gap in the Community's democratic deficit: because of the scope of powers and the quality of its officials, the Commission plays a major role in the Community which some observers consider to be extreme. The Council of Ministers is too fragmented, despite the important role played in the decision-making process by the Committee of Permanent Representatives (COREPER). Even though members of Parliament are elected on the basis of universal franchise, they only play a secondary role in handling legislative and budgetary problems. To make matters worse, the stands they take often prove to be unrealistic. In any case, France is committed to European economic integration come what may. Her intent is to orchestrate her foreign and security policy with European unity in mind wherever possible.

The purpose of this book is to show how France's attitudes towards these problems have developed. On the eve of the drafting of new community texts, and faced with the deadlines that have been set for the implementation of the European economic zone; the applications for membership coming from some of the Eastern European countries and the South's appeals for aid, the French views on these matters had to be summed up. The aim of this book which our colleagues and friends François Bilger, Pierre Gerbet and Max Peyrard have agreed to co-edit with us, is to do just that.

Note

1. The equivalent of the judiciary committee of the House of Lords.

PART I: ECONOMICS

Chapter 1

The impact of the Single Market on the French economy — strengths and weaknesses

Alain Buzelay

The slowing of inter-community trade and growth within the EEC, observed from 1975 onwards, is considered in this chapter. Such slowing has been caused by an Economic Community that has become increasingly fictitious. Although customs barriers have been progressively dismantled, they have been replaced by other barriers, such as differences in technical standards, fiscality, subsidies and calls for tender. Plans for the 'post 1992' Europe involve reducing or even abolishing all such barriers. Member-states should then constitute a single market, complying with the original project for a 'Common Market'. As a result, French companies ought to be able to reduce costs, given an increase in outlets. This should result in greater efficiency in scale of production and in increases in competitive investments, following more intense competition once the single market has been created.

A more efficient production strategy is a function of effects on supply and relates to how producers adapt to the single market. Such effects should become apparent as soon as member-states open their markets. Once implemented, the single market should be able to support the economies of member-states, as illustrated in an analysis based on Keynesian economics.[1]

In this analysis the impact of the single market on the French economy evaluated and highlighted how French companies have already adapted to progress in Community construction.

Table 1.1 The 40 sensitive sectors identified by the methodology

NACE code	Sectors	Removal of customs control and tax harmonization	Technical standards	Subsidies and public procurement	Flow of capital and company law	Global score
330	Office and data-processing machinery	0	1	1	1	3
334	Telecommunications	0	2	2	1	5
372	Medical and surgical equipment	0	1	2	1	4
257	Pharmaceutical products	1	2	1	0	4
315	Boilermaking	0	2	1	1	4
362	Rolling stock	0	1	2	1	4
425	Champagne, sparkling wines	1	2	1	0	4
427	Brewing and malting	1	2	1	1	5
428	Soft drinks, water	1	1	0	1	3
341	Insulated wires and cables	0	0	2	1	3
342	Electrical machinery	0	1	2	1	4
361	Shipbuilding	0	0	1	0	1
417	Spaghetti, macaroni, etc.	0	2	1	0	3
421	Cocoa, chocolate, sugar confec.	1	2	0	1	4
247	Glass and glassware	0	1	0	0	1
248	Ceramic goods	0	0	0	1	1
251	Basic industrial chemicals	0	2	0	0	2
256	Other ind. & agric. chem. prods	0	2	0	0	2
321	Machine & other tools	0	1	0	1	2
322	Textile mach.	0	1	0	1	2
323	Mach. for food, chem. & related ind.	0	1	0	1	2

Table 1.1 contd.

NACE code	Sectors	Removal of customs control and tax harmonization	Technical standards	Subsidies and public procurement	Flow of capital and company law	Global score
324	Agricultural machinery	0	1	0	1	2
325	Plant for mines, etc.	0	1	0	1	2
326	Transmission equipment	0	1	0	1	2
327	Equip. for spec. branches of industries	0	1	0	1	2
345	Radio, TV	2	2	0	1	5
346	Domestic-type electrical appliances	1	0	0	1	2
347	Lighting	0	0	0	0	*
351	Automobiles	2	2	0	0	4
364	Aerospace equipment	0	0	1	1	2
431	Wool industry	0	1	0	1	2
432	Cotton industry	0	1	0	1	2
438	Carpets	1	0	0	0	1
451	Footwear	1	0	0	1	2
453	Ready-made clothing & access.	2	0	0	0	2
455	Household textiles	1	0	0	1	2
481	Rubber goods	0	0	0	1	1
491	Jewellery	1	1	0	0	2
493	Photog. & cinemat. labs	0	0	0	0	*
494	Toys & sports goods	1	1	0	0	2

Note: Score per criteria: 0 = slight or no impact; 1 = major impact; 2 = very major impact.
Global score: 0 or 1 = slightly or not sensitive, 2 = sensitive, 3 and above = very sensitive.
* These sectors were included as sensitive because there are non-tariff barriers at Community level.

Sector-by-sector breakdown of performances

Methodological approach

Initially the approach identified those sectors most sensitive to competition within the twelve. It evaluated the extent to which such sectors were subject to protectionism, rate of imports from community members, price differentials and potential for achieving economies via scales of production. Secondly, the performance of such 'sensitive' sectors was evaluated using the customary indices. Indices included the rate of cover of imports from both within and outside the Community, production and export indices.

However, it should be noted that the sensitivity and performance of selected sectors were considered nation-wide and can, therefore, mask intense regional disparities. This is especially the case in a market where regional components, as opposed to nations, will experience greater difficulty when confronting competition and specialization. It should also be noted that the effects of supply mentioned previously were not incorporated in the approach. This was because it was not possible to perform quantitative extrapolation concerning the impact of modifications to the behaviour of producers and macro-economic adjustments made by official organizations.

Inventory of sensitive sectors and performances with respect to current employment[2]

The Commission of European Communities detected 40 sensitive sectors in France and evaluated the effects of abolishing non-tariff barriers for each (see Table 1.1).

It should be noted that the 40 sectors identified within France were the same as those specified at Community level. Their effect on certain key values in the French economy is illustrated as follows (see Table 1.2).

When considering the performance of sensitive sectors, the following observations can be made:

- Unlike the United Kingdom, French sectors credited with good performances in accordance with selected indices represented 29.6 per cent of industrial employment. This was greater than sectors with poor performance records (16 per cent of industrial employment). However, when assigned, statistics provided more concentrated or scattered results. Thus, 9.3 per cent of French industrial employment concerned sectors with extremely poor performance records such as machinery, shoes and clothing. However, 12.8 per cent of such employment concerned sectors credited with high performances such as drinks, aeronautics and railway equipment, etc.

Table 1.2   Importance of sensitive sectors identified at national level

Sensitive sectors	Share of industrial value added (1985)	Share of industrial employment (1985)	1987 imports intra ———————— 1987 exports extra[1]	Intra-penetration rate[2]
High NTB[3]	22.7	22.0	137	12
Average NTB[3]	30.7[4]	28.8[4]	146	25

1 1987 imports (intra-EC)/imports 1987 (extra-EC)
2 1987 imports (intra-EC)/internal market 1985.
3 Total score 3 in Table 1 for high NTB and total score <3 for average NTB.
4 Not inlcuded: household textiles

Note: The 40 sensitive sectors identified at national level after analysis are the same as those adopted at Community level.

• In France as in the United Kingdom, Belgium and Spain, employment was distributed fairly equally. This was not the case in Germany and Italy where employment is concentrated in high performance sectors. In Denmark, the Netherlands and Ireland employment was concentrated in activities credited either with extremely high or extremely poor performances. In Greece and Portugal most employment was dependent on low performance or even totally non-productive activities.

The relatively weak French position with respect to 1992[3]

Establishing strong and weak points on a sector by sector basis

In identifying the 40 sensitive sectors of French industry the Communities Commission calculated the average cover rate for imports within the community for the years 1985, 1986 and 1987 (1980 = 100) and consulted the Balassa specialization index for 1987. The results of this are provided in Table 1.3 below.

French Industry can be optimistic in 10 out of 11 strong sectors of the economy when they confront the increased competition resulting from the single market. There are reservations, however, concerning the continued strength of the French pharmaceutics industry, as companies in this sector are not sufficiently large or have not developed their activities on an international scale. In addition, such companies are protected to a greater degree than in other member-states, which means that high degrees of research and development cannot be justified.

Table 1.3 The weak and strong points of French industry in sensitive sectors

NACE code	Weak points Sectors	CR	ΔCR	SI	NACE code	Balanced position Sectors	CR	ΔCR	SI	NACE code	Strong points Sectors	CR	ΔCR	SI
372	Medical equipment	55	123	79	344	Telecommunications	90	115	101	330	Data processing, office machinery	120	140	118
341	Insulated wires & cables	63	52	72	342	Electrical equipment	97	88	124	257	Pharmaceutical products	151	87	118
417	Sphagetti, macaroni, etc.	11	63	30	247	Glass & glassware	95	83	131	315	Boilermaking	134	108	88
421	Cocoa, choc., sugar confec.	63	92	83	345	Radio, TV	91	96	115	362	Rolling stock	150	75	111
248	Ceramic goods	44	127	77	351	Motor vehicles	101	60	101	425	Champagne, sparkling wines	265	213	178
251	Basic industrial chemicals	86	95	118	453	Ready-made clothing	100	88	83	427	Brewing & malting	128	135	125
256	Other chemical products	71	96	106						428	Soft drinks, water	135	59	193
321	Agricultural machinery	39	85	84						361	Shipbuilding	166	106	78
322	Machines & other tools	40	82	56						364	Aerospace	192	44	111
323	Textile machinery	57	124	72						431	Wool industry	195	85	163
324	Mach. for food, chemical & related industries	43	94	64						481	Rubber goods	139	104	170
325	Plant for mines, etc.	68	73	101										
326	Transmission equipment	82	111	113										
327	Equip. for special branches of industry	39	86	49										
346	Domestic electrical appl.	51	74	80										
347	Lighting	50	118	84										
432	Cotton industry	78	95	94										
438	Carpets	25	50	34										
451	Footwear	43	61	49										
455	Household textiles	42	65	56										
491	Jewellery	56	155	20										
493	Photograph. & cinematogr. equipment	67	188	119										
494	Toys & sports goods	56	84	74										

CR = Average intra-Community coverage ratio for 1985, 1986 and 1987.
ΔCR = Variation in coverage ratio between 1980 and 1987 (1980 = 100).
SI = Balassa specialization index in 1987.

In the six sectors featuring neither strong nor weak points — dynamic activities such as telecommunications, electrical products, radio — TV and cars may result in them obtaining strong sector status. However the competitive rating for 23 sectors remains low and these constitute the weak points in French Industry.

The sectors at the bottom or in the middle of the 'league table' produce either plant or consumer goods. Their failure to compete is often the result of insufficient specialization. This is especially the case for machine tools, agricultural plant, machinery for the food industry, shoes, electronic equipment and television — everyday consumer products. In fact, exchanges within the community are already relatively high and competition from non-EC countries is increasing.

Analysis of exchanges within the community alongside data in Table 1.3 demonstrates that France is in a difficult position in so far as 23 sensitive sectors are concerned. These account for 16.5 per cent of industrial employment and more than 17 per cent of industrial added-value. This should be compared against only 12.4 per cent of employment and 16 per cent of industrial added-value for sensitive sectors featuring strong points.

When it broke down sectors in the French economy into strong and weak points, the Commission evaluated the static competitive position of such sectors. It subsequently placed them in the context of the dynamic situation arising from 1992 development. In addition, the room for manoeuvre in every sector was taken into consideration along with current product ranges. The parameters selected were the cover rate, specialization indices and prices. Partial and then overall values were then calculated to establish forecasts and specify key advantages (see Table 1.4).

Table 1.4 confirms the difficult position of post-1992 France in so far as numerous sectors were assigned low or even negative marks.

The marginal role of economies of scale and the real sources of comparative advantages for France

There were further advantages for certain sectors of French Industry other than those caused by abolishing non-tariff barriers. Arguments in favour of the single market claimed that there would be beneficial effects on supply through increased competition and economies of scale linked to the greater number of outlets. Therefore, several sectors of activity would see their positions improved or favoured. This was because they would benefit from increased exchanges between EC member-states. In cases where large-scale production was advantageous, an increase in trade between EC member-states should be observed. However, such trade would be increased in different ways depending on whether homogeneous

Table 1.4 French industries in the context of 1992

NACE code	Sectors	Coverage ratio[1]	Positioning from the point of view of:					Global score
			Special index[2]	Price index[3]	Companies[4]	Products[5]		
351	Motor vehicles	0	0	0	0	0		0
342	Electrical equipment	0	1	na	2	0		3
453	Ready-made clothing	0	-1	0	0	0		-1
345	Radio, TV	0	1	0	1	0		2
364	Aerospace equipment	1	0	1	0	1		4
344	Telecommunications	-1	0	-1	2	2		2
481	Rubber goods	1	1	0	0	1		3
251	Basic industrial chemicals	-1	1	na	0	-1		-1
315	Boilermaking	1	-1	1	0	0		1
257	Pharmaceutical products	1	1	1	-1	-2		0
256	Other chem. prod. for industry & agriculture	-1	0	na	0	-1		-2
451	Footwear	-1	-1	0	0	-1		-3
432	Cotton industry	-1	0	-1	0	0		-2
325	Plant for mines, etc.	-1	0	1	0	1		1
247	Glass & glassware	-1	1	-1	2	2		3
330	Office and data-processing machinery	-1	1	-1	1	-1		1
346	Domestic-type electrical appliances	-1	-1	-1	1	1		-1
361	Shipbuilding	0	-1	0	0	0		-1
324	Machines for food & chemical industries	-1	-1	-1	0	0		-3
321	Agricultural machinery	-1	-1	0	0	0		-2
421	Cocoa, chocolate & confectionery	-1	-1	-1	0	0		-3
431	Wool industry	1	1	-1	0	0		1
248	Ceramic products	-1	-1	-1	-1	0		-4

Table 1.4 contd.

NACE code	Sectors	Coverage ratio[1]	Positioning from the point of view of:				Global score
			Special index[2]	Price index[3]	Companies[4]	Products[5]	
322	Machines & other tools	-1	-1	0	0	-1	-3
326	Transmission equipment	-1	-1	na	0	0	0
341	Insulated wire & cables	-1	-1	-1	2	1	0
494	Toys & sports goods	-1	-1	0	-1	-1	-4
347	Lighting	-1	-1	0	0	0	-2
362	Rolling stock	1	1	-1	2	2	5
372	Medical & surgical equipment	-1	-1	0	-2	-1	-5
425	Champagne, sparkling wines	1	1	0	0	2	4
427	Brewing & malting	1	1	-1	1	0	2
428	Water, soft drinks	1	1	0	0	0	2
491	Jewellery	-1	-1	-1	-1	0	-4
323	Textile machinery	-1	-1	0	1	1	0
327	Equipment for special branches of industry	-1	-1	-1	0	0	-3
438	Carpets	-1	-1	0	0	0	-2
493	Photographic & cinematographic labs	-1	-1	0	0	-1	-1
417	Spaghetti, macaroni, etc.	-1	-1	-1	1	0	-2
455	Household textiles	-1	-1	1	0	0	-1

1 Intra-Community coverage ratio (CR): $-1 = \text{CR} < 90$; $0 = 90 \leqslant \text{CR} \leqslant 110$; $1 = \text{CR} > 110$.
2 Specialization index (SI): $-1 = \text{SI} < 90$; $0 = 90 \leqslant \text{SI} \leqslant 110$; $1 = \text{SI} > 110$.
3 Price index (PI): $-1 = \text{PI} > 105$; $0 = 105 \geqslant \text{PI} \geqslant 95$; $1 = 95 > \text{PI}$.
4 Companies: the higher the score, the stronger the capacity for manoeuvre of the companies (score of -2 to 2).
5 Products: the higher the score, the greater an asset the product range (score of -2 to 2).

or heterogeneous products were concerned. In the case of homogeneous products, abolishing non-tariff barriers should increase French national production on a restricted number of sites identified on a geographical basis. This would be a function of the comparative advantages of every member-state. There would be then an increase in trade between industries. However, in the case of heterogeneous products, several production units could be maintained within the various member-states, each specializing in different kinds of products. There would then be an increase in trade of the inter-branch type.

As in the United Kingdom, Belgium, Germany and the Netherlands, France has a high level of inter-branch trade. In fact, France should experience an intensification of such trade in sensitive sectors; but it should increase as a function of vectors different from those concerning economies of scale. Research work has demonstrated that France possesses comparative advantages in capital-intensive sectors and in research and development, but is at a disadvantage in labour-intensive sectors where economies of scale only play a marginal role. Authentic comparative advantages for France, therefore, should be increased capital investment and research and development in specific areas subject to poles of specialization. These will be a function of partner demands.

It appeared that this conclusion complied with research undertaken by Hanel and Roncin.[4] Their research involved determining features of exchanges. These were differentiated in accordance with the type of products and the geographical areas of partners in accordance with community zones, the United States, Japan and developing countries. This would indicate that France's position overall should be relatively strong for capital-intensive products that have achieved a certain maturity in the production cycle.

1992 — policies for adjustments in France

At company level

Although French Companies were reluctant to provide information on their policies for confronting the single market, this did not signify that no such strategies exist, but that they preferred to keep their policies confidential to confront competition more effectively. Several companies have realized that even total abolition of non-tariff barriers would not be sufficient to boost or increase exports, so they have attempted to reduce their cost structures, adapt their products to the new situation and multiply co-operation agreements. Such agreements should involve both small and medium-sized companies and will include setting up subsidiaries within partners' countries. It should be noted that the changes which have occurred in 1992 have led to an increase in the number of mergers and acquisitions of majority-holdings. In France, figures for such mergers and majority-holdings are comparable to those in Germany but lower than in Italy. French companies have also increased the number of subsidiaries in member-states where France and Germany are ranked joint second behind the Netherlands.

Efforts to adapt to the new situation may nevertheless be slowed by an over-pessimistic reaction. French companies forecast that in 1991, export growth would be limited to 4 per cent, i.e., a lower rate than imports. It was thought that this would be caused by a reduction of demand in Germany caused by re-unification, the market recession in the United States and Britain and the reduction in the competitiveness of the French economy due to lower dollar rates. Other factors include the stagnation of household consumption, caused by relatively high levels of capital investments, and the slowing of salary increases.

These factors should not encourage companies and other organizations to continue investing because their profit margins, calculated at 37.5 per cent in 1988, dropped to 30.5 per cent in 1991. In addition, the savings rate, calculated at 17.4 per cent in 1988, dropped to 14 per cent in 1991; and finally, interest rates have led to heavier financial burdens and produced significant levels of indebtedness.

French banks and other financial institutions, however, influenced by deregulation, hope that like their German counterparts, they will be able to participate in financing fixed assets of French companies. The reform of the 'Bourse' (French stock exchange) which is currently underway should facilitate such a development. It is planned to incorporate banks into companies operating on the Bourse.

Public authorities[5]

After 1992, the activities of public authorities will diminish in many fields. The process of creating a single market implies a certain degree of harmonization in the parts played by public authorities in national economies. There was an increase in public authority activity in France in the early 1980s. Now although there will be an attempt to reduce their influence, they will still play an important role. In 1988, the public sector represented 24 per cent of non-agricultural companies, 17.6 per cent of salaried employment, 34.9 per cent of fixed assets and 19.5 per cent of added-value French Companies taken as a whole.

This should be compared with 12.6 per cent in Germany and in the United Kingdom and this burden is even heavier when the public industrial sector is considered separately. In France, this has been calculated at 18.2 per cent against an average of 7 per cent in the remainder of member-states. This is probably the reason why France is attempting to create privatized subsidiaries of mother companies (see France Telecom, UAP and AGF etc.).

The single market also entails abolishing differences or discrimination in fiscality. Although French VTA complies with legal harmonization standards, it does not comply with economic law. In the case of savings taxation, apart from discrimination on the basis of resident or non-resident status, French rates are still high. If this situation persists in the short term, a flight of capital will occur. This will not affect *épargne logement* (similar to building societies in UK) which benefit from fiscal benefits, but investments in property will be affected. The Conseil National de Crédit has estimated that flights of capital amounting to FRF 100 million (10 per cent of capital authorized for such withdrawals) would be sufficient to raise interest rate by 2.3 per cent in the short term. This would reduce investment in Companies by FRF 40 million. This risk of flights of capital forced France to take swift action to reduce disparities in this field. It is presently continuing such action.

The single market has also resulted in a positive policy for creating new standards in France, mobilizing French companies and renovating the national certification system. To date, French Companies were the least active in contesting abusive standards to which they were subjected in export markets, while German and Italian companies took more effective action with regard to the Brussels Commission or tribunals. Certification should be the essential factor, as it is no longer necessary to simply supply products that comply with even European standards. Today, there must be proof of such conformance issued by an organization whose credibility cannot be put into doubt.

Conclusion: significance for France of opening European frontiers

As our approach was simply limited to industrial activities, service industries were not taken into consideration although some of these will be greatly affected as a result of 1992.

Generally, the results of this analysis confirm that the opening of frontiers will not necessarily signify greater consumption — at least over the short term — despite there being greater levels of competition. There will, of course, be winners and losers among companies, as will be the case with sectors and regions, in so far as costs and advantages of the single market will not be distributed evenly.

If the opening of frontiers is to be beneficial, France and other member-states must transfer a minimum amount of benefits in order to compensate losers before gaps become significant enough to have an adverse effect. There must also be a minimum number of rules even if they are restricted to competition. This is because even in countries that traditionally have centralized structures, de-regulation does not always signify a complete absence of rules. Opening of frontiers, symbolised by 1992, cannot simply be restricted to exchanges. The opening must also cover national policies and politics within a pragmatic and humanistic framework as opposed to a doctrinal or dogmatic structure. On this point the single market appears to be moving towards French philosophy.

Notes

1. See 'La Nouvelle Economie Européenne: une évaluation des effets économiques potentiels de l'achèvement du marché intérieur de la Communauté Européenne (The New European Economy: Evaluating the potential economic effects of establishing the single market within the European Community)'. Report directed by Michael Emerson and published in *Economie Européenne*, No. 35, March 1988.
2. See 'L'impact sectoriel du marché intérieur sur l'industrie: Les enjeux pour les Etats membres (Sectorial impact of interior market on Industry: stakes for member-states)' in *Economie Européenne*, numero spécial, 1990.
3. As for Note 2.
4. Hanel and Roncin, *Le rôle des facteurs de production et du facteur technologique dans les échanges internationaux de produits manufacturés. Application à l'analyse du commerce extérieur de la France (Role played by production and technological factors in international exchanges of manufactured goods as applied to the analysis of international French Trade)*. Association Française de Sciences économiques, Paris, November 1977.
5. See: Poncet, Jean-François and Barbier, B.: 'Les conséquences pour l'Economie Française du marché intérieur européenne. (Effects of the Inner European Market on the French Economy)'. *Economics*, Paris, December 1988.

Chapter 2

The EC industrial policy and its impact on French and European industries

Philippe Rollet

The debates on a necessary industrial policy — and more widely on necessary structural policies — have taken on some importance in most of the great industrial countries during the last few years. Its supporters thus put forward the necessity for the public authorities to orientate the productive structures (investment, production in each branch) in order to integrate in a better way the technological changes in industry, deal more satisfactorily with the new trends in demand and in international competition, and reinforce the weight and competitiveness of some sectors considered essential — especially because technical evolution and economic growth are based on them.

This concern also exists at the EC level; and though the various institutional texts rarely deal with industrial policy, numerous and varied EC actions have tried to modify the spontaneous trends of the industrial structures in declining sectors as well as in sectors using advanced technology.

So does this imply the existence of a real EC industrial policy? Are the actions carried on by the EC efficient not only for France but also for the other member-countries? Which orientations have to be chosen in the now well-advanced perspective of the economic and monetary union? Such are the issues tackled in this chapter.

Is there a European industrial policy?

The answer to this question is rather negative for two reasons:

1. an industrial policy is difficult to implement (at the national level and even more at the European level); and
2. the EC didn't provide itself with the means for such a policy and the

recent orientations, which especially give priority to the single market and the competition mechanisms, seem to indicate that this situation is far from changing.

Difficulties in implementing an industrial policy

An economic policy is defined by its instruments and goals. In that respect, the industrial policy is rather vague compared with the other economic policies, and its implementation is therefore difficult. We could attempt to define it as the set of actions co-ordinated by the public authorities and aimed at trying to modify the industrial productive structures, i.e., essentially the production techniques, the size of the firms and their degree of integration, the evolution of employment, of production and foreign trade in each branch. Even so, however, in order to reach goals such as improving industrial competitiveness, employment or economic independence, two sharp issues arise.

First, its instruments (aid to research, or investment, regulation, aid to export, trade and non-tariff barriers, etc.) are mostly part of other economic policies such as regional or scientific research policies, foreign trade or competition policies. It would be more accurate, then, to speak about industrial strategy, i.e., the co-ordination of several economic policies for the purposes of influencing the industrial structures, rather than about an industrial policy. The difficulty in implementing such a strategy is clear — at least if it is not to remain marginal — since it must be certain that the various authorities' interventions are coherent not only in regard to purely industrial goals but also to goals specific to every economic policy. There are additional difficulties at the EC level. This is because the interventions of the member-states in favour of their own industry have to be co-ordinated while they are most often competing with each other (faced with external constraint, each country often considers its European partners as competitors they have to challenge), and also, these national interventions have to be limited in order to establish specific European actions. This gives rise to the issue of the relationship between the European and national industrial goals.

Secondly, implementing a real industrial strategy clearly implies defined goals. In that respect, too, when we look beyond the 'great principles' on which there is necessarily a consensus — the lifting of the foreign constraint and the improvement of competitiveness, for example — the goals and consensus are less obvious. For instance, does seeking to improve the competitiveness of industry only mean to act on production costs — through actions on wages, or in favour of productivity, by the implementation of an energy policy to reduce the supply costs. Or does it mean to go further, by considering that the weight of the external constraint, the development of exports and the ability to limit foreign penetration into the internal market, also depend on the nature and quality of the international specialization — that is to say, the orientation of our productive system, to a greater or lesser degree, towards sectors of advanced technology or those with world-wide markets? In the latter case, which industrial activities have to be promoted? And based on which criteria? The goal of economic or technological independence, sometimes put forward by countries such as France which expressed a wish for an industrial policy, of course brings up similar issues: why is a national or European electronics industry, or even a machine tool industry, required? Conceiving an industrial policy implies, at least, a sufficiently precise idea about what is the right specialization for a country, and the answers to some difficult questions: for example, should we only have to exploit our comparative advantages? Should we have to prepare the future — i.e., the comparative advantages to come which are not necessarily the present ones — and how? Should we have to create those comparative advantages and, if so, in which fields and how?

At the European level, the problems are even more acute, for the optimal productive structure — or specialization — of the whole EC is not necessarily the aggregation of all the optimal productive structures of the member-countries. If the electronics industry is considered as a strategic activity, should it be located in a large number of EC countries (but in that case, are the advantages provided by the specialization, and the European dimension with the possible economies of scale, really exploited?), or, on the contrary, only in a few countries (the others could thus consider that they do not benefit from the intra-EC division of labour). On which criteria should the choice of location be done among the different countries?

All those issues are complex and much debated; and though the crisis in the 1970s tended to bring the member-states closer, their philosophies on that matter remain rather different. The lack of any common medium- or long-term industrial plan (and then of precise and clearly defined goals) and the difficulties in implementing an industrial strategy (undoubtedly because the theoretical reflection on this has only been recently initiated) account for the limited attention given by the EC to the definition of a European industrial strategy.

Varied European actions, but no industrial strategy

It is notable that the importance given in the EC budget to industry and to actions favouring Research and Development remains limited, and that the various European interventions are only, in the best of cases, the beginnings of a consistent policy.

The direct financial intervention favouring industry is of limited extent:

- In 1989, it represented 1.5 billion ECUs, which is less than 0.4 per cent of the EEC GDP and less than 20 per cent of the European budget;

• As emphasized by J.F. Marchipont,[1] European aid is low compared to national aid. For example, national aid is ten times more important in France and Germany; and

• Even if in the framework of the structural fund reform the expenses are noticeably increasing (those structural funds should double in real terms between 1988 and 1993), this will not fundamentally modify the situation, and the weight of European intervention in favour of industry will remain low.

It appears obvious, then, that the EC has not given priority to action on industrial structures, but this judgement has to be seen in context, for European intervention is not merely in the form of direct aid and loans. On the contrary, they are numerous and vary from sector to sector. Indeed, the EC can influence the evolution of the industrial structures by influencing the European environment of the firms (through the implementation of the single market, through taxation and the legal framework, and through its competition policy), and by influencing their foreign environment through the common trade policy. During the last two decades, those means have been differently used according to the sectors and time spans involved.

The European policy was first a defensive-type policy, aimed at partly preserving the relatively declining sectors such as textile, steel or shipbuilding industries; they all required substantial restructuring because of the slowing down of world demand and the intensification of the international competition. The European action then mainly consisted of controlling and checking national aid. In the steel industry — where this organization of national aid can be considered as late since it only was implemented in the early 1980s, while the crisis had been obvious since 1974 — it was accompanied by a quota policy and fixed minimum prices. This enabled the European firms to avoid the worst, but did not solve all the problems, for the present situation is far from excellent: the production over-capacities remain, and the national aid is not yet suppressed. In the textile industry, the aid-rationing policy went along with the trade policy (multifiber agreement, General system of preferences) in order to limit the competition from low-wage countries.

During the last ten years, then, the European policy has become more offensive, and has been dealing more and more with advanced technology activities.[2] Simultaneously, its modalities have been changing too. First, the EC endeavoured to stimulate transborder co-operation between some European firms; in its early stages this process concerned the aerospace industry, and much later — through the implementation of programmes spread over several years — to stimulate research in the sectors of information technologies (ESPRIT, programme launched in 1984), telecommunications (RACE, 1987) and biotechnologies (BAP, 1985). But, above all, the completion of the single market has been increasingly seen as the main instrument of the industrial restructuring.

Since the removal of the non-tariff barriers, the opening of government procurements and the extension of the markets should intensify competition, enable the exploitation of economies of dimension, and boost ongoing changes profitable to the international specialization of the member-states.

The EC intervenes in the industrial field in various ways, and sometimes with appreciable impacts (in the steel or aerospace industries, for example) but for several reasons, such as the following, this is not sufficient to constitute a real industrial strategy:

- The interventions remain too selective and only concern some activities. In the past, it was the declining sectors which, as we are aware, represented a noticeable part of the industrial added value. Nowadays, there are just a few really advanced fields which are in high technology sectors.
- There is no overall view of the expected evolution of the EC productive structures (which specializations within the EC? Which specialization of Europe against the rest of the world?), and the EC has not yet, except very vaguely (its intention would be to restructure the declining sectors and promote the high technology ones), any common industrial plan. The very late reactions of the EC in the high technology sector — strategic in terms of international competition — are the expression of this lack of plan.
- Similarly, competition policy remains the main instrument used by the EC as its industrial policy. In the past, the objective consisted of controlling aid. Today, the growing priority is the completion of the single market. Although it is an essential element of a European industrial policy, as J. Mazier and C. Couharde noticed,[3] for example, its sectorial impact should not be overestimated. Indeed, the single market will concern the sectors in which the non-tariff barriers are high (a few sectors of high technology — telecommunications, computer sciences, medical appliance — pharmaceuticals and some other sectors including the railway industry), or about 15 per cent of the industrial added value. Its impact will be all the more important since it will be accompanied by other structural instruments — as is the practice of foreign competitors — in order to make the best of the EC advantages. But there is, at present, no such seeking of any coherence with those other essential instruments, as the lack of any common trade policy in crucial sectors such as car and electronic industries demonstrates.

However, the difficulties of the European industries and the advantages which could be provided by a common industrial policy justify a more voluntarist approach from France and the other countries.

Assessment of the outcomes and suggestions

Assessment

It is obviously difficult to assess the effects of a common policy which does not exist yet, or more precisely, which is only at its start. However, we will initiate some reflections on its possible impact on economic policies, and on the French and European economies.

As far as the economic policies are concerned, the present French and European conceptions can be considered as very close. Like the European policy, the French one, which was a sectorial policy (and not merely a defensive policy since it aimed at promoting a few important strategic sectors), is now a policy focusing to a greater extent on the competition mechanisms, on Research-Development, and on the co-operation between dynamic firms. It is regrettable, maybe, that the ideas put forward have been following their present trend, and that the French ideas about a medium-term industrial programme have been put aside.

The impact on industrial structures is more difficult to assess. One may possible consider that the French economy benefited from some actions at the EC level — the positive impact of the Airbus programme, for example, is undeniable (the French market share was multiplied by four), and shows how, in some fields, common actions are useful to increase national or European competitiveness, though the outcomes of pluri-annual programmes initiated mid-1980s cannot be assessed yet. As for the Davignon plan, its impact is much more questionable. It did improve the situation of the French steel industry, but at what cost? The same question arises for the whole set of the declining sectors. Though national and European policies did enable essential and necessary adjustments — unforeseen by the firms — and limited the social costs of those adjustments for wage-earners and old industrialized regions, a pertinent question would be whether the sums spent would not have been more useful in promoting other activities. Also, the implementation of defensive policies finally led to the curbing of adjustments and damage to competitiveness by maintaining too high a degree of specialization in sectors where comparative advantages have decreased.

However, to come out of this debate, we should be able to refer to a precise industrial plan defined on economic criteria (improvement of competitiveness), on political criteria (economic or technological independence) or on social criteria (employment situation, difficulties specific to one particular region). Nevertheless, a first assessment can be made from the analysis of the condition of the French and European industries against the international competition. All the studies on the quality of the international specialization of the European countries lead to converging outcomes,[4] and show that structural competitiveness is inadequate — not in terms of control on production costs, but the ability to orientate our resources towards the dynamic sectors of high technology, or with a large world market. Three aspects may be more particularly underlined.

First, despite a real evolution, most of the European countries, including France, still remain too specialized in old sectors (textile, clothing or consumption goods industries), despite the comparative advantages of the New Industrialized Countries. Comparative advantage ratios (share of branch in the world market weighted by the share of the whole industry in the world market, 1989) show that this specialization is higher than the average level in developed countries, and especially higher than the level in the United States and Japan. In the textile industry, those indices are 1,1 (EC), 0.9 (France), 0.4 (United States) and 0.5 (Japan). In the clothing industry, they are 0.9 (EC), 0.7 (France), 0.2 (United States) and 0.06 (Japan). This can of course reflect the weight of defensive national and European policies implemented in the 1970s.

Table 2.1 Balance of the EC exchanges with the rest of the world in the main sectors of high technology (billion dollars)

	1970	1986
Pharmaceutical products	+ 0.60	+ 3.56
Data processing and office automation equipment	− 0.27	− 7.34
Telecommunication equipment	+ 0.29	+ 2.14
Consumer electronics	+ 0.39	− 6.10
Aerospace industry	− 0.52	+ 1.96

Source: Economie Européenne, n°39, March 1989.

In addition, every EC country has been delayed in the advanced technology industries. The data on the evolution of the trade balance in the main high technology sectors illustrate these European difficulties (Table 2.1), since on the whole the trade deficit of the EC against the rest of the world significantly increased from 1970 to 1986. This deficit is due to data processing, with office automation equipment (7.3 billion dollars), consumer electronics (6.1) and the EC strong points (especially chemistry, telecommunications) only affording partial compensation. The comparative advantage indices also reflect those difficulties: for example, in 1983, they are about 0.8 for the whole EC (0.84 for France, 0.97 for Germany) which is far behind the United States (1.26) and Japan (1.36). Once again, this probably reflects the late reactions of the European and national authorities. There is insufficient co-ordination between the various national policies (which continue to compete with each other) in the areas which the importance of the economies of dimension — at the production as well as at research levels — binds to thinking at least at the EC market level.

Finally, the productive system of the European economies is insufficiently adapted to world demand. Some studies analyse the impact of international specialization on the evolution of market shares, by distinguishing between three components:

1. The shares gained or lost in the elementary market — defined by the imports of a particular product by a specific geographical area — which express the evolution of competitiveness.
2. The impulsing or specialization effect indicating the more or less adequate sectorial and geographical adaptation of exports to international demand at the beginning of the period.
3. Finally, the adaptation effect which assesses adaptation of these exports to international demand variations during the period.

With this method, G. Lafay and C. Herzog,[5] for example, analysed the role of the specialization effect over a long period — since 1967. They underscored the gradual worsening of the situation in the European economies, shown in Table 2.2. The results of the EC countries, which had been very good over the period 1967—73 (except for the United Kingdom), have slowly deteriorated. The French economy has been following this trend: after relatively good results in the 1960s and 1970s, the 1980s have shown an obvious degradation in its competitiveness in terms of adaptation to world demand. During the last few years, the Asian New Industrial Countries have moved into the lead, while the European countries have known negative results.

Table 2.2 Classification of the countries according to the initial specialization effect 1967—86*

	1967—73	1973—80	1980—86
France	6.6	4.5	− 5.8
Germany	8.7	0.4	− 2.6
British Isles	− 0.8	4.2	− 1.7
Italy	6.6	2.4	− 2.4
Netherlands	5.4	− 1.2	− 2.6
Belgium, Luxembourg	4.4	− 0.7	− 3.5
United States	− 13.3	3.1	− 1.8
Japan	3.1	3.3	18.2
South East Asian NIC	1.5	0.3	15.3

* Variation in thousandths of the market share, following from the evolution of the partners' exports, taking into account shares initially acquired in the elementary markets.

Opponents to an industrial policy may consider that such results do reflect the market strengths and the nature of our comparative advantages (most of the European economies, except perhaps the German economy, would be in an intermediate situation between the advanced economies — such as the United States and Japan — and the New Industrialized Countries); but this would be to forget that the main competitors do intervene in favour of their industries, and that there is no reason why the most advanced EC countries would have comparative advantages different from their main competitors. The fact that they do have an industrial policy (much more easy to implement in their national framework) does not explain all the difficulties in the past; but it at least justifies, despite the difficulties described above, the endeavour to implement a real industrial strategy, which can only be a European policy.

Short plea for a common industrial strategy

An industrial strategy has to be supported by the implementation of the single market; under no circumstances can it act as a substitute for it. This is what our Asian competitors have clearly understood: their internal markets remain highly competitive, but they have mobilized all their sectorial means as well as their macro-economic policies in order to support their manufacturers and exporters. Accompanying the internal market, such an industrial strategy can be but a common strategy, and for a few simple reasons. Purely national strategies may be conflicting; it is necessary to avoid national aid, granted without any concern for community coherence, which may distort the working of internal competition and introduce new market divisions. Also in such fields as Research-Development, in which a European dimension is essential, some co-operation is required in order to avoid overlapping which prevents crucial sizes being reached and creates inefficiency.

A European approach provides advantages. It makes possible operations which a priori exceed the capacities of a single country (the aerospace industry, for example). It enables standards to be defined which will allow competition with Japanese or American firms in the world market; and it will, above all, enable each country to carry weight in international negotiations.

Finally, the will to set up the European monetary union requires a strong and coherent industrial basis. The evolution of the medium- and long-term exchange rates not only depends on the mastering of the prices and costs but also on structural competitiveness[6] (i.e., on the quality of international specialization, for it highly influences external results and outcomes in terms of balance of payments). From an external point of view, then, the EC requires an efficient productive system (in terms of competitiveness costs, adaptation to world demand, ability to develop sectors of high technology, etc.) in order to have a strong currency; and from an internal point of view, the EC needs sufficiently converging economic results (prices and growth, as well as a good international specialization of the productive systems) in order to avoid any important imbalances in the current payments which would affect the stability of the exchange rates between the member-states.

This, however, pre-supposes the EC countries will agree on a common industrial project, and set up the means to co-ordinate the various economic policies in order to reach this goal. This is a hard task, but is the only condition to setting up a real integrated zone rather than a simple free exchange space.

Notes

1. J.F. Marchipont 'La stratégie industrielle de la Communauté pendant et après l'achèvement du marché unique' Revue du Marché Commun, no 334, Février 1990.
2. On the presentation of the EC industrial policy, see P. Maillet and P. Rollet 'Intégration économique européenne: Théorie et pratique', ed. Nathan Sup. (especially chapters 7 and 9), 1988.
3. J. Mazier and C. Couharde, 'Growth and comparative costs of structural policies in EC', Second Integration symposium, Structural policies in Europe. Confederation of European Economic Association, University of Lille, September 1990.
4. For a detailed presentation of those studies, see P. Rollet 'Spécialisation international et intégration économique européenne', Ed Economica, 2ème édition, 1990.
5. G. Lafay, C. Herzog, 'La fin des avantages acquis', Ed Economica, 1989.
6. See P. Rollet, op. cit, on the relations between international specialization and exchange rates.

Chapter 3

The European Community R&D policy and its impact on the French R&D policy

Patrick Cohendet and Patrick Llerena

The European Community's intervention in the field of Research and Development (R&D) is relatively recent. For many years, the EC activities in favour of research were limited to coal, steel and nuclear energy, according to the EC, ECSC and EURATOM Treaties. In January 1984, a resolution on a first-action programme in the field of research and technology was passed by the Council, but it was not until 1987 that policy measures in this field were given a legal basis in the Single European Act (Title VI). This legitimized an increased effort which had begun in the early 1980s. This was when the strategic significance of R&D for industrial competitiveness was realized, as well as Europe's accumulated delay compared to the United States and Japan in generic technologies (such as micro-electronics, bio-technology, new materials).

R&D programmes of the European Community

The need to co-ordinate the R&D activities of the EC member-states was translated into the implementation of framework programmes, starting in the mid-1980s. The first one extended from 1984 to 1987, the second from 1987 to 1990 and the third one, which was adopted on 23 April 1990 will cover the period 1990—94. These framework programmes rely partly on major technology programmes (e.g. ESPRIT, RACE, BRITE-EURAM, BIOTECHNOLOGY programmes, etc.), which consist of a concerted and intensive effort aimed at promoting joint ventures between universities and enterprises for pre-competitive projects, with a view to reinforcing Europe's industrial competitiveness. The framework programmes aim at other objectives as well, such as stimulating the mobility of researchers within Europe in order to reinforce the co-operation between European researchers (on the Science Programme) and

Table 3.1 EC framework programme 1990—94

	1990—92	1993—94	Total
	in million ECUs		
I. Generic technologies			
1. Information and communication technologies	974	1247	2221
• information technologies	1352		
• communication technologies	489		
• telematics systems of general interest	380		
2. Industrial and materials technologies	390	498	888
• industrial and materials technologies	748		
• measurement and testing	140		
II. Management of natural resources			
3. Environment	227	291	518
• environment	414		
• marine science and technology	104		
4. Life sciences and technologies	325	416	741
• biotechnology	164		
• agricultural and agro-food research	333		
• biomedical research and health	133		
• life sciences and technologies for developing countries	111		
5. Energy	357	457	814
• non-nuclear energies	157		
• nuclear fission safety	199		
• controlled thermonuclear fusion	458		
III. Valorization of intellectual resources			
6. Human capital and mobility	227	291	518
• human capital and mobility	518		
Total	2500	3200	5700[1]

1 Including 57 million ECUs for centralized diffusion and valorization activities levied on each programme and 550 million ECUs for the Common Research Centre, of which 180 million ECUs for 1993—94.

to promote access to big scientific equipment of European interest (1989 EC Plan).

The new framework programme 1990—94 (see Table 3.1) provides for global resources amounting to 5,700 million ECUs and has the following main characteristics:

• it concentrates on research in the field of environment, biotechnology, agricultural and industrial research, development of telematics systems of general interest, and valorization of intellectual

resources (Human Capital and Mobility). On the other hand, the relative weight of research in the field of fission energy is decreasing.
• a new principle was introduced, that of subsidiarity. According to this criterion, the EC only does 'what is best done at Community level as opposed to the national, regional or local levels'. This principle, together with the principle of 'degression', according to which the rate of EC participation decreases as one gets nearer to the market (applied research) and increases as one gets away from it (fundamental research) defines a priori the limits of EC intervention. However, if pre-competitiveness remains the favoured field, it can be foreseen that the EC will progressively extend its participation to research activities which are closer to the market, as is the case in the EUREKA programme (see p. 36).

It should also be mentioned that a number of measures taken by the EC outside the framework programmes described above, can nevertheless be connected to the objectives of the EC R&D policy. This is so, in particular, in the cases of the SPRINT programme (concentrating on technology transfer) or the ERASMUS and COMETT programmes (Education policy).

Despite the growing efforts of the EC in the field of R&D, the EC budget remains very low compared to the budget of the member-states. In 1986 for instance, the EC contribution to research or co-operation programmes amounted to 661 million ECUs, i.e. 2.2 per cent of the public funds allocated to non-military R&D in all EC member-states.

French R&D policy

The main characteristic of French R&D policy is the relatively important public funding (higher, as a percentage of the GDP, than in Germany for instance) which is strongly focused, with two-thirds of French public subsidies devoted to aeronautics, space and defence electronics. On the other hand, the funding of industrial research lags behind compared to the major western countries.

Therefore, according to ERGAS's classification (1987), which suggested classifying industrialized countries according to the nature of the technology policies the public authorities implement, France clearly belongs to those countries whose objectives are defined with a view to asserting their national sovereignty and whose first priority is to support major innovations which promote industrial aims of national significance (e.g., *plan calcul* in 1966). From this point of view, the French R&D policy (bearing close resemblance to that of Great Britain) differs from those countries (Germany, Sweden, Switzerland) whose technology policies rely on the fundamental objective of diffusion, i.e. on making a technology potential available to all firms in different industries in order to allow them to adopt new technologies as fast and as efficiently as possible. Japan has an intermediate position between the first and the second category.

The 1991 research budget puts special emphasis on this French characteristic. Indeed, 35.7 per cent of the budget is devoted to big programmes. Industrial research, i.e. diffusion programmes, represents only 10.9 per cent.

The benefits of the EC R&D policy for France

It seems, then, that the EC R&D policy, despite its limited financial volume, has a globally positive impact on the French situation for the following reasons.

- The EC policy is no substitute for the French R&D policy. It reinforces the horizontal co-operation networks between universities and enterprises around pre-competitive projects, and stimulates the development and diffusion of 'generic' technologies (micro-electronics, biotechnology, new materials etc.) These are technologies to be assimilated to public goods presenting a lack of appropriability; from this point of view the EC programmes in a way compensate for the negative aspects of mainstream French R&D policy, which relies more on vertical connections between major R&D projects and may promote 'barriers' to innovation on the side of the participating firms.

- In some fields, such as generic technologies, the EC policy provides the critical mass necessary to get a chance to hold a competitive position world-wide. In many instances, even at the level of France, no single European country would have had a chance to reach a competitive position on its own.

- The EC R&D policy enables French companies which get involved in an intensive European collaborative project to better understand the prerequisites for successful innovations — according to the various European contexts — and thus to better prepare their future marketing policy on a European level. Be it different standardization procedures, local practices or specific regulations on environmental protection, for instance, these are all elements which play a critical role for successful marketing, but which have often been neglected by French firms. Contacts established during pre-competitive research work, often enable French firms which have entered into research co-operation to extend it beyond — but thanks to — the EC funding in order to improve their outlets in terms of market shares.

- The subsidies, which are sometimes quite substantial for firms, generally complement national programmes. They could be considered as 'marginal', but in fact they provide for the creation of links between laboratories and industrialists from different countries, which can later be transformed into a stronger co-operation. However, over the past few years, a progressive reversal of the situation can be observed: in some fields the themes of national programmes, in particular French ones, originate more and more frequently from the EC. This is the case for the non-priority fields in France (i.e. those other than space, aeronautics and nuclear energy), for which national subsidies use EC programmes as levers, in order to adapt these programmes to the specificities of the French industry.

The EUREKA Programme

The EUREKA Programme was proposed by France and adopted in November 1985. It gathers 20 countries: the 12 EC countries, the Scandinavian countries, Iceland, Switzerland, Austria and Turkey. The main objective of the programme is to follow up on R&D in order to hit the market and its actions are therefore more downstream than the EC programmes. The implications for industrialists are all the more important. In addition to reinforcing Europe's technology potential, this programme makes it possible to tackle transborder problems such as environmental problems (Eurotrac, Euromar, Eurocaire, Eurosylva) or infrastructure problems (transport). The Tables 3.2 and 3.3 give a general view of the scope of topics under study, as well as of French participation.

Even if it is difficult at this point to assess the programme, it seems that its results are generally positive. Already some patents have been taken out. Nevertheless this programme must become more efficient and

Table 3.2   French participation in EUREKA

| | Projects with French participation | | | Projects without French participation | | Total EUREKA | |
	Number	Total cost (FrF m.)	French participation (FrF m.)	Number	Total cost (FrF m.)	NB	Total cost (FrF m.)
Hanover	7	2,063.5	586.5	2	242.2	9	2,305.7
London	38	17,478.5	6,347.4	19	1,479.8	67	18,958.3
Stockholm	15	3,163.2	1,325.7	22	1,078.0	37	4,241.2
Madrid	21	2,629.1	914.4	35	2,568.3	56	5,197.4
Copenhagen	21	1,205.1	492.0	33	1,292.0	54	2,497.1
Total	102	26,539.4	9,666.0	111	6,660.3	223	33,199.7
ECU m.		3,791.3	1,380.9		951.5		4,742

Source: French Ministry for Research and Technology

Table 3.3 Topical distribution

	All projects (213)	Projects with French participation (102)
Information technologies	35	15
Production technology, robotics	46	26
Materials	21	10
Transport	11	5
Ocean, environment, urban planning	12	4
Biotechnology, medical field	40	16
Laser	13	7
Energy	10	6
Communication	11	5
Micro-electronics	14	8

Source: French Ministry for Research and Technology

more open to projects of lesser importance (shorter and/or less expensive), accessible to SME.

In conclusion it can be said that EC R&D policies stimulate and complement French policies. In particular, they allow the creation of important synergies (common big equipment for research purposes, etc.), co-operation habits and national research activities which complement each other better. This resolutely optimistic presentation must, however, be qualified. Indeed, any co-operative venture carries the risk of being imitated. This is a real risk, implying that caution is necessary in choosing projects and partners, but it must in no way hold up the participation in, and the development of, European policies in the future.

Chapter 4

French energy policy and the impact of the European Community energy policy

Guy de Carmoy

There are two reasons why any policy on energy requires mid- to long-term horizons. First, time is required to install the equipment. Five years are necessary to develop a new oilfield and at least seven years for the installation of a nuclear plant. Secondly, the reserves of oil may be exhausted within the next 30 to 40 years, given the increasing rate of transport use world-wide, and despite the extension of exploration. These two reasons prompt an analysis of the French energy policy in a historical perspective by separating the 1960—73 period of cheap oil supplied to Europe, the 1973—86 period, marked by the oil shocks, and the 1986—92 period of preparation for the 1993 deadline following the adoption of the European Single Act in 1986. The influence of the Community on French policy increased with time. In order to understand this influence, it is important to recall the basic facts of the French energy economy.

Basic facts

France is poor in terms of fossil-fuel resources. Its reserves of coal amount to 450 m.t., one-hundredth of those of the United Kingdom, its reserves of oil are negligible and the reserves of natural gas in France's South West will be exhausted by the end of the century. Its hydro-electric resources are notable, but barely extensive. On the other hand, France is relatively rich in fissile resources having 3 per cent of the uranium world-wide reserves at low production costs.

The bulk of the energy sector is nationalized: Charbonnages de France (CDF), Gaz de France (GDF) and Electricité de France (EDF) were founded in 1946 and the Commissariat à l'Energie Atomique (CEA), was created at the end of 1945 and has a predominant role in the civil and military nuclear fields. The state holds 35 per cent of the capital of Compagnie Française des Pétroles (CFP) and 70 per cent of that of the oil Group Elf Erap. The latter holds the third position behind Royal Dutch and British Petroleum among the oil companies based in the EEC; it has reserves in Central Africa and in the North Sea and a subsidiary in the United States. Total-CFP holds the fourth position in the EEC. It mainly exploits in the North Sea and also has an American subsidiary but its financial results tend not to be as good as those of Elf Erap.

The state regulates the supply of crude oil, the refining and the distribution of oil products in accordance with a 1928 law. Its four-year development plan defines the objectives of the national companies in the energy sector in agreement with the Ministry of Industry.

The 1960–73 period

In 1960, coal represented 52.3 per cent of domestic energy consumption, imported oil 32.1 per cent and hydraulic energy 12.8 per cent. The rate of energy independence was 59 per cent.

In 1973, the place of oil was such that it supplied 71.3 per cent of domestic energy consumption. France imported 134.5 m. tep (million tonnes of oil equivalent) of which three-quarters came from the Middle East, the surplus being shared between North Africa and Central Africa. CFP had, since its creation, a minority participation in the Arab Petroleum Company. Government policy was to have franc-zone hydro-carbons, so CFP and Elf Erap were encouraged to carry out explorations in Algeria. This led to important discoveries of oil and natural gas, but Algeria nationalized the majority of the assets of the French companies in 1971. Meanwhile, in 1973, Gaz de France, the sole supplier, imported 7.5 m. tep of natural gas of which more than four-fifths came from the Netherlands and the surplus from Algeria.

Coal's share as an energy resource was reduced sharply. Charbonnages de France gradually reduced their exploitation from 1960 onwards and benefited from subsidies from the French government and from the ECSC (European Community for Steel and Coal). Taking into considera-tion the technical cost and the social cost of the decrease of coal-mining during this period, imports of coal remained stable at 10 m. tep. With a view to using the domestic resources of uranium or, if possible, remaining independent of the United States for the supply of enriched uranium, the government decided in 1952 to build nuclear reactors according to the graphite-gas-natural uranium method. However, as the cost of running these reactors was high, it opted in 1962, at EDF's request, for the American PWR method. In 1972 it launched the construction of an uranium enrichment factory (Eurodif) using the gas diffusion process; it did this with the help of Belgium, Spain and Italy, CEA being the main shareholder. An experimental supergenerator factory, Phenix, was launched in 1970, on a national basis. In 1971 CEA associated with qualified English partners in a company called United Reprocessors in order to control the European supply market. However, the share of electricity coming from nuclear energy was still negligible in 1973 in France. Following the decrease of coal production, the surge of oil imports and the unavoidable time delay for starting the first nuclear reactors, the domestic production of energy in 1973 covered 22 per cent of domestic needs compared to 59 per cent in 1960.

During this period, the co-operation of France with ECSC was on the whole satisfactory, but the relations with Euratom remained tense with France wanting to keep its total independence in the nuclear domain. In 1968, after the closure of the Suez Canal, the EEC Council invited member-states to constitute a security stock up to the level of 65 days of oil consumption. France conformed to this recommendation.

The 1973—86 period

This period is marked by two oil shocks and the oil price fall in 1986. Oil remained the dominant energy and its sudden changes in price, upwards then downwards, affected the prices of other sources of energy and prompted considerable changes in domestic policy and an increase in the role of international institutions.

The United States, after their intervention in the Middle East to promote negotiations between Israel and Egypt, proposed in 1974 the creation of the International Energy Agency (IEA) within the framework of the OECD. The IEA's objectives were defined as being to strengthen the co-operation of member-states in order to reduce their excessive dependency on oil, to implement an information system on the international oil market and to establish a security plan for supplies.

France, fearing that this institution might compromise the relations between the industrialized countries and the Arab oil producing countries, was the only state of the EEC not to become a member of the IEA. However, the close collaboration between the IEA member-states alleviated the inconvenience of the French absence.

In 1980, the Council of the EEC asked the Commission to give an appreciation on the convergence of domestic energy policies of member-states. In 1981, the Commission listed the actions requiring development within the framework of a 'Community energy strategy' which would include aid to research and development projects and loans for the financing of infrastructure. The objectives included the reduction of the share of oil in energy consumption, the reduction of the share of electricity produced from hydrocarbons, and the increase in the share of coal and nuclear energy. Measures aimed at reducing pollution, in particular in the field of car emissions were to be adopted.

The French policy conformed to the orientations of the common policy in regard to hydrocarbons. Its singularity lay in its forceful promotion of nuclear energy in order to reduce external dependence.

In March 1974, the government decided on the construction in 1974—5 of 13 nuclear plants of 900 MW each, and later of 5 plants each year to raise nuclear capacity by 1985 to 55,000 MW (which is the equivalent of 60 m.t. of oil production per year). The implementation of the programme was the responsibility of Framatome, the only constructor of boilers for nuclear reactors, in whose capital the CEA and the public industrial sector held a strong interest. The CEA was in charge of the fuel cycle and of the development of fast breeder reactors.

By 31 December 1985, on the eve of the fall in world oil prices, France had at its disposal an electronuclear capacity of 39,000 MW, the second in the world after that of the United States, so that 70 per cent of the electricity produced in France was of nuclear origin. France's nuclear plant, compared to foreign competitors, provided a brief turnaround time and economies of scale as a result of the size of its reactors. Sections of 1,300 MW were brought into service from 1985 onwards. In 1976, the CEA founded NERSA, a company with German and Italian participants to build in Creys-Malville a prototype fast breeder of 1,200 MW under the name of Superphenix.

The oil-price collapse, resulting both from a fall in oil demand to OPEC and from the depreciation of the dollar, prompted France to modify its nuclear policy. The pace of building reactors was notably reduced. In view of the fall in the growth rate of electricity consumption, a surplus of equipment in nuclear plants was foreseeable by 1988 and effective in 1990. As for the fast breeder reactors, their construction appeared less urgent, because world-wide demand for uranium was increasing much less than forecast following the slowing down or closure of the nuclear industry in many countries of the Community and of the OECD.

However, studies had started in order to build at Creys-Melville a new commercial prototype called European Fast Reactor (EFR) with the help, alongside the CEA and EDF, of qualified English and German organisms, and with the financial and technical support of the Community.

The French electro-nuclear programme gave rise to a variety of criticisms. The opposition of the environmentalists was foreseeable, the cost of the programme seemed too high, and concern was expressed that too large a part of savings had been drained towards the energy sector at the expense of the modernization and competitiveness of industry, as a deficit of manufactured products appeared in the foreign trade. Others claimed that the development of nuclear energy would promote other branches of the domestic industry. However, public opinion, on the whole, accepted the increase of electricity production of nuclear origin.

Electro-nuclear plants have a cost advantage compared to electrical plants using coal. According to a study from the OECD, the cost price of coal KWh in France was, in 1984, 80 per cent above that of nuclear

KWh. This gap decreased with the increasing cost of managing waste and the reinforcement of security measures, but has not disappeared.

The production of electricity did not go along with an increase in coal consumption. The production of domestic coal was reduced by half from 1973 to 1987, as the economically exploitable reserves became exhausted. Imported coal represented almost half of the consumption of this resource.

Important modifications also occurred in the origin, the uses and the imports of oil and of natural gas. As nuclear power came on stream, the public authorities reduced the use of oil in thermic plants. The share of oil, which represented 69.1 per cent of the supply in primary energy for France in 1973, had fallen to 40.3 per cent in 1986. Imports of oil were reduced by half: 135 m. tep in 1973, 70 m. tep in 1986. Their geographical origin was diversified: the Middle Eastern share fell to 38.1 per cent; North Sea and Central Africa represented respectively 17.2 per cent and 18.0 per cent, North Africa and the Soviet Union respectively 10.2 per cent and 8.9 per cent. Despite their efforts, the French oil companies registered a decrease of their productive potential. Exports of the paraoil sector, however, enabled France in 1986 to cover 33 per cent of its oil deficit.

As far as natural gas was concerned, there was both an increase in consumption from 13.3 m. tep in 1973 to 23.8 m. tep in 1986 and a diversification of supply. The Soviet Union and the North Sea provided half of the imports, with the usual suppliers, the Netherlands and Algeria, supplying the other half.

The government encouraged energy savings in three sectors: industry, the residential-tertiary sector and transport. Energy intensity improved at rates of 24 per cent between 1973 and 1982, but stagnated between 1982 and 1986.

Public opinion was for a long time quite unconcerned about environment problems, notably during the 1971—86 period marked by the creation of 15 new nuclear plants. The awareness of the environment only appeared in 1980 with a substantial reduction of sulphur dioxide and of carbonic gas emissions.

With the growth in nuclear output, domestic production has more than doubled. Energy substitution further pushed the rate of energy independence to 46.3 per cent in 1986. Finally France, because of its nuclear overcapacity, has become an exporter of electricity to the United Kingdom, the Federal Republic of Germany, Switzerland and Italy. Framatome has exported three PWR reactors to China, to Korea and to South Africa.

The 1986—92 period

The adoption of the European Single Act in February 1986 is due in large part to French insistence to strengthen the European Council's deliberations. The Act aims to strengthen the European Union, through the completion of the internal market. The latter is defined as 'a space without internal frontiers in which the free circulation of goods, persons, services and of capital is assured'. Its realization is facilitated by the more generous adoption of the rule of qualified majority. The implementation date is the 31 December 1992. Obstacles to the unification of the energy market and the solutions proposed to surmount them are mentioned in the Commission document on the internal energy market of May 1988.

Among the obstacles to trade which derived from the French import regime, is the fact that France, in exception to its partners, does not recognize the origin of oil products by refinery, but defines the origin in terms of the oilfields the products are supplied by. France also imposed the obligation on oil traders to buy back a proportion of the oil acquired by the state.

Monopolies having a commercial character are submitted to Article 37 of the Treaty, which imposes the exclusion of all discrimination between nationals of member countries. The French monopoly on oil was adapted in conformity with the Treaty, the government having accepted to replace, by objective criteria, the conditions of discriminatory character imposed on refining and distribution activities. Two problems arose concerning electricity and gas transport and distribution monopolies. The first one deals with free transit within the Community. The Commission proposed that competition conditions were to be negotiated between the companies concerned, in accordance with the competition rules of the Treaty. The second problem deals with the access right for third parties to transport channels (common carrier principle). This right can only be implemented under certain conditions which remain to be determined.

Companies from the energy sector, since the adoption by the Council in 1990 of a Community directive, will have to conform to the rule of opening the public procurement markets for civil engineering and supplies, in line with the more open policy on tenders throughout the Community. This rule includes dispensation for concessions dealing with the prospecting and production of coal, oil and natural gas. It is applicable to equipment supply. In the electricity sector, the supply of power is not covered by the directive, but the Commission keeps the right to open it to competition from 1995 onwards. This measure will satisfy France, which is a permanent exporter of electrical power and therefore favours a fluid market in this energy source.

Aids from the states to the production of coal do not alter exchanges between member-states and have been approved by the Council since 1986. Also, the principle of mutual recognition of technical standards, included in the Single Act, will be applicable to every sector, including energy, from 1993 on.

Tax harmonization is one of the factors which most affects the competition within the Community. Proposals from the Commission published in 1987, tend to narrow the differences in the VAT rates and to unify the excise taxes. France is one of the member-states with the highest VAT rates, and it could not accept a substantial drop of its tax revenues. Since then, the Commission has softened its position, but the question remains open.

Taxation can be oriented to support the objectives of energy policy, either with a view to reducing the energy consumption or to restricting pollution for which it is responsible. France, after some delay, agreed to less taxation on unleaded oil and diesel because of its lower pollutant features. The Community regulation to this effect was introduced gradually between 1988 to 1993.

The expected economic gains of the unified market have been evaluated in Paolo Cecchini's book *1992: the Challenge*. They will only be attained if, in the coming years, the member-states adopt coherent political and technical decisions. These may be grouped around six main ideas.

The first one consists of improving energy efficiency through the co-ordination of investments, the development of infrastructure and price transparency. Concerning investments and infrastructures, the French contribution is and will be substantial. It seems less assured in the field of price transparency.

The second theme consists of matching resources to needs through energy savings and substitution. France could use more natural gas in the production of thermic electricity, following the decline of domestic sources of coal. But energy-saving measures are not necessarily popular. They involve the reduction or at least the stabilization of oil consumption. This could be obtained through the development of collective transport in cities and the production of low-energy consuming cars, encouraged by tax incentives.

The third theme deals with the protection of the environment. The report on the environment presented at the request of the Finance Committee in the National Assembly in April 1990 shows that French public opinion is now aware of the importance of environmental problems.

The promotion of technical innovation is the means to satisfy an increasing demand, by limiting outside dependency and by reducing pollution and this is the fourth theme. The field for desirable innovations is vast. France contributed actively to the THERMIE programme adopted by the Community Energy Council in September 1989.

A fifth theme deals with economic and social cohesion. Its objective is the reduction of inequalities between regions. Such a policy on a Community basis corresponds to the policy undertaken by France at the national level. Its application to energy could be beneficial.

The last theme is the one of international relations. The Community is the prime importer of energy in the world and it must contribute to the harmony of international relations in this field. Three points are to be mentioned. One is the result of French membership of the IEA in 1992, the role of which will remain important in regard to the cohesion between its members and to the co-operation with energy producing countries. The second point is that of the relations with Eastern European countries which are much in need of aid. On the one hand, they are exposed to an increase in the price of hydrocarbon imported from the former USSR and on the other hand are subject to a level of pollution unknown in the Community. The third point deals with the co-operation with Third World countries for energy planning. One part of the credits provided by the Lomé Agreements associating the 68 countries from Africa, Caribbean and from the Pacific (ACP) with the Community, could be allocated to the exploitation of local energy resources.

In 1991 France joined the United States, the United Kingdom and several Arab countries in a coalition against Iraq which had invaded Kuwait and was therefore in a position to threaten the bulk of the Middle East oil reserves. The Gulf War led to a military and political victory by the United States under the aegis of the United Nations and demonstrated the limits of the influence and action of the European Community in the area.

Meanwhile, France pursued its action in the field of enriched uranium and proved its capacity to start selecting fissile material through the use of lasers. The merger of CEA industries and Thomson decided at the end of 1991 is expected to stimulate nuclear energy research.

Conclusion

All energy policies aim at ensuring the adjustment of resources to needs. This adjustment is world-wide in scope and has three characteristics: it is related to geology by the location of resources; to the environment through the behaviour of populations confronting pollution; and to the calculus of geopolitics informed by the exploitation of important energy resources.

Every energy policy entails uncertainties concerning prices — this is the case for oil, the main energy; risks for health — nuclear radiations; and for the protection of nature and of the climate — emissions from the use of coal in thermic plants.

The increase in needs for comfort and for transport acts in the direction of an increase in oil consumption. The oil crisis, for a brief period of time, has put a brake on its development. Has France, which has no hydrocarbon reserves nor a powerful oil group at its disposal, made the right choice by fully playing the nuclear card? In the perspective of the exhaustion of oil reserves in 40 years, barring a major discovery, the French choice could only favour coal or nuclear power, the two long-run and large-quantity resources. Nuclear energy has the advantage for France of ready sources of supply for the medium term. It also provides access to advanced technology, and underwrites France's military and geopolitical ambitions.

The chosen strategy is a defensive strategy in the sense that it aims to reduce energy dependence. Other states have chosen an offensive strategy, trusting the market's mechanisms to compensate for the expensive dependence on fossil fuel imports by increased exports of manufactured products. Such is the case for Japan, which has not, however, neglected the nuclear card. The French choice has its justifications, though it has been pushed too far, as shown by the exaggerated production of electricity of nuclear origin. It carries risks, in the possibility of an important accident in one of the plants, and there are only two precautions against such a risk. The first one is in the reinforcement of security measures in nuclear plants, whether they are in or out of use; the second is in the solidarity, as far as energy is concerned, between states of the Community in a unified internal market. A debate at the National Assembly on French energy policy, in December 1989, gave rise to a widespread agreement on the parliamentary control of nuclear security and on the promotion of a European energy policy.

References

Paolo Cecchini (1988), *Studies on the Economics of Integration: The Cost of non Europe*, Commission of the European Communities.

Energy Policy Vol. 13 no. 1 January, February 1990, John Surrey, The Single Market and European Community Energy Issues.

International Energy Agency, Paris, Annual Reviews.

The Royal Institute of International Affairs, (1989), *A Single European Market in Energy*, London.

Chapter 5

Transport policy

Jean A. Belotti

Because the transport industry links producers and consumers, it plays an essential part in the economic activity of a country. As far as the European Community is concerned, transport represents more than 7 per cent of the community's GNP. This is why, as early as the Treaty of Rome, transport was considered a primordial common policy to be implemented.

This policy is subject to the 1986 Single European Act. This document materializes the political intent expressed by heads of state and government to better relationships between member-states to finally attain a European union. In such a way transport shall contribute to the creation of a broad market which would be beneficial not only to the producers and consumers but also to the communities, to the states and, finally, to the entire European Community.

Several conditions must be fulfilled before this vast European market can exist:

* companies must adapt to new market conditions;
* states must take measures to attain harmonization in the technical, social, fiscal, training and standards domains, for example. Such action implies a change from national policies to a common policy which will come into being once the various regulations, forged by history, and all the national idiosyncrasies are either eliminated or adapted; and
* the institutions of the European Community will have to assume fully their extremely complex mission.

It is intended that the transformation of the various national markets into a large European market shall be accomplished by creating sound competition between all concerned. As for transport, this means that all barriers to the free exercise of transport services must be eliminated gradually.

Treating transport policy in a few pages is a challenge, unless it solely entails highlighting certain particular characteristics and interrelating them to obtain a more comprehensive view of the subject and this is our purpose here. We shall briefly present the areas concerned and discuss a few of the conditions required to ensure the success of the European project.

Road transport

In France, road transport of goods is a dynamic branch of industry whose main characteristic is the diversity of its constituents, ranging from the self-employed transporter to industrial transport groups. Also, more and more companies are branching out their activities, so that the notion of a main activity has become obsolete for grasping the economic reality of these very versatile companies.

As far as European traffic is concerned, until 1992 there was a quota on most road transport operations between the EC states, the vehicles having to circulate under bilateral or community transport authorizations. As of 1992, the quota system is replaced by a market access system based on quality criteria; however, the phase of granting and withdrawing community authorizations can only be terminated once the following conditions are fulfilled:

- standardization of vehicle weight and size specifications and creation of community regulations to replace the present directives which allow individual countries to apply their national rules;
- specific regulations concerning driving hours and rest periods; and
- harmonization within the European Community of a specific fiscal system for road transports taking into account the overall expenses borne by transporters. The particular case of France where insurance-related taxes are non-deductible must be considered; for example, the French road tax disc (vignette), the lorry axle tax and the tax on fuel (including full deduction of the VAT).

The EEC has already processed a great many files which have been approved by the qualified majority. For example, cabotage has been authorized under a quota.

Beyond the temporary quota agreement, it is necessary to bear in mind that cabotage will lead to the multiplication of agencies and subsidiaries of EC companies and even to the buying up of existing companies in the countries where they wish to expand. The process is already started. It answers the essential requirement for efficiency and profitability of the logistic system to be installed. Then will arise the question of nationality. For example: a company installed in France, whose majority of capital belongs to a Swiss holding, supplying Italy using German lorries and Turkish drivers.

As far as inspection procedures are concerned, many proposals have been made by the French Board of Transport (Conseil National des Transports — CNT) to solve the problems involving the performance of heavy goods vehicles. These proposals concern safety, drivers' living and working conditions, and equality in the face of competition. This means that inspection must be carried out without discriminating between the self-employed, small and medium, and large transport companies, as well as between national driver teams and teams from other countries.

Previous to the Single European Market, European traffic regulations were still in an embryonic stage because of the multiplicity of the problems to be solved. The Commission, of course, has already proposed certain measures but this approach does not yet have the necessary coherence for the development of a common policy. The evaluation of the investments, choices to be made, financing means, are essential points which will be discussed further on.

As concerns competition — the key market condition — the entire trade is well aware of the fact that excessive competition generating speed excess, overload and poor working conditions for drivers would only lead to a waste of means and would jeopardize company existence.

Railway transport

In France, the recent agreement between the French National Railway Company (SNCF) and the government has set forth the overall strategic orientations of its programme and mentions the intention of the authorities to contribute to its development. The long-standing problem of debt has also been satisfactorily solved and, after considerable efforts to improve productivity and thanks to the development of the high-speed train (TGV), the SNCF has broken even and is now ready to implement its development plan.

In the agreement, large investments (totalling 100 thousand million Francs over 5 years) have been approved. Parts of this investment are to be made by the government, the public communities and the regions as well as being self-financing. The remainder shall be provided by a loan. This loan, although it will increase the company's debt, will no longer serve to compensate a deficit but to finance investments which will generate profits.

The SNCF, therefore, is ready to expand beyond the frontiers of France, according to a general development plan which retraces all possible railway connections for the next 20 years.

As far as goods transport is concerned, the first aim is to offer the customer more and more 'full door-to-door service' (transport, paperwork, insurance, storage), and this by the combined use of rail, road and even air transport.

The overall purpose is to integrate transport and company logistics.

This complementarity of transport modes shall also lead to an effort in standardization (multifunction platforms, containers, swap bodies, TOFCs, low-loader wagons, etc.). This type of co-operation is already effective (standardization, compatibility of traffic systems, Europe wagon pool, Eurofima, Interfrigo, Intercontainer, etc.). However, the governmental and administrative constraints which delay forwarding goods will have to be alleviated (for instance, customs, sanitary and technical inspections could be effected in a single operation, if possible, on departure).

As far as passenger transport is concerned, the TGV because of its high speed is a significant tool for the economical promotion. Moreover, it is highly adapted to Europe where the populations are dense and accustomed to travel by rail.

The TGV should enable France to benefit from its geographical location and technical advance to develop as the centre of high-speed railway junctions. The 14 new projects currently under study by the French Transport Board will require a financing of 250 thousand million Francs. Two of these projects are already in process, these being the Trans-Channel TVG via the tunnel to Great-Britain, and the Paris—Brussels—Cologne—Amsterdam line towards BENELUX and Germany. The future Paris—South-East, —Atlantic and —North junctions and subsequently the Eastern TGV are already preparing the opening to Europe. As far as the rough lines of the International Union of Railways (UIC) European high-speed network development plan are concerned, they will be completed in function of the development in Eastern Europe.

The fact remains, that due to the competition with other modes of transport, railways will have to overcome certain problems because of the rigidity of railway systems, of certain constraints to which they are still subjected and of their handicaps as far as social security contribution and infrastructure costs are concerned. It is also necessary that the cost borne by the various companies be comparable, in order to accelerate harmonization on a national basis (retirement, social security, etc.), not only within each mode of transport but on an intermodal basis.

As far as the EEC is concerned, railways have always been considered as a basic factor in the future common transport policy.

One of the main targets is to increase efficiency of railway services and make them more attractive by adapting them to the new market conditions, rather than protecting them by tightening the restrictions to which the other transport modes are subject.

Another concern of the EC institutions is to render the relations between member states and their railway companies more transparent in order to better pin-point their possible economic incidence and repercussions on the overall transport industry. Because of the poor results obtained, this target was modified in favour of that of self-management and financial equilibrium after financial rehabilitation.

Although the 1984 proposals and their approval in 1986 by the French cabinet have still not yet been voted, the Commission goes on applying their principles. It is true that today's significant development of high-speed trains in Europe depends more on the political intentions of the member states than on that of the Community.

Sea transport

The French fleet ranks 12th in the world, on an international scene of persistent overcapacity and insufficient freight rates. With four sea fronts — the North Sea, the Channel, the Atlantic and the Mediterranean-France is in a position to satisfy the maximum oceanic expansion capacity which Europe will require. This means that French ports, in the Community's service, should become economic poles of attraction.

As far as the market is concerned, after 10 years of an over-abundant offer, 1988 was a year of marked recovery, thanks to an exceptional increase in new and second-hand ships and a significant increase in freight rates for bulk transport. On the other hand, the French ship-owners and managers central commission (CCAF) is not sure that this recovery will last, considering the rate of growth of the Western world, the renewal of inflation and perturbations on the foreign exchange market, the very heavy social security contribution which penalizes the French fleet in comparison to their main European competitors some of which are foreign companies established in one of the EC states.

Other apprehensions concern the world-wide dimension acquired by certain companies. With a considerable capacity, they are capable, by a simple transfer of their potential to quit a market which shows signs of weakness and to position themselves on another where better opportunities are available, thus devitalizing a situation in record time.

The phenomenon of market permeability is already well known for bulk, but also reaches the area of regular lines and even gains new amplitude because today large companies also operate on the land portion transporting from one end to the other. In fact, shipowners and managers can no longer concentrate their activities on ships and sea transport alone, they must increasingly offer their customers full transport services, including short or long nautical portions. Therefore, because containers are preponderant, long-haul carriage of all types of goods is today inter-modal. This will result in certain in-depth changes. For example, the regrouping of means, not only on the sea but on land, to answer constraints of area and size and to face the considerable technological investment required to optimize container management.

Finally, it is a fact that the scope of economy is gradually becoming world-wide and sea transport companies are definitely assuming an international aspect, whatever the nature of the goods they carry or the services they offer. Furthermore, there is a marked tendency for restructuring and concentration: certain shipowners and managers are structuring their companies financially; certain freight-forwarders are gaining control of ocean lines; and sea transport companies are continuing to diversify their action. Several of these operations include international regrouping.

As far as Europe is concerned, the Commission has been implementing measures of assistance to fleets of the EC states to ward off competition coming from outside countries. It is giving its approval to study financial and fiscal measures, cabotage, shipments of food aid and group exemption for consortiums, as well as the transfer of ships from one country to another.

The EC Commission in Brussels favours the strict application of regulations, applying the rules of competition to sea transport. Therefore, when considering the problem of Euro-African relations, it would appear that commercial interests were not given enough consideration. At this point shipowners involved in this traffic, with the support of the administration of most EC states, requested that specificity of traffic be taken into account. Likewise, as the entire nautical world recognises the need for consortiums as an essential tool to rationalize traffic, the commission considers that this type of regrouping restrains competition a priori and wishes to submit all consortiums to an individual exemption procedure which is long and costly. Within the European Shipowners and Managers Commission (CAACE) this attitude has almost been unanimously adopted. However, the Union of Greek shipowners were not in agreement with the other EC states.

All these incidents set aside, therefore, the fact remains that it is up to Europe to define a common nautical policy, the largest fleet in the Community having in fact totally different economic interests than those of the other EC states. However, the integration of Southern Europe has given Europe renewed energy and high prospects for its transport activities, and also, transport plays a structuring part, i.e. helping to develop a tangible Mediterranean contribution to the European Community, more balanced and therefore more powerful on a world scale.

The presence of Europe in the domain of sea transport remains essential to international trade and economic exchange. An important harmonizing effort remains to be accomplished, however, notably as far as fiscal questions — raising capital and employment of labour from countries outside the community — are concerned.

Inland waterway transport

The future of inland waterways lies in the answer to the following question: must a certain number of missing links in the high-tonnage network be developed (the Seine-North, the Seine-East and the Saone-Rhine links)? These were already listed in the 1984 waterway development plan but the answer is not yet clear. In view of the huge investments this project would entail, it appears that the rate of profitability would be less than that of other programmes, the TGV, for instance.

The French Government will make a decision after examining recommendations regarding the development of large infrastructures, their financing possibilities and the cost of the maintenance and renovation of the existing network.

Therefore 3 types of consequences must be considered:

1. Consequences on the general economic environment — as all other areas of national economy, the waterways will also bear the consequences of the social, commercial and financial broadening related to the opening of the Single Market. Inland waterway transport may encounter competition problems if the harmonization does not take their own particular requirements into consideration: entirely tax-free fuel, etc.
2. Consequences on transport — the problem of European waterway transport is overcapacity. How can there be fair competition with its main competitor, railway transport?
3. Internal consequences on waterways — the problem of the 'each in turn' system is incompatible with a common policy, because it eliminates the user's freedom to choose, and allows marginal companies to survive, companies that no longer answer demands, not only from the point of view of operation but also that of equipment available. (The 'each in turn system' consists of distributing traffic between vessels which are registered at the chartering exchange bureau in the chronological order of their availability after unloading. It only covers transport subject to trip contracts and does not affect tonnage type transport.) There is also the question of whether the Treaty of Rome should or should not be pre-eminent over the Mannheim Acts.

As early as 1989, on a European level, the Commission adopted a 'rehabilitation' programme for the inland water transport system, mainly aimed at the Rhine fleet where overcapacity was rampant. Thanks to its advantages (low economic cost, river ports which are the most natural multimodal platforms, creation of a European network), waterway transport is called to play a part in the transport chain providing that it becomes more aggressive commercially and is able to integrate modern logistics.

Air transport

The organization of the world air transport market, contrary to the desire for multilateralism expressed at the 1944 Chicago Conference, has developed on a basis of bilateral relations. Therefore the traffic rights, which are negotiated by the governments and applied by the airway companies have been exchanged bilaterally.

This profession has always been surrounded by a high number of regulations from various organizations, but after the American experiment of eliminating regulations, Europe is following in the three following phases:

- 1988 — introduction of a more flexible bilateral system between the member-states;
- 1990 — definition of a common policy which would result in a total EC market integration; and
- 1993 — denationalization of the national EC member-states companies, the European Commission then being solely competent to negotiate with non-EC countries.

In 1987, the 'Paquet' Act of the French Transport Board was signed. It supplies the legal basis for a common air transport policy, appointing the European Commission competent for the rules of competition according to the Treaty of Rome, inside and outside the EC.

Aside from the problems existing in various areas (legislative, social, cultural, administrative etc.) there are also numerous specifically aeronautic problems:

- adaptation of the bilateral air traffic agreements of the member-states with countries outside the EC;
- co-ordination of the aeronautic policies of the member-states in relation to countries outside the EC;
- choice of the scope: the 12 EC states or the 22 ECAC (European Civil Aviation Conference) states;
- reciprocity of traffic rights; and
- appointment of the company by agreement with a country outside the EC; etc.

Therefore the task of standardization undertaken is gigantic. In very complex fields, choices must be made to preserve a harmonious EC development without cutting off the rest of the world. Many European long-distance air transport companies depend in large part on international traffic.

One thing is sure. Only a slow and painstaking process will enable concentrations to develop (temporarily authorized) and lead to the preparation of group regulations which, step by step, should replace national regulations. There will be great upheavals: transformation of existing agreements and restructuring of relations between partners and competitors, implying a radical change in deeply-rooted habits and attitudes. As far as the expected results are concerned, they will also depend on decisions made regarding the creation and the renovation of airports, air traffic control, personnel training (crews, air traffic controllers, technical personnel, etc.).

Infrastructures

Certain concerns, for instance those pertaining to infrastructures, are common to all types of transport.

The share of infrastructure investments in the European countries' GNP has steadily decreased during the past 15 years (1.5 per cent to 0.9 per cent) whereas traffic has increased more than 50 per cent and this is a very considerable discrepancy. Moreover, the technical revolution which affects almost all forms of transport to varying degrees is issuing desperate and urgent signals for the improvement of existing structures and the development of entirely new infrastructures and it is now time to raise the delicate question of criteria for evaluating the nature and the magnitude of these investments. The possibility of modal overcapacity due to competition, the need for economic and financial coherence at the macro and sector levels and financial constraints inherent to each mode, require that the evaluation and programming of projects or infrastructure networks be subject to great stringency. But in the face of such complex questions, methods are far from being harmonized.

The evaluation of overall infrastructure requirements reaches huge sums: for the SNCF alone, almost a billion Francs for the next 15 years. Therefore, public communities and managing companies probably will not have sufficient means to finance these requirements. Neither shall the French Government be able to assume such a burden without jeopardizing the balance of the budget and this results in the necessity to resort to the financial market which implies a profitability rate capable of attracting potential investors.

The following essential points are also under study:

- harmonization of sharing the burden of infrastructure construction and maintenance between public communities and transport companies; and
- financing the cost of environmental protection which in many cases is heavier than the construction of the infrastructure itself.

These are points which lead to the question of arbitration:

- between national and regional development and the financial profitability for operators in a system which includes national and regional, public and private, as well as European partners;
- between competitive transport modes; and
- between projects depending on priorities selected.

In fact, the problem of evaluating transport-related policies resides in the fact that the institutional frame of analysis appears to be too narrow as it is not possible to dissociate national and regional, European and even world targets. In France a study group has been created (EUREQ)

in which several administrations participate to determine the medium-
and long-term requirements of infrastructures in Europe. The
Community itself has appointed a group of experts to analyse the question of infrastructures and environment and to set up an overall coherent
community policy regarding transport infrastructures.

All of the above goes to show that it is urgent that the notion of a
transport system be reinstated, and a consensus is emerging in the various
European countries. The French National Transport Orientation Law
(LOTI) of December 1982 already brought about an overall transport
approach and recommended the creation of development plans and
certain orientations for the evaluation of infrastructures. This notion of
'transport system' emphasizes the importance of the interlinking of
networks, the balance between modes and the interdependence of
participants.

If an overall and coherent apprehension of transport systems is
desirable today, the matter of pricing is to be considered in a new light
and must take into account the following points:

- coverage of costs related to environmental protection;
- adjustments between profitable and non-profitable links within a
  network, in particular when a border is crossed;
- the cost of network accessibility and the articulation between the
  various networks (urban and interurban, high-speed networks, the air
  traffic and highways, tunnels and regional and international accesses);
  and
- the diversity of tariff structures which in a large Single Market makes
  more complex, if not impossible, the presently applied price policies.

For its interventions the EC refers to an infrastructure which is to the
advantage of the Community, and arrived at this with the assistance of
quality criteria. However, multiple possible combinations must be
considered before thinking in terms of a European network. This
corresponds, in fact, to a finer description of the share of European traffic
concerned and the adjustments which could intervene between links of a
same line with very poorly matched cost and traffic characteristics.

Also, the present trend is to be considered because of its effect on the
transport area. This is due to the development of logistic chains and the
part played by transport as a link in the chain; and manufacturing
companies' new strategies based on global raw material and goods flow
management, the development of information and communication
technologies.

Conclusion

The evolution of the nature of trade, the increasing complexity of manufacturing processes and the present world-wide scope of economy will bring about very significant changes in the transport field during the next 15 to 20 years. Segmentation of activities (modal segmentation, segmentation by professions) as practised until now, is doomed to disappear to give way to a new operator concept, multifunctional, multimodal and on an international scale. The regulation modes will have to be renovated to enable the public authorities to concentrate their efforts on those aspects for which they are really responsible, leaving the partners free to establish their own commercial contracts. With, at the start, a great variety of situations from one state to another, along with a confrontation of space structured by different regulations, the transition will be made to a more homogeneous and more competitive European space. The French Ministers of Transport have clearly expressed their intentions to limit environmental threats and to promote 'clean' means of transport.

The imperative need of harmonization should lead to the following:

- safeguarding of the interests of the EC transport companies in the face of outside competitors; and
- distribution of traffic between the various modes of transport to best serve the interests of the customers and the communities.

In this context, companies must ensure their own durability. To this end, a strong trend toward co-operation, collaboration contracts, coordination agreements and participation is pervading all modes of transport. This trend shows a will to rationalize and optimize the means implemented, and this seems to portend that competition is no longer a prime factor.

In view of the above, companies are raising a question and voicing concern. Their basic question is to ascertain if harmonization and liberation can live together, while their concern is to witness, allegedly on behalf of sound competition, a technocratic side-slip which would tend to centralize the Community and would superimpose its effects on the national framework.

As far as Europe is concerned, the will to attain harmonized competition conditions is without any doubt one of the Commission's main concerns, because it will constitute a frame, in which market forces can be active, for the best distribution of traffic between different modes of transport and for the elimination of all existing discriminations and restrictions.

Of course, states and regions will still have essential parts to play, but the results obtained will depend on the power delegated to the present institutions: the Council of Ministers, the Commission and the Parliament, and the evolution will begin to take shape like a federal structure in which, for example, the Brussels Commission could be replaced by a European Executive Council responsible unto the European Parliament, such as Claude Henry de Rouvroy, Count of Saint-Simon (1760—1825) had already suggested some time ago. In his words: 'Europe would have the best possible organization, if all the nations it includes recognize the supremacy of a general parliament, above all national governments, and having the power to judge all their controversies'.

References

Thousands of articles have been devoted to transport. The reader may consult the following organizations in France:

1. Conseil National des Transports (CNT — French Board of Transport)
2. Direction des Transports Terrestres (DTT — direction of terrestrial transports)
3. Institut National de recherche sur les transports et leur sécurité (INRETS — French research centre on transports and related security questions)
4. Institut du Transport Aerien (ITA — air transport institute)
5. Laboratoires d'Economie des transports (LET — transport economy research centre)
6. Observatoire des Transports (OEST — transport observatory)
7. TRANSPORTS Magazine

Chapter 6

Costs and benefits of the Common Agricultural Policy for France

Catherine Pivot

Since the beginning of the European Economic Community, agriculture has been considered as an unavoidable necessity and a symbol of European integration. France, for its part has always insisted upon the importance of a common policy in this field and for a long time its farmers have hoped to solve their problems with the common agricultural market; their hopes have even been falsely represented or interpreted. Many have then naturally assumed that the Community, globally deficient in many products from the start, would absorb French products integrally. Moreover, the Common Agricultural Policy (CAP) should reduce French agricultural subsidies and, in consequence, relieve the French budget. Obviously, the French farmers expected much from the Common Market.

Traditionally, the analysis of costs and benefits of a policy tends to rest upon the whole of the practical methods of optimal choice in the matter of policy obeying the criteria of the net maximum social profitability. More precisely, the study of benefits aims to locate all the rewards brought by decisions taken in the name of a given policy to individuals, as well as the national collectivity. A macroeconomic approach is therefore favoured to the detriment of microeconomic particularities. Two major difficulties then remain: the evaluation of the advantages; and measuring their value in the frequent absence of market prices.

So, after nearly 30 years of existence, what about the results expected by France? How does one compare the results specifically attributable to the CAP upon French agriculture and those linked to the general economic evolution? As an attempt to answer such questions, it is necessary to examine first the principal result common to all member-states, namely the Europeanisation of agricultural problems and, secondly, the costs and benefits arising from the CAP specifically for France.

The CAP: or the Europeanization of macroeconomic problems

All the agricultural policies of market economy countries devote priority to the defence of their agricultural activity. However, they also tend to make this sector contribute to the fundamental economic balance (self-sufficiency in foodstuffs, balance of payments, stability of labour market, savings etc.) and in consequence, to the growth and the general development of economics.

These aims, generally of qualitative nature, are equally present in the CAP. In fact, the Treaty of Rome (1957) conferred five general targets to this policy:

- increase agricultural productivity;
- ensure a good standard of living for the farmers;
- stabilize markets;
- guarantee supplier's security; and
- ensure reasonable prices for consumers.

To achieve such targets, the CAP was constructed around three fundamental principles: unity of markets; community preference; and financial solidarity. Based on these, the community organization of the market and the policy of agricultural prices lie, definitively, on simple rules. These are: the abolition of quantitative obstacles towards inter-community trade; a uniform system of pricing (indicative price, intervention price and threshold price), and equal guarantees applying to all the producers in the Community; common front regarding Third World countries; and, finally, common management of markets and budget. Also, though no measures of the Treaty of Rome contemplate a regional policy explicitly, this aspect was underlying it because the reduction of the economic inequality between different regions, by the process of catching up by the less prosperous regions, was explicitly indicated in the prelude of the treaty so as to reinforce the economic unity of Europe.

Clearly, Europe has thus organized its policy around means aimed at the protection of an operation still socially important and controlled by specific rules of performance (the *homo-rusticus* opposes, in many aspects, the *homo-economicus*), when at the same time the United States was trying to reach the same goal by means of a different strategy, that is to say, the quick integration of agriculture into the heart of food processing. However if, since the beginning of the 1980s, perceptible alterations have been brought to the CAP so as to allow the pursuit of its functions, its aims have not evolved even when the political and economic context have done so profoundly. The Green Book of 1985 presented by the Commission also confirmed this, reasserting its will to maintain a large agricultural development analogous to that of the United States consisting, for example, of large areas but few farmers.[1]

A resources management that is often collectively irrational

ACCUMULATION OF SURPLUS

European agriculture is at present characterized by multiple surpluses leading people to question the wisdom of the desire to modernize farms rapidly. These surpluses are:

- production surplus. In the European area, the global growth of production has exceeded internal demand by nearly 1.4 per cent a year. This corresponds to a growth of self sufficiency of 97 per cent in 1974 to 126 per cent in 1989. The pursuit of these tendencies during the next decade would lead to a supplementary growth of 15 per cent of the self sufficiency's level, thus doubling the present surplus. Since few changes are to be expected on the side of demand, adjustments should be made on the side of supply, particularly by reduction of productivity; but nothing guarantees a slowing down of the flow of technical progress. The slower growth of productivity factors observed during the last decade seems due rather to a less efficient use of factors (disguised unemployment, milk quotas) than to a reduction of technical possibilities.[2] Only in the very long run could environmental constraints and price policies prevail.

- land surplus. The policy of the 'freezing of land', the abandoning of a lot of activities in mountain regions, the massive departure of farmers and the intensifying of systems of exploitation lead to the greatest abandonment of land. The use of new technology often results in a decreasing need for land, particularly in mountain areas and near the Mediterranean coastline which thus become marginal zones. A destruction of the social network of rural areas might well result since the spread of fallow land has negative effects upon other activities (for example, tourism). Thus, from now until the 2000s, between 15 and 20 million hectares of arable land will become fallow.

- labour surplus. Of 320 million people living in Europe, some 18 million live from farming; but only 9 to 10 million have agriculture as the main activity, the mechanization of most agricultural tasks have reduced the need for human labour. Since the beginning of the 1980s, however, employment of manpower has stabilized in most countries with the exception of France, Denmark and Ireland. According to the zones, this signifies either the development of pluriactivity (Germany, Spain, Portugal) or the maintenance of disguised unemployment (elderly or mountain farmers surviving thanks to subsidies). So from this point, the European farming population can be divided into three types of rural areas, these being: a centre with flourishing farms and more than 50 per cent of full-time farmers (Denmark, Benelux, parts of Germany and France); peripheral zones with farmers' majority just surviving (Southern Europe); and intermediary areas half way between the both (Ireland, North Germany).

DEGRADATION OF ENVIRONMENT

The decline in the use of arable land accompanied by a stronger degree of land intensification has resulted in a dangerous growth of the use of fertilisers per hectare. Between 1970 and 1989 this meant 70 per cent more chemical fertilisers, 15 per cent more phosphates and 20 per cent more potassium. This phenomenon is one of the main causes of environmental degradation. Northern Europe has increased its consumption of fertilisers the most and this can be interpreted as the result of industrial agriculture whereas Southern farms are still more traditional in their methods.

The rise of restrictions due to successive expansions of the Community

The inertia of basic principles and global targets of the CAP has led to the emergence of a multitude of regulations with the purpose of maintaining the daily functioning of this policy and the increasingly complex decision-making process in order to attempt the European integration. But, equally, the working of the CAP has been complicated by the successive widening of the European Community.

With the Great Britain addition (1973), the first market expansion brought about the end of political consensus because of the British tradition in favour of the maintenance of reference to the market rules with limited price support. On the other hand, the French and the Germans are more in favour of the indirect intervention system through pricing and a deep commitment of the Community in the agricultural field to guarantee higher revenue.

The joining of Spain and Portugal (1981) then Greece (1986) to the Community has led, as far as they are concerned, to an increase in the heterogeneousness of agricultural production's conditions and, in the attempt, the integration of two types of farming: those that are traditional and often not very productive with low revenues (situated essentially in Southern Europe); and the others modernized and very productive, ensuring on average high revenues (essentially in Northern Europe). However, upholding the financial solidarity principle, which has the result that the financial costs of the CAP are supported by the least agricultural members, has become difficult to sustain. 1988 was therefore marked by the intention of the members to finish with a policy which, in spite of all evidence, was financially dangerous — the increase in community farming expenses having exceeded 164 per cent between 1975 and 1987. The acceptance of an upper limit of expenditure had aimed at the rationalization of the CAP by introducing the co-responsibility principle of the farmers by means of taxation of production exceeding the maximum quota (if the threshold of production was exceeded, the prices guaranteed to farmers diminished). This measure was rounded off by the freezing of land. But such a decision runs the risk of having the return to a demand for specific national aid as a corollary.

The temptation to renationalize agricultural policy to the detriment of the CAP

The permanent existence of a policy with quasi-identical foundations since the beginning of the Agricultural Common Market contrasts strongly with the instability and rapid evolution of its environment. Moreover, it is made up of contradictions between four opposing concerns which shape the decisions. These are:

- a social concern which leads to keeping food prices as low as possible for the consumer;
- an economic concern of rationalization which requires a profit-making agricultural activity to render it competitive;
- an electoral concern which encourages the granting of important subsidies or guarantees to farmers; and
- a growing concern about the defence of the environment which tends to increase the control of the farm modernization process.

The decision-making institutions are thus places of CAP development where different rationalities clash, where uncertainty over the results plays a large role and where the rules of decisions are preponderant. This policy results, then, in a sequential process of development in the short term directed by conflicts of interest between politicians and professional pressure groups and in the long term affected by fundamental economic forces (rate of growth, market evolution, etc.). However in the European Community the most important farmers' organizations are in the majority general organizations and not sector-based organizations. The main area of intervention by these pressure groups is thus that of national institutions. In consequence, at the European level, any decisions become necessarily the result of a compromise between 12 governments which leaves a very narrow margin for manoeuvre to the Commission. From this, because of the establishment of growing community control over agriculture and the heterogeneity of the situations, the farming representatives are tempted again to obtain from their governments direct interventions in the place of more and more limited and selective community intervention. The temptation to renationalize agricultural policies is all the stronger as the new protectionism rests on a resolve of national promotion of agricultural exports.

During the establishment of the Agricultural Common Market, the farms' heterogeneity helped justify the choice of Community borders protection by means of a levy technique (variable duty collected daily at the border so as to compensate for the discrepancies between the internal and external supply prices). However, the growing surpluses are not in favour of the maintenance of such a system. In effect, the sale of agricultural products on the world market becomes continually more costly and the development of a commercial policy is from then on shaped by the future measures that the GATT is now implementing so as to limit the obstacles to borders which are under considerable American pressure. Moreover, 'green' Europe has still many gaps to fill in the implementation of a genuine internal market, because the abolition of the customs tariffs alone does not suffice. This is due to the innumerable new forms of protectionism the state members issue to hamper agricultural exchanges, for example: protection of product quality, hygiene standards, environmental protection, etc.

The CAP or a short-term strategy for France

The research of short-term national advantages due to the CAP

As early as 1945, France had opted for a policy of modernization of its agriculture. Its entry into the European Community facilitated this task by the reinforcement of the policy of support for prices and revenues. A rapid evolution of farms ensued which permitted favourable results on the plane of revenue and the quantities produced. Therefore, a strong progression in the size of farms (an enforced condition for reaching economies of scale) was achieved: 37 hectares on average in 1987, the second best performance though far behind Great Britain (with an average of 118 hectares). This progression had, as a corollary, a reduction of the active farming population and a heavy intensification of productive systems. Incomes were regularized but large farms — especially the grain producers — benefited most from the European support.

France thus became the first European agricultural nation with nearly 25 per cent of the whole community production. From then, the national production was based on four productions: grain, dairy produce, beef and wine. The preponderance of products for which community support was strongest should be noted, showing that the hierarchy of supported prices has had a major structuring effect on the choice of specialization by French farmers. The efficiency of the productive results, however, should hide neither the rise of farmers' debts nor their difficulty in mastering the costs of production. If the French unit costs have remained relatively low[3] because of the maintenance of an important labour factor of unremunerated family type, a 'scissor' effect resulting from the conjunction of a rapid rise of the intermediary consumptions purchased, and a slowing down, if not a real decrease, of the prices of delivered products, has resulted in a lesser progression of revenue in the last few years.

The production of growing quantities of agricultural products by France, even though domestic demand has stagnated, has been facilitated by the opening up of large solvent markets in Europe (320 million inhabitants), few of the member-states being self sufficient at the start of the Common Market. So France focused its efforts on exports to European markets and specialized in the exchange of important basic farm products. The French commercial balance has greatly benefited by this, grain alone bringing in, on average, more than 25 to 35 thousand million francs since 1980. The CAP has thus helped facilitate the flow of the French products and, as a consequence, the modernization and specialization of farms, a function indispensable to the progress of productivity. Also, community preference has played to the full in favouring the growth of inter-European exports by giving numerous products a solution to the surplus problem without France having to worry for a long time about the method of insertion of its agricultural production system into the dynamics of world economy.

The weakness of the long-term French strategy as a result of the necessary evolution of the CAP and the rise of European competition

For a long time, many farmers assumed that the securing of high prices was a guarantee for survival or a condition of modernization. So France had accepted high prices without fear because of its natural advantages and its important productive potential under German pressure. However, if at first French exports had automatically benefited from the lack of self sufficiency of many European markets, this is due more to the export of surpluses than to real specialization based on actual comparative advantages.[4] Also, when under the effect of a uniform price support policy, nearly all the member-states became self sufficient in terms of basic agricultural products, and the possibilities for intra-EC exports were reduced. Progressively, France has lost out on many markets because of the collective export of mass products and is only competitive in oleaginous products and wine, clashing more and more with the generalization of European self sufficiency. Certainly at present, the European outlet remains a privileged one for France because the principle of community preference does not seem truly endangered, in spite of internal and external pressures exerted on the CAP. On the other hand, this outlet might be reduced as a result of production rising faster than consumption inside the Community. But from now on, France is forced to find new outlets on Third World markets, even though it is difficult for it to reduce the prices because of the heterogeneity of French agriculture. Many farmers are close to the poverty line, making all lowering of price a delicate matter. Equally, the CAP has contributed to the illusion of European protection and to equality as regards price support. In fact, various products do not benefit from the same levels of support; and in the same way, despite the principles of price unity, the levels of agricultural prices have been different from one country to another due to divergences of monetary evolution. These distortions of competition have been unfavourable to France, particularly in the area of pork and poultry, because of great differences in technology and cost-structuring at the heart of the Community. The explanation of these distortions is also to be found in the structure of tariff protection common to all member-states,[5] particularly concerning intermediary consumption necessary to farms (fertilisers, tractors, animal fodder etc.). Thus, the Netherlands and the Federal Republic of Germany have benefited from an effective protection (that is to say the impact of the tariff structure upon the added value by branches and no longer only the impact of the effects alone upon the sale prices of the exchanged products). This protection has been higher in those countries than in France because of massive recourse to products imported from the Third World and lower duties.

Furthermore, the CAP has comforted France with the traditional and restrained vision of agriculture and as results, it has not known how or wanted to take into account all the facts of the food sector, thus ignoring the food industries. Because of this, industries organized themselves according to their own requirements (search for cheap supplies, narrowing of distribution to secure tighter control of the markets, setting up plants close to the consumers etc.). France no longer controls the main outlets of its own agricultural products and cannot hope to have a real influence on the common food market, the achievement of which should be accelerated by the implementation of the Single Market in 1993 (especially if monetary union is set up).

Moreover, the general reorientation of the Community rationale, from now on no longer based upon harmonization of national regulations but on competition, threatens to give preference to the least restricting regulations, thus opening the way to deregulation. Thus, with the Community rationale becoming, above all, a rationale of competition, French weaknesses, both in the area of agriculture and foodstuffs, might well be accentuated and compensated for by a strong internal restructuring. The creation of the Single Market should equally bring back into question the very process of decision which presides over the CAP and should be unfavourable to the French style concept of 'decentralisation' and promote a German style 'decentralisation' approach, leaving more power to local authorities. Despite its policy of decentralisation, France would then be at a disadvantage, because of a traditional policy scarcely favourable to such a rationale; and because of a risk of increased marginalization of some French regions, disadvantaged both by natural environment and financial resources, with the implementation of the freeze on land and regional production quotas increasing the dangers of dualism at the heart of French agriculture.

As a whole, it appears that the CAP procured many advantages of security for France at the start (price support, outlets, currency sources etc.); but at present, the global cost of creating agricultural Europe is becoming higher and higher because of false specialization linked a long time to concentrated efforts around production of the most supported productions and ignorance of the true restrictions of international competition. The evolutionary perspectives of the CAP will thus accentuate the numerous difficulties of French farmers. In the long run, all solutions rely on successfully opening up world agro-alimentary markets, and this cannot be achieved without a genuine Common agro-alimentary policy.

Notes

1. Philippe, B. (1986) *P.A.C. et marchés mondiaux*, Paris, Economica, p. 239.
2. Henrichsmeyer, W. and Ostermeyer-Schloerder, A. (1989) Croissance de la productivité et adaptation dans l'agriculture de la CEE, *Economie rurale*, no. 189, p. 18.
3. Commission des Communautés Européennes (1988), The use of agricultural forestry resources in Europe, *Fast Programm*, Vol. 6, p. 14.
4. Bultault, J.P., Charles, R., Hassan, D. and Reigner, E. (1988), L'efficacité comparée des agricultures européennes, *Bulletin INRA-Recherches Sociales*, Juillet.
5. Courgeon, J. and Mahe, L.P. (1986) Distorsions de concurrence dues à la PAC, *Colloque SFER*, Paris, Printemps.

Chapter 7

European environmental policies and environmental protection in France

Corinne Larrue and Rémy Prud'homme

Introduction

Over the past 15 years, the EEC has been developing an environmental protection policy, which has become increasingly comprehensive and effective. The first directives in this area were issued in 1972; now more than 130 directives have been adopted by the Council of Ministers of member-states, and must be applied by these states.

These directives, which are mandatory, influence *de facto* as well as *de jure* environmental policies conducted in each of the EC countries. Such policies were developed in the early 1970s in most European countries. Institutions were then created, laws were passed and strategies were elaborated in an effort to protect the environment. In France, a Ministry of the Environment was created in 1971. Major laws were enacted in the years that followed in the areas of air pollution, waste disposal, natural environment protection (other bills, in the area of water protection, had actually been passed in the 1960s) and a new administration was developed. Policy objectives were defined and specific instruments were utilized.

The European environmental policy was thus grafted on a tree already planted. The question that arises is therefore: how did EEC directives influence pre-existing national policies? Did they strengthen, or did they undermine strategies and instruments already in place? Did they accelerate or hinder the development of national policies?

To properly answer these questions, it would ideally be necessary to compare the policies effectively implemented in France with the policies that would have been implemented in the absence of a European policy. The second term of the comparison is of course unknown. The analysis of the impacts of the EEC policy is therefore necessarily somewhat arbitrary and speculative. It is not entirely impossible, however.

Before attempting such an analysis, it is useful briefly to describe the main features of the European environmental policy. We shall afterwards examine cases in which the European policy did strengthen or accelerate French environmental protection policies, and then cases in which the European policy had a negative impact, or no impact, upon French policies. A concluding section will attempt to provide a global appraisal of the impact of EEC policies upon environmental quality in France.

EC environmental policy

The environment is not mentioned in the Treaty of Rome as an area of EC competence, yet as early as 1972 the Heads of State and government recognized the importance of a common policy in this area; and in 1973 the Council of Ministers approved the first action programme in the area of the environment.

Until 1986, the European Community based its action in the environment on articles 100 and 235 of the Treaty of Rome. These articles made it possible to issue directives aiming at harmonizing laws and rules in member countries, where the use of different national norms or standards is a potential obstacle to the free circulation of goods. Similarly, the imposition of different national taxes or constraints upon enterprises can lead to trade distortions, and harmonizing environmental constraints between European countries is a necessary step to the construction of a European market. European environmental policy therefore came about as a by-product of European trade policy.

In 1986, with the Single European Act, the environment became explicitly an EC competence. The Single European Act devotes an entire chapter to the subject. The objectives of the Community environmental policy (defined in the new article 130R of the Treaty of Rome) are as follows: to preserve, protect, and improve the quality of the environment; to contribute to the protection of human health; and to ensure a prudent and rational use of natural resources.

The European policy is founded on several basic principles:

- prevention of pollution at source principle: Community policy must be preventive rather than curative;
- polluters pay principle: costs associated with the prevention and elimination of environmental damages must be borne by polluters; and
- subsidiarity principle: in each area, decisions must be taken at the most appropriate level, that is the level at which decision and action will be most efficient.

In addition, environmental policies must be compatible with economic and social development. In certain cases, its implementation will require compromises or transition periods.

The main lines of European environmental policies are defined in 'action programmes'. The first three programmes, launched in 1973, 1977 and 1983, were mostly focused on pressing issues. They aimed at defining common ambient standards relative to acceptable pollution levels in air and water, or common emission standards for motor vehicles. The fourth programme, now in progress, aims at strengthening the set of measures taken so far. It tries to issue stricter environmental norms and standards. It tries to develop anti-pollution investments, either directly through the European Investment Bank, or indirectly through the structural agricultural and regional Funds. It tries also to better integrate environmental policies and other European policies, in particular by means of environmental impact statements.

The directives set up by the Commission cover many environmental areas. In order of importance, one can mention air, inland waters, sea, protection of nature, wastes, chemicals and noise. For each of these areas, the commission issued between 10 and 30 directives or decisions.

These directives determine either ambient standards (maximum concentration of specific pollutants) for air or inland or sea waters; product standards for specific products (motor vehicles, fuels, etc.); or procedures designed to take into account the environment in decision-making processes (environmental impacts statements, authorizations for polluting activities, etc.). In the area of natural protection, directives specify species to be protected, and how they should be protected.

Furthermore, either through directives or through specific programmes, the commission seeks to improve the information available on the state of the environment and its evolution. The EEC seeks to disseminate this information between countries as well as among the public at large.

Finally, the action of the Community is assisted by decisions taken by the Court of Justice in Luxemburg, When member countries fail to apply an EEC Directive, or do so inadequately, the Commission can take to the Court the faulty state or states.

The European environmental policy relies primarily upon rules and regulations. Less than 1 per cent of the EC budget is devoted to environmental protection. It is true that the European Investment Bank grants loans for waste or water treatment plants, or for the development of clean technologies and that, in addition, in recent years, the structural Funds are allowed to finance investments that can contribute to environmental protection. But the financial amounts involved remain small. The impact of the European environmental policy upon the French environmental policy will therefore be felt more in terms of regulations than in terms of expenditures.

Beneficial impacts of European environmental policy

There is no doubt that the policies briefly discussed above have had, in a number of areas, a desirable impact upon the French environmental policy. It is important to note that there was no contradiction between the two policies, as the European policy is not basically different from the French one. The 'prevention at source' and the 'polluters pay' principles are also part of the French approach. This similarity complicates the analysis of the impact of the European policy and probably also limits the scope of this impact.

Despite this, however, in several areas decisions taken at the European level happened to be stricter than similar decisions taken at the French levels. A number of European directives imposed norms that were more restrictive (for potential polluters, or for consumers of natural resources) than the norms imposed by French laws. It follows that stricter norms were adopted, and must have led to an improvement in the quality of the environment, relative to what would have happened in the absence of these Directives.

It is in the area of air pollution that French policies were most influenced by EC policies. The EEC set ambient air standards for sulphur dioxide and dust (Directive no. 80/779), for lead (Directive no. 85/884), and for nitrogen oxides (Directive no. 85/203). The setting of such maximum acceptable concentrations of pollutants was in contrast with the approach developed by the French administration up to this point. Until the early 1980s, French authorities considered that ambient air standards of this type amounted to the granting of 'rights to pollute' in the zones where air quality was better than these norms. On this basis, the Ministry of the Environment refused to set such norms and relied upon emission standards, and direct negotiations with would-be polluters, to decrease pollution levels wherever it was desirable and feasible.

The introduction of European norms had several beneficial impacts. First, it led to the development of air quality monitoring networks in French cities, or at least to a marked improvement of existing networks. In the case of lead, for instance, in 1980 only two or three stations monitored lead concentration in the air and its evolution. After the issuance of Directive no. 85/884, more than 25 stations were created to meet the EEC requirements. Similarly, the introduction of European ambient standards for SO^2 and dust led the French Ministry of the Environment to review the monitoring system for these pollutants and to take control of networks so far managed by independent organizations.

Second, and more importantly, the introduction of ambient air quality standards gave additional muscle to the French authorities in charge of air pollution abatement, particularly in the case of SO^2. French administrators were strengthened in their fight with polluters, particularly in zones where the standards were exceeded. The definition and imposition of a standard common to all member countries cuts the argument — often put forward by French industrialists — of unfair competition ('We can't do it if our competitors don't do it'). The standard being the same for everyone, no one appears discriminated against, and the conditions of international competition are not violated. In that sense, directives that contribute to the necessary harmonization of national legislations in order to achieve the common market happen to be quite effective.

Again in the area of air pollution, another clear example of the beneficial impact of the European policy on French policy is provided by the case of the directive on fossil fuel combustion stations. In 1983, the Commission proposed to the Council of Ministers a directive regulating the emissions of pollutants by large boilers (mostly power stations, and large industrial burners). This directive proposed standards stricter than those which were then in force in France. The French Ministry of the Environment took this opportunity to anticipate the decision of the EEC Council, and issued a ruling which incorporated the main constraints of the (not yet formally accepted) directive, and applied to the burners the legislation of 'classified installations'. As a result, Regional Industry and Research Agencies (Direction Régionales de l'Industrie et de la Recherche or DRIR), the administrative entities responsible for the implementation of air pollution abatement policies at the local and regional level, were much better equipped to impose stricter constraints, particularly for new industrial installations.

More generally, it can be said that the French administration in charge of the environment, at both national and local levels, tends more and more to anticipate European regulations in the definition and implementation of its own environmental policy. This is true for air, but also for water and for wastes. This means that a simple comparison of the chronology of European and French laws is a poor indicator of the impact of the former upon the latter. A French law issued in 1985 may well be explained by a European directive issued only in 1986; the preparation of the European directive may have started in 1984, and induced the French government and parliament to take in 1985 a decision that was considered inescapable.

The most spectacular case of reinforcement of the French environmental policy is probably the case of automobile pollution abatement policies. The introduction of the 'clean car', i.e. the imposition of severe emission standards for motor vehicles, and more precisely of catalytic converters (devices added to motor vehicles to treat exhaust gases) in 1989, is a good example of how French policies were made more severe by European policies.

In 1984, under pressure from the German government worried about the state of its forests, the Commission proposed to stiffen exhaust standards for automobiles. Until then, car emissions were being progressively reduced, at the speed made possible by technological progress, but in negotiations between European countries, there was an implicit agreement to avoid using catalytic converters, in contrast with the policy adopted in the USA and in Japan in the 1960s and the early 1970s. The Commission proposal therefore shattered the consensus established between member countries. On this point, France, Italy and the United Kingdom were opposed to Germany, the Netherlands and Denmark, who supported the proposal of the Commission.

In 1985, an agreement (called the Luxemburg compromise, and later incorporated in Directives nos 88/76 and 88/436) was reached. It made catalytic converters mandatory for big cars (with engines of more than two litres) while for small cars, member countries have not yet reached an agreement. As a result, since 1 July 1989, all new big cars (with an engine of more than two litres) sold on the French market must be fitted with a catalytic converter, an achievement which would never have taken place in the absence of a European directive. The impact of these stricter norms on environmental quality in France is still very modest. It will increase in the future, with the share of 'clean cars' in the stock of vehicles. Furthermore, since vehicles fitted with catalytic converters cannot use leaded fuels (such as ordinary gasoline or premium gasoline), lead free gasoline has had to be progressively introduced in France, in keeping with Directive no. 85/210. There is no doubt that the introduction of lead free gasoline in France would have been much slower had it not been for European environmental policies.

It is therefore fair to conclude that the European environmental policy has had an important impact on French air pollution abatement policies in general, and on automobile exhaust policies in particular. Air quality in France is somewhat better than it would have been in the absence of EEC policies, but air is not the only area impacted upon by European policies.

EEC directives in the area of water also had important consequences on the content of French policies. Here again, a key role was played by the imposition of ambient standards. The standards and norms introduced by directives on the quality of bathing water (Directive no. 76/160), on the quality of surface water for human consumption (Directive no. 75/440) or on the quality of fishing water (Directive no. 78/659), are used in France as reference data to prepare the quality objectives maps of the various French rivers. These maps are then utilized to define priority actions for water pollution abatement.

The case of the European directive on the quality of potable water (Directive no. 80/778) is probably the best example of the influence of EEC policies on French policies. This directive sets a 'guiding value' (25 mg/l) and a 'maximum value' for the nitrate content of water used for human consumption. Following the adoption of this directive, the French Ministry of Health undertook a survey of the quality (including the nitrate content) of water distributed in France. The survey revealed that more than 3 per cent of the population was receiving water with a nitrate content exceeding the maximum value prescribed by the EEC. This led the Ministry of Environment to develop an effective policy against water pollution by nitrates of agricultural origin. Without Directive no. 80/778, this policy would most probably have been delayed, because of marked opposition by farmers at that time.

In the area of nature protection, it can again be said that the two directives under preparation on the protection of natural habitats of wild flora and fauna will influence the entire French policy of nature protection.

It is interesting to emphasize, also, the role played by repressive actions taken by the Community. France has been one of the countries most often taken to court by the European Commission, although things have improved in recent years. This procedure tends to accelerate the implementation of Community directives by member countries, and implies therefore a greater influence upon member countries' policies.

Last, but not least, it can be said that European directives bring an essential support to the Ministry of the Environment, both *vis-a-vis* pressure groups affected by environmental policies and *vis-a-vis* the other ministries interested. When a European directive can be invoked, the action of the Environment Minister appears more legitimate to the Industry Minister, or to the Agriculture Minister, or to the Finance Minister. The policy of the Environment ministry, and its implementation, are thus strengthened.

Negative impacts of European environmental policy

The impacts of the European environmental policy are not always positive, however, and some of them are clearly negative. Negative impacts seem mostly associated with the 'compromises' that are characteristic of Community decision processes. European policies are the outcome of joint decisions, taken by 12 partners and such decisions necessarily involve negotiations and compromises between the differing positions of member countries. The final compromise does not always reflect the position taken by France. This does not facilitate the implementation of the decisions taken.

The case of the EEC directive on the sulphur content of diesel oil and domestic fuel (Directive no. 75/716) illustrates this point. The sulphur content of diesel oil and domestic fuel had been progressively reduced by the French government before the introduction of standards at the European level. When Directive no. 75/716 was enacted, the French administration followed suit and the sulphur content was reduced from 0.9 per cent in 1967 to 0.3 per cent in 1980. The French Ministry of the Environment wanted to reduce it further to 0.2 per cent and, although discussions were held at the European level in 1987, member countries could not reach an agreement, and the revised directive leaves member countries free to set this product standard between 0.2 per cent and 0.3 per cent. As a result, the French Ministry of Environment could not use the argument of a common norm to mandate the oil industry to produce diesel oil and domestic fuel with a sulphur content of 0.2 per cent.

This example illustrates the importance of decisions taken by the Community in national decision-making processes. When the compromise reached in Brussels is not in line with the positions taken by the French environment administration, the latter is weakened relative to its own domestic partners.

In addition, decisions taken on the basis of negotiations and compromises between member countries do not always lead to coherent or optimal policies in each of these countries. Thus, for instance, the decision to introduce in France non-leaded gasoline for vehicles equipped with catalytic converters did slow down the process of reducing the lead content of ordinary and premium gasoline. When Directive no. 83/351 imposed the availability of non-leaded gasoline, the French administration was negotiating with the oil industry a reduction of the lead content in gasoline from 0.40 to 0.15 grams per litre, and an agreement was about to be reached. Business interests took the pretext of the introduction of non-leaded gasoline to refuse the overall reduction, arguing that the simultaneous introduction of the two constraints was technically and economically impossible. Instead of having only gasoline with a 0.15 lead content, France ended up having a lot of gasoline with a 0.40 lead content plus some gasoline with a zero lead content, an outcome which, for the environment, was undoubtedly an inferior solution. A partial reduction for all gasoline would have been better than a total reduction for some gasoline. In the first case, air quality would have been improved immediately but in the second case, air quality improvement will be a function of the number of vehicles that use non-leaded gasoline, and that number will increase only slowly, as the total stock of vehicles is renewed.

Another possible negative impact of the European policy (associated with decision-making processes at the European level) can be found in the case of the Luxemburg compromise on the 'clean car'. This compromise has two features. First, it prescribes a specific technology (the catalytic converter); and second, it is restricted, at least for some years, to specific types of cars (cars with engines of more than 2 litres). It can be argued that these decisions are detrimental for (i) the international community; (ii) the French automobile industry; and (iii) the air quality in France.

The Luxemburg compromise can be considered undesirable for the international community at large because the prescribed technology is not necessarily the best one. Catalytic converters offered the most easily available technology, but not the only possible technology. Other technologies were conceivable, and were being studied in the automobile industry research laboratories: the technology of the 'low mix', aiming at reducing pollution at the level of the engine itself (as opposed to eliminating pollution already produced) can be cited as an example. It is possible, and even likely, that these technologies were more cost-efficient than the prescribed technology. They would probably have made it possible to reach the same environmental results at lower costs, which would have been beneficial for everybody. On the other hand, it is fair to say that this is only a possibility because these technologies were not yet fully operational and their costs were not well known. Of course, the research on the development of these technologies was abandoned so they will probably never be operational, and their costs will never be known. There remains the possibility that a technological opportunity was missed.

The Luxemburg compromise is more clearly detrimental to the French automobile industry. French firms were working on alternative technologies, and were not ready to produce catalytic converters meaning that most of them will be imported. In addition, catalytic converters cause greater increase (in relative terms) to the price of French and Italian cars than to German cars. The reason is that French and Italian cars are on average smaller and cheaper than German cars, and the cost of a catalytic converter is largely independent of the size and price of the car it is fitted to. If a catalytic converter costs 1,000 ECUs, it costs 10 per cent of a 10,000 ECU car, and 5 per cent of a 20,000 ECU car. The imposed technology should therefore impact, in terms of sales and profits, the French and Italian industries more than the German industry. This is, of course, the reason why the Luxemburg compromise applies only, at least in a first stage, to large cars.

But this is also precisely why this compromise is not good for air quality in French cities. The cars used in France (just as the cars produced in France) are mostly small cars, and they will continue to pollute.

What would have happened if the EEC, under the pressure of the German government — acting under the pressure of German 'Greens', and of German businessmen — had not intervened vigorously in the 'clean car' issue? One can imagine the following scenario: research and development in process would have been successful; less-polluting cars would have been produced at a smaller surcost, particularly for small and medium-sized cars; and this would have made it possible to adopt exhaust standards stricter than the standards which have been adopted. Everybody would have gained: city dwellers, who would breath a cleaner air; vehicles consumers, who would pay less; and automobile producers, who would have strengthened rather than weakened their competitive position.

Of course, no one can tell for sure that this scenario would have prevailed. French research and development could have failed. Roqueplo (1988) believes that French auto makers, who had started research on this theme in the late 1960s had stopped it in the mid-1970s, for lack of an appropriate regulatory pressure. The French automobile industry denies it vigorously, and says that its research was about to be successful. It is difficult to find out, and to rewrite history with 'ifs'. Nevertheless, this scenario is plausible, and implies that the EEC-driven policy can be associated with serious negative impacts.

More generally, can one argue that the EEC environmental policy has negative impacts for French enterprises? Depollution is also a market. This market is less developed in France than in other countries, particularly Germany. An acceleration of environmental policy in Europe creates or accelerates the development of this market. It probably benefits more the enterprises and countries which are already more developed and more efficient in this area. This is why some people have criticized the European environmental policy for favouring the interests of German businessmen who were more advanced in this domain. However, this reasoning neglects three points. First, that stronger German firms in the anti-pollution sector merely reflects stronger environmental policies in this country. But sales of anti-pollution enterprises are also purchases and costs for polluting enterprises. What is an advantage for some is a disadvantage for others. Second, that in certain areas, such as water purification and treatment, French enterprises appear to be quite competitive. And thirdly, that a strengthening of norms and standards introduced by the European policy should induce a large-scale development of the demand for eco-products, and therefore of this sector in the entire community, including France.

Finally, one should envisage the environmental impacts of European policies conducted in other (than the environment) sectors. A recent report (EEC 1990) tried to estimate the direct and indirect consequences of the suppression of borders between member countries. Among the undesirable impacts cited in this report appears the increase in exchanges of wastes, including toxic and dangerous wastes. The abolition of borders is likely (in the absence of specific measures to the contrary) to increase transborder trade in wastes. France is already an important net importer of such wastes and might become unable to limit or control wastes imports, which could potentially be dangerous in terms of transportation and disposal. Similarly, the suppression of controls on land purchases by foreigners might favour developments hazardous to the environment, particularly in touristic areas in France. More generally, the completion of the common market calls for a parallel implementation of a more rigorous environmental policy at the European level. In the absence of such a policy, pressures on the environment, particularly in France, will be strengthened.

Conclusion

Is it possible to sum up our main findings on the impacts on France of the European environmental policy? A first point would be that this European environmental policy is not basically different from the French policy, and that both have similar principles and objectives. However, in several of the environmental areas discussed above, European norms and standards are stricter than French norms. The European policy therefore contributes to the strengthening or the acceleration of regulatory pressure in France in favour of the environment. More generally, and perhaps more importantly, many of the EEC directives reinforced the French Ministry of the Environment both relative to its industry partners and to the other — often competing — ministries. Because it is a relatively young ministry, the Ministry of the Environment is generally weaker than other ministries, and than business interests. The help given by the European environmental policy is therefore particularly welcome, and facilitates or strengthens the implementation of environmental protection policies, most of the time to the benefit of environmental quality.

In addition, the European environmental policy did play a significant role in the improvement of environmental monitoring. The norms and standards introduced by the EEC for a number of pollutants led member countries, and France in particular, to create or reinforce surveillance systems for these pollutants. Furthermore, the creation of a European Environment Agency, recently decided in order to improve environmental monitoring contributed to the creation by the French government of a French Environment Agency that will be the counterpart of the European one.

However, these benefits of the European environment policy are limited by the 'compromises' produced by the European decision-making processes. When negotiations conducted at the European level do not condone the French government position, the implementation of French policies is made more difficult, because the position of the Ministry of the Environment is weakened at home. This is also what happens when interests successfully defended by French representatives in Brussels are more favourable to the other ministers concerned than to the Minister of the Environment.

In the future, it is likely that the positive impact of European environmental policy will be more and more important in France. As mentioned in the fourth EEC programme, the objective of the Community is to adopt norms that will be more and more severe. Moreover, European environmental policy is more and more comprehensive, and covers now almost all the many dimensions of environmental concerns. This beneficial impact, however, will only be reaped if member countries accept these stricter policies. The importance allocated to environmental protection by the general public, as shown in surveys, but also in recent elections, suggests that environmental protection will remain in the coming future a major policy goal for member countries.

References

European Communities Commission (1990), *1992 The Environmental Dimension, Task Force Report on the Environment and the Internal Market*, Commission des Communautés Européennes.

Haig, N. (1984) *EEC Environmental Policy and Britain*, Institut pour une Politique Européenne de l'Environnement, Environmental Data Services Ltd.

Larrue, C. (1987) *La mise en oeuvre en France des Directives européennes pour la protection de l'air*, Institut pour une Politique européenne de l'Environnement.

Lavoux, T. (1985), *Impact des Directives eau et déchets en Allemagne Fédérale, France et Pays-Bas*, Institut pour une Politique européenne de l'Environnement.

Roqueplo, P. (1988), *Pluies acides: menaces pour l'Europe*, Economica, Paris.

Chapter 8

Effects of the Community regional policy in France: appraisal in compliance with a cost-benefit approach

Alain Buzelay

Despite its existence for the past thousand years, France has yet to experience harmonization of growth in all sectors of its economy. Regional disparities remain significant even where enlarging the community to include less developed countries with greater geographical disparities has reduced such phenomena to a certain degree.

When considered overall, such disparities divide France into four distinct segments. These are:

- the Paris region (Ile de France) is the richest region — more than 20 per cent of the French population is concentrated here, an area representing only 2 per cent of French territory. Ile de France has an income-per-head that is 50 per cent higher than the national average;
- Eastern France is the second geographical region — it can still be considered as being industrialized, even though the northern section of the region has been struggling with re-deployment problems over the past few years. The income-per-head is presently slightly lower than the French national average;
- the third area comprises Western France and is economically less developed — this region represents half of all French territory with 34 per cent of the population. However, the income-per-head is 20 per cent lower than the French national average;
- the fourth region, even less favoured, comprises Corsica and the 'Outre-Mer Departements' (Overseas French territories) — such territories include Guyanne, Guadeloupe, Martinique (French Caribbean Islands) and Réunion Island (Indian Ocean).

Regional disparities are less pronounced than in Italy but greater than in

Germany. In 1954, France implemented a regional policy that aimed to relieve pressure on the Paris region and promote development in the west, north and north-east. This was known as a national and regional development plan and its purpose was to facilitate the exploitation of potential growth in these regions.

Despite some encouraging results, reductions in regional disparities remained insufficient following the operation of the plan over 20 years. Both the recession in the 1970s and early developments in Community integration contributed to maintaining such disparities. It was therefore necessary to extend the scope of the plan to a Community scale in accordance with the Treaty of Rome. The preamble to this treaty provides for harmonious development and in addition, following reports established in 1963 and 1964, a Directorate General for Regional Development was set up. Following this development, the Council adopted a resolution for co-ordinating regional aid to member-states. It was necessary to define an authentic European policy and as a result the European Regional Development Fund was established in 1975.

Initially, the EEC regional policy was simply a continuation of national policies. However, with the membership of new member-states having greater regional disparities with ERDF reform, the policy became more autonomous. Directives became stricter and aid more selective. Ways in which such community action is still compatible with the objectives of French regional policy will now be considered.

French regional action

Continued significant regional disparities

A SLIGHT REDUCTION

The index used by Brussels to evaluate regional differences highlighted significant disparities within France (see Table 8.1). From 1981 to 1985, Corsica was credited with a rating that was 80 per cent lower than that of the Paris region (Ile de France). In addition, 12 out of the 22 regions specified were credited with a rating equal to, or higher than, the average. For the 1977—81 period, nine regions were credited with a rating that was higher than the national average (97.9). Corsica was assigned a rating that was 136 per cent lower than that assigned to Ile de France. Therefore, gaps between regions have narrowed slightly, although some such regions have benefited from regional policies to the detriment of others. A comparison of the periods 1977 to 1982 and 1981 to 1985 illustrates the privileged position of regions such as Ile de France, Alsace and Rhone-Alpes. Ile de France moved from 9th to 5th position, Alsace from 22nd to 13th position and Rhone-Alpes from 55th to 22nd

Table 8.1 Synthetic regional index in metropolitan France

Regions	1977/79/81			1981/83/85		
	Index EEC = 100	rank Fr/22	rank EEC/131	Index EEC = 100	rank Fr/22	rank EEC/160
Ile de France	135.3	(1)	(9)	151.5	(1)	(5)
Alsace	125.3	(2)	(22)	136.4	(2)	(13)
Rhône–Alpes	116.7	(3)	(35)	130.1	(3)	(22)
Franche–Comté	115.3	(4)	(36)	115.0	(5)	(45)
Centre	110.1	(5)	(43)	117.0	(4)	(37)
Champagne–Ardennes	108.1	(6)	(47)	112.2	(6)	(51)
Haute–Normandie	106.7	(7)	(49)	104.5	(14)	(72)
Bourgogne	105.0	(8)	(55)	110.9	(7)	(53)
Lorraine	103.9	(9)	(56)	106.0	(13)	(55)
Picardie	97.1	(10)	(66)	103.7	(14)	(76)
Pays de la Loire	96.6	(11)	(69)	100.6	(15)	(87)
Limousin	94.6	(12)	(74)	109.2	(10)	(62)
Auvergne	94.3	(13)	(76)	108.5	(12)	(64)
Provence–Côte d'Azur	89.9	(14)	(83)	110.4	(8)	(56)
Aquitaine	89.2	(15)	(86)	109.1	(11)	(63)
Basse Normandie	87.8	(16)	(89)	95.3	(19)	(10)
Midi–Pyrénées	87.4	(17)	(90)	109.8	(9)	(58)
Nord–Pas de Calais	86.9	(18)	(91)	96.6	(18)	(94)
Bretagne	86.0	(19)	(92)	98.1	(17)	(90)
Poitou–Charentes	85.6	(20)	(93)	90.7	(20)	(108)
Languedoc–Roussillon	76.8	(21)	(104)	87.2	(21)	(111)
Corse	57.2	(22)	(120)	84.2	(22)	(113)

Source: Periodic reports of the Commission on situation and socio-economic evolution of EEC regions (131 to 160 regions with the EEC widening).

position. Conversely, improvements in the positions of low-ranking regions such as Poitou-Charentes, Languedoc-Roussillon and Corsica are not simple to interpret. Improvements in rankings were the result of the increasing size of the Community, as statistics then took into consideration even less developed regions, such as Andalusia (Spain) and Thrace (Greece).

Regional disparities are less than in Italy, Spain and the United Kingdom but greater than those in the Netherlands and former West Germany. Regional disparities in France are even more pronounced when French Overseas territories (Départements d'Outre-Mer) are considered. In 1983, the GDP index calculated in European Currency Units was 57 for Calabria at current price and exchange rates (Community average of 100). Ratings dropped to 52 for Martinique, 44 for Guadeloupe and Réunion and 41 for Guyanne.

When considering employment, disparities reflect the major rankings illustrated by the Brussels index. However, regional unemployment rankings are subject to significant differences in so far as underdevelopment and migration can reduce unemployment statistics in underdeveloped regions and increase unemployment in more prosperous areas. In 1985 the national average of unemployment in France was 10.2 per cent, but the rate in Provence-Côte d'Azur was 12.2 per cent against 11.8 per cent in Corsica.

INFLUENCE OF FRANCE AND EEC ON DISPARITIES

Regional disparities in France were initially caused by national factors. Generally, distances play an important role. As transportation costs are added to the price of products, this tends to isolate urban economies and reduce the competitiveness of areas on the periphery. In addition, as productive structures are inadequate, such areas cannot attract new activities. This is due to insufficient infrastructures in localities. Here again there is close interdependence between crises of a regional and sectorial nature. Such crises are linked to insufficient diversification of activities, initially caused by early industrialists who did not wish to compete on local employment markets. Finally, France is traditionally a centralized country that privileges the centre and creates problems of distance. This adversely affects the remainder of French territory.

The continued presence of, or even increases in disparities may be linked to the European integration process that has been operating over the past 30 years. French regions are thus not only subjected to competition from other French regions but also to competition from other member-states. This is especially the case with France's highly developed near-neighbour, Germany. Such pressure is even more significant when it is considered that specialization will be greater at regional than at national levels. In addition, monetary integration is an even greater burden for regions in difficulty. This is because such integration operates by adjustments that are a function of the most privileged regions in Germany.

In conclusion, it should be noted that mobility of labour and especially capital are more beneficial to prosperous regions than to those in difficulty.

State and local administration action

ADAPTING THE SYSTEM

Over the past few years, France has adapted regional policy by placing greater emphasis on local authorities in three significant areas of action.

Action in favour of developing French territory and economic development of regions was simplified in 1981. It has now been decentralized in so far as responsibility is now shared with the local public authority (APUL). Two categories of premium result from this change. One such premium stems from 'national solidarity' sources that benefit regions; and the second consists of sums assigned by regions as a function of their participation in goals.

Aid granted by the state consists of the Prime d'Amenagement du Territoire (Territory Development Premium — PAT), the purpose of which is to promote activity in certain areas. A list of such areas is officially issued following consultations with the regional authorities concerned, and companies in these regions creating or maintaining employment can benefit from the PAT. To benefit, the minimum number of jobs to be created is 20, for industry, but organizations creating or re-starting activities can also benefit (however, the rate is modulated according to the region involved). In service industries, the minimum number of jobs required drops to 10. At present, the state can grant aid to improve the social and economic context in which a company operates with such aid known as Fonds Interministeriel d'action territoriale (Inter-ministerial Funds for Territorial Action — FIAT). Two other kinds of aid can be granted: the first is Fonds interministeriel de développement des aires Rurales (Inter-ministerial Funds for development of Rural areas — FIDAR), and the second the Fonds Interministeriel d'aménagement de la Montagne (Inter-ministerial Funds for the development of mountain activities — FIAM).

Aid available to all French regions but allocated on a regional basis, is as follows:

- Prime Régionale à l'emploi (Regional Premium for Employment — PRE) which operates in the same manner as the PAT except that it can be granted to all French regions; and
- Prime Régionale de la création d'entreprise (Regional Premium for the creation of Companies — PRCE).

In addition, in certain cases, regional authorities are authorized to grant long-term and attractive short-term loans. They can also guarantee funds, participate in assets and grant tax exemptions.

Action in favour of crisis regions undergoing industrial changes led to setting up centres of redeployment in areas where dominant activities were identified as sensitive to world competition. Such activities include iron and steel, mining, shipbuilding, cars and telecommunications. Aid for modernizing and diversifying industries can be granted. The regional and national development premium was granted to a third of French national companies between 1984 and 1990 and these benefited from redeployment centres. Further aids of a social nature are available. These include exceptional financial aid known as Programmes Contractuels de Développement (Contractual Development Programmes) granted to provide better equipment and a more convivial human environment. All such aid is granted by a regional committee headed by the Préfet de Région — Comissaire de la République (Regional Local Authority Head — Commissioner for the French Republic).

Action in favour of transport infrastructures led to programming state action and specifying the long-term investments required by the various ministries involved. As from 1983, such finance was granted following consultation with regional authorities.

QUANTITATIVE ASSESSMENT

Following increases up to the early 1980s, finance for regional planning has since stagnated. In 1990 direct investment by the state and local authorities amounted to approximately FRF 162,000 million. This represented an increase in current value of 25 per cent since 1984 (+14 per cent for the state and +26 per cent for APUL it accounted for 90 per cent of the total). However, when monetary erosion is considered, progression is almost nil.

State aid to regions fell dramatically from 1984 to 1989. During this period, aid dropped from FRF 3,000 million to FRF 1,364.3 million. The development of PAT proves this. From FRF 1,475 million in 1984 it fell to FRF 254 million in 1987. It increased to FRF 1,023 million in 1988 but fell back to FRF 680 million in 1990.

Since implementation, regional and national development premiums benefiting small and medium-sized companies have been directly distributed by the regions using state funds; and premiums paid to large companies have been distributed at national level. Decentralization premiums were discontinued and now only state-allocated premiums are available. The French state wished to concentrate its efforts on large companies and leave regions with the task of financing small and medium-sized companies. However, only three regions were able to take over from the state using their own resources; these were Nord, Limousin and Bretagne.

It should be noted, however, that when the statutory order updating

Table 8.2   Budget 1990 for regional development (in million current francs)

	1989	1990 (as available)
Current expenses and others	218.4	229.7
Programme authorizations		
Territory planning premium	220.0	680.0
Interministerial funds for territorial actions	634.3	738.3
Interministerial funds for the development of rural areas	340.0	375.0
Interministerial funds for the development of mountains activities	20.0	35.0
Interministerial groups for mining zones	150.0	150.0
Total	1,582.7	2,208.0

Source: DATAR

the Finance Act was voted, it enabled the budget for developing territory in 1990 to attain customary levels granted in the early 1980s. The sum voted, FRF 2,208 million, was an increase of 39 per cent with respect to the budget for 1989 (see Table 8.2).

It is difficult to assess the exact amount of sums granted as state supervisory and control authorities have ceased their activities in this field. However, it can be assumed that regional aid has slightly decreased over the past few years. Regions are now tending to use their resources upstream of activity rather than downstream and have therefore, replaced the regional employment premium and the company creation premium with financing infrastructures and training. Regions are also anxious to acquire assets in Companies.

Impact of the common market

Aid in favour of France (1975–86)

ERDF FUNDS ARE MAINLY NATIONAL RATHER THAN COMMUNITY FUNDS

Following the Paris conference that recognized the necessity of an authentic community regional policy, the European Regional Development Fund (ERDF) was set up in 1975. Apart from co-ordinating national action in this field, its purpose was to grant financial aid to regions in difficulty. France was granted two types of aid from the ERDF.

Aid is a function of quotas, i.e., predetermined shares of funds that

Table 8.3   Community assistance for France (in million ECUs)

	1975—86 ERDF	1981—85			
	ERDF	ERDF	EAFOF	BEI-NIC	CECA-Euratom
Ile de France	0	—	0.8	250.7	0
Alsace	7.54	2.7	4.3	65.9	0
Rhône-Alpes	43.51	34.7	21.7	690.5	428.8
Franche-Comté	0.35	0.1	0.7	49.6	0
Centre	4.32	3	8.5	290.2	156.9
Champagne-Ardennes	19.68	10.6	5.6	43.9	0.1
Haute-Normandie	1.79	1.4	8.6	60	0
Bourgogne	0.70	0.2	3.4	44.3	8.1
Lorraine	124.98	82.2	4	98.6	398.8
Picardie	3.47	2.8	2.6	67.5	0.2
Pays de la Loire	100.97	51.3	24.9	149.4	0.1
Limousin	95.11	63.3	6.6	34.7	0
Auvergne	119.73	71.2	4.3	80.1	0.2
Provence-Côte d'Azur	12.83	12.2	47.9	196.3	20.4
Aquitaine	118.64	74	37.4	136.5	0
Basse Normandie	36.61	25.3	7.1	244.9	110.1
Midi-Pyrénées	211.03	185.9	28.9	150.6	0.7
Nord-Pas de Calais	125.83	65.7	10.2	424	241.2
Bretagne	282.77	163.4	27	185.2	0
Poitou-Charentes	63.58	36.8	6.4	50.4	0
Languedoc-Roussillon	132.06	100	108.2	78.2	0.4
Corse	56.21	41.7	14.1	21.6	0
Département d'Outre Mer	395.21	314.5	7.1	0	0
Total	1,956.92	1,343.0	390.3	3,413.1	1,366.0

Source: EEC and DATAR

finance certain state expenditure. During the first few years of operation, this industrial and infrastructure support system was simply a method of re-financing the national budget.

Off-quota aid since 1979 has not exceeded 5 per cent of the total funds to which they apply. Unlike previous aid, off-quota aid is not predetermined and is not linked to national policies; France was granted such aid for its south-west region to consolidate the region's ability to confront the tougher competition that followed enlargement of the EEC. It concerned textiles, clothing, shipbuilding, fishing and the iron and steel industry. It was granted to facilitate economic redeployment in areas experiencing difficulties.

Between 1975 and 1986, ERDF granted 1,956.91 million ECUs to France, the majority of which covered the period from 1981 to 1985 (see Table 8.3). Regions that benefited the most were Outre Mer (French

Overseas Territories) 20 per cent, Bretagne 14 per cent, Midi-Pyrénées 11 per cent, Nord-Pas-de-Calais 6 per cent and Lorraine 6 per cent. Ninety-five per cent of such aid was granted in accordance with the quota system and was distributed on a financial and geographical basis as determined in 1975. However, action undertaken may possibly fail to comply with Community standards.

OTHER COMMUNITY LOANS ARE SCATTERED MORE THAN CO-ORDINATED

In addition to the ERDF funds from which France benefited, there was also aid from the European Social Fund during the period under consideration. Such aid is dependent on geographical criteria and was created to favour less prosperous regions (see Table 8.3). In 1986, 357 million ECUs were granted to finance plans for the north-east and south-west regions of France. In addition, there was finance from the orientation section of the European Agricultural Guidance and Guarantee Fund (EAGGF). Such finance was significant between 1981 and 1985 for the following regions: Languedoc-Roussillon (108.2 million ECUs); Provence—Côte d'Azur (47.9); Midi-Pyrénées (28.9); and Pays de la Loire (24.2). The European Bank of Investment and the New Community Instrument (NCI) also provided loans that were especially significant in the Rhone-Alpes regions. Finally the ECCS (European Community for Coal and Steel) and Euratom provided finance mainly for the Rhône-Alpes, Lorraine and Nord-Pas-de-Calais regions.

Much research has highlighted discrepancies in granting such funds on a regional basis. In France, it was observed that orientation aid from the EAGGF was in some cases granted to fairly prosperous regions or to those already receiving aid (see Table 8.3). Moreover, prior to the implementation of the European Single Market Act, the various funds were managed by the Communities Commission assisted by management committees in which representatives of member-states could block propositions for decisions emanating from the commission and appeal to the European Council. This possibility could lead to even greater discrepancies.

The effect of reforms and enlargement of the Community

STIMULATING REFORM IN FRANCE

The 1985 reform removed the reliance of the ERDF on national authorities. A system involving margins replaced the previous quota-based system. It put states into competition in so far as the upper limit was an incentive to present programmes that complied as far as possible with committee requirements. The lower limit represented the minimum resources guaranteed to each state provided that a sufficient number of admissible requests for aid were addressed to the commission. Granting of premiums within upper and lower limits is dependent on implementation by member-states of Community priorities and criteria. It should be noted that the 'off-quota' principle has been maintained via Community Initiative Programmes (CIP).

The purpose of the reform was also to enhance co-ordination of action at all stages of decision-making. Several programmes have been implemented including the Mediterranean Integrated Programmes (MIP) which are directly linked to fulfilling Community objectives; and the National Programme of Community Interests (NPCI) which should ensure co-ordination between national and Community policies. Five goals now govern financial arbitration at Community level. These are as follows:

1. Aid for developing less advanced regions;
2. Aid for industrial redeployment areas;
3. Aid for social redeployment (goals 3 and 4);
4. Aid for assisting agricultural structures to adapt to new conditions and rural development (goals 5a and 5b).

In the interests of greater efficiency and coherence of Community action, reforms have indirectly complied with French regional policy. Competition between national demands for finance resulted in the implementation of the margin system. This has caused decisions concerning selection of national projects to be taken with greater discernment.

ERDF reform appears to have benefited France. Indeed, programmes submitted in 1988 obtained an aid of 2,700 million francs — the highest amount granted by the fund since its creation. The Midi-Pyrénées region received almost 23 per cent of the total. It was followed by Languedoc-Roussillon (17 per cent), Franche-Comté (17 per cent), Aquitaine (12 per cent), Nord-Pas-de-Calais (8 per cent) and Lorraine (8 per cent).

Reforms of such structural funds implemented on 1 January 1990 should enhance coherence. The major part of such reforms consisted of multiplying real-term amounts by two for the period covering 1987 to 1993. They also provided for higher concentration of activities from geographical and operational standpoints. These included: technical interventions via two-yearly programmes rather than ad hoc projects; participation or creation of partnerships with regions; and preparation and performance of programmes. Finally, it involved enhancement of an integrated approach by encouraging mergers in areas experiencing difficulties (aid from ERDF, EDF, (European Development Fund) and the EAGGF (European Agricultural Guidance and Guarantee Fund)), directing action through loans from the EBI (European Bank of Investment) and from the ECCS where implementation of integrated operations is an example.

The reform of structural funds transferred the principle of community support structures to the French economy. Such funds are the commission's response to requirements expressed in national plans. The technique of 'contract plans' is now implemented. This technique is used to facilitate extending such plans to regions by co-ordinating the orientations of the regional plan with the national priority implementation programmes (PIP). With the contract plan, finance is released during the first year of implementing the national plan (1984) and throughout the five-year period to which it applies. The two partners, i.e. the state and the region, each have executive powers and separate budgets.

ENLARGEMENT OF THE COMMUNITY HAS ADVERSELY AFFECTED FRANCE BUT HAS CREATED NEW SYNERGIES

As the Community has been enlarged to include countries with even greater regional disparities, French plans that are eligible for Community aid have recently been slightly reduced. This can be illustrated by the total of Community aid that was granted to France over the period extending from 1989 to 1993. Aid granted to underdeveloped regions in France was estimated at 883 million francs which was 2.6 per cent of Community funds. This can be compared with 28 per cent for Spain, 22 per cent for Italy, 19 per cent for Greece and 19 per cent for Ireland. Such aid is now restricted to Corsica and the Départements d'Outre Mer (French overseas territories), as Table 8.4 indicates.

Table 8.4 Aids to development of less advanced regions: community aids to the benefit of France (millions of francs)

Régions	ERDF	EAFOF	EOF	
Corse	80.5	35	22	137.5
Guadeloupe	79.3	23.3	63.4	166
Guyanne	33.8	12	27.6	73.4
Martinique	78.4	20	66.1	164.5
Réunion	134	69.7	142.9	346.6
Total	406	160	322	888

Source: DATAR

Aid in favour of industrial redeployment amounted to 700 million francs for the period extending from 1989 to 1991. This was 18 per cent of Community funds, compared with 38 per cent for the United Kingdom and 18.6 per cent for Spain. Half of such aid granted to France went to the Nord-Pas-de-Calais and Lorraine regions.

Aid for social redeployment amounted to 872 million francs (16 per cent of Community funds) against 19 per cent for the United Kingdom and 11 per cent for former West Germany, Italy and Spain respectively.

In addition, aid to promote agricultural structures and rural development was granted to many regions of all member-states, except for the United Kingdom. Such reduction in aid may appear to adversely affect France as it now contributes more to the Community than it receives and this situation will continue, given the levels of income-per-head in France. However, Community reforms and enlargement of the Community more than compensate for these disadvantages by creating other synergies.

First, the concept of partnership that was introduced with the reform of structural funds had favourable repercussions on the French economy via the contract plans which rendered national action and planned synergies more coherent.

Next, at national level the Community now tends to treat the causes of regional disparities rather than their effects, i.e. it evaluates the efficiency of the productive process and environment rather than the creation of employment which is the result of such action. Therefore, unlike objectives over the period extending from 1980 to 1985, activity in France is no longer restricted to increasing employment by maintaining or creating companies or promoting industrial redeployment. Action now emphasizes modernizing activities, developing human resources, encouraging research, and innovating and developing communications. Rather than grant aid dependent on opportunities, such opportunities are now themselves promoted. If this was not the case, national and community grants would be in danger of being inefficient and might overburden budgets unnecessarily.

Finally, the most significant expected effect produced by Community finance will be on underprivileged European countries. The development of less prosperous countries should accompany, but not slow, that of more privileged member-states. Countries must be integrated in development processes and must take advantage of opportunities via the community trade multiplication which should apply to all states and regions within the Community. This is especially true for France which is close geographically to Spain and Portugal. The most commonly acknowledged hypothesis is that there will be economies of scale produced by geographical redeployment over the entire Community. Redeployment will concentrate production over wider areas.

The most likely effects of ERDG reforms will be on structural funds. The Community regional policy is not directly favourable to France, yet it will have an indirect impact as there will be greater coherence and novel synergies will be created. Such phenomena will undoubtedly have a positive effect on the French economy. This is important when considering that competition and specialization within the single market will be on a regional rather than on a national basis, which means that differences in productivity and costs will be less obvious in statistics.

Chapter 9

The French financial system

Josette Peyrard

In France, as in most industrialized countries, the financial market has altered considerably in the course of the last few years. The system of financing the economy has undergone an important change which can be described as passing from an economy of debt to one of financial markets, i.e. businesses resort less to borrowing money from the banks and more to issuing shares on the markets.

The proposal to construct a large, internal European market and the European directives to this effect have been the cause of these changes.

With effect from January 1993, the free movement of capital and the free availability of services on offer in the banking, financial and insurance field will have an appreciable impact on the financial markets of the Community. Achieving one, single European financial zone exerts an influence at intermediary levels: for example, at the levels of the market authorities, compensation methods, carrying out complex operations etc. Profound changes have already taken place.

In the first section of this chapter, we shall study the way the financial environment is evolving; the second section will be devoted to the changes in the French financial market. Finally, the consequences of the reforms undertaken will be assessed.

Evolution of the financial environment

Numerous reforms have been carried out in the course of the last few years and they have helped the French financial system to adapt to evolution in the economy. Certain reforms were more or less dictated by fluctuations in the international financial environment, such as significant changes in interest rates and exchange rates, and other reforms were influenced by consideration of the single European market.

This study will examine in succession the stages in the process of evolution and then the reform of the monetary market.

The process of evolution

At the same time as inflation was weakening, the financial environment underwent successive modifications which can be expressed under three headings: deregulation, the removal of intermediary levels and a policy of liberalization.

DEREGULATION

Deregulation, i.e. changes in the rules, became necessary because of evolution in the financial markets. It began in the USA, has spread to the European countries, first to Great Britain, then to France and Germany and is reaching Japan.

In France, deregulation has taken the form of:

- getting rid of exchange control (getting progressively less and less since 1986 and finally achieved in 1990);
- removing restrictions on deposits;
- allowing banks to fix the value of short-term deposits as well as long-term ones; and
- allowing commercial banks to take control of business banks, a procedure which has resulted in a process of integration, particularly in Great Britain.

Several Community directives have enabled a 'single market' to be achieved in the banking sector and these can be grouped in three sections:

- freedom for banks to set up business under the jurisdiction of the host country (directive dated 19 June 1989);
- free commercial use of financial services: since 1989, the OPCVM (unit trust for trading in stocks and shares) can canvass customers throughout Europe; and
- setting up prudential guidelines within the Community: banks will have to have a solvency ratio of 8 per cent by the end of 1992.

The establishment of a single market in services and capital funds creates a new competitive situation to which banks have had to adapt. Numerous deals have taken place linking banking firms with insurance companies (for example, BNP and UAP, CIC and GAN, Compagnie bancaire and Groupama) to such an extent that a new term is used: 'bankinsurance'.

The public authorities in France have played an essential part in the process of change in the financial system. The French state, at first strongly interventionist, has gradually withdrawn from the scene and France has moved from an economy of debt towards a market economy. Financial intermediaries have emerged and now provide the essential elements in financing the economy.

DISINTERMEDIATION

In using the expression 'disintermediation', we are describing what occurs when a part of the currency flow which used to pass through the traditional financial institutions, in particular the banks, from now on is handled by the capital markets.

The system of intermediary stages in France has evolved. This evolution is as much the result of new technologies in the field of information technology as it is of changes in regulations and of innovations in financial products. Businesses resort less and less to bank loans and more and more to market finance.

THE OPENING UP OF FINANCIAL CIRCUITS

There has also been an opening up of the markets: the monetary market, the bond market and the mortgage market.

Right up until 1985, the mortgage market was regarded as a specialized section of the monetary market, sealed off from agents not specifically trained in financing. This market was short of liquid funds and did not allow loan companies to mobilize resources over the long term.

The law of 11 July 1985, altered the juridicial framework of this market area and created the Mortgage Refinancing Bank (CRH). The bank underwrites for its shareholders promissory notes which have the value of creating funds available to the mortgage market. On the other hand, it creates long-term bonds, quoted on the Stock Exchange and benefiting from State guarantee.

The trend is towards a single market of capital funds covering all transactions and open to financial and non-financial agents alike.

Reform of the monetary market

In 1985, reform of the monetary market had these objectives:

● the creation of a new monetary policy on the basis of an open market policy; and
● the introduction of new financial procedures.

THE NEW MONETARY POLICY

For a long time, the French monetary market was a closed market in which financial institutions exchanged money from central funds totally disconnected from the other capital markets. This isolation prevented confrontation with the others in the supply and demand of capital funds.

Deregulation and financial innovation have had important consequences on monetary policy. In fact, monetary policy is based on a narrow relationship between growth in the money supply and growth in the economy. Right into the 1980s, people's reactions were geared to the interest rate: a rise in interest rate resulted in a slowing down in money circulation and also of growth.

Since 1980, financial innovations have made control of the money supply (variation in interest rates, market integration) much more difficult. For example, monetary measures (money supply and its various elements, establishing interest rates etc.) and their relationship with the rest of the economy are much more difficult to evaluate. The effectiveness of interest rates as a tool in monetary policy becomes appreciably weaker.

THE INTRODUCTION OF NEW FINANCIAL INSTRUMENTS

These instruments, as follows, are of short- or medium-term duration, negotiable and capable of being underwritten by all economic agencies.

- Certificates of deposit are short-term negotiable instruments and issued by commercial banks, lasting from 10 days to seven years, of a value per unit of at least one million French francs. The only people authorized to issue these certificates are banks licensed to receive from the public short-term deposits of at least two years duration and who are obliged to have compulsory levels of reserve funds.
- Commercial paper — commercial paper is a promissory note issued by businesses (limited companies at least two years old with capital funds equal at least to those of societies using public savings), lasting from 10 days to two years. Their unit value is one million French francs.
- Negotiable treasury bonds — negotiable treasury bonds are issued by the State Treasury. They have a fixed interest rate and last from 10 days to five years. Bonds with a fixed, preassessed interest rate (BTF) are issued with a discount for durations of 13, 26 or 52 weeks and, in exceptional circumstances, for durations of 24 or 28 weeks. Bonds with a fixed rate of interest and an annual rate of interest to be paid on due dates (BTAN) are issued for durations spanning from one to seven years. They are auctioned weekly.
- Bonds from specialized financial institutions and bonds from financial societies — these bonds are issued by the CEPME (Bank for small and medium-sized companies), the National Credit Bank and the SDR (Societies for Regional Development). They fall due over a period of two to seven years.

Financial innovations, by increasing the range of choice available to borrowers and lenders, are an effective element in the allocation of saving-resources at the heart of the European Community.

Evolution of the French financial market

In step with the setting up of Community regulations, the financial market has considerably modernised itself.

Community rules for financial markets

In taking such a large interest in financial markets, the European Community had two principal aims. These were to safeguard the smooth running of the money markets in all countries in the Community, and to permit widespread mutual penetration of each other's markets. The community authorities have taken great care to publicize the directives with the aim of improving communications and the supply of adequate information, and to assure a certain degree of co-ordination between the rules of member countries.

These directives have been successively concerned with:

- the conditions for listing stocks and shares to the Official List of a Stock Exchange (5 March 1979);
- the conditions for setting up, supervizing and diffusing the prospectus to be published, giving details of entry requirements to the Official List of a Stock Exchange (17 March 1980);
- regular information concerning entry requirements for stocks and shares to the Official List of a Stock Exchange (5 March 1982);
- the legal, regulatory and administrative requirements needed as regards certain organizations which purchase stocks and shares collectively (OPCVM) (20 December 1985); and
- regulations needed for established operations.

The proposals in the directive, presented by the Commission on 3 January 1989, concern investment services in the field of stocks and shares. They ought to achieve the creation of a 'European passport', operating in the field of investment services but they have not yet been adopted. These directives have had a considerable influence on the reform of the French financial market.

The modernization of French stock exchanges

IMPROVEMENT IN THE SERVICES OFFERED TO USERS

Improvement means that investors can place their savings in better conditions, since information is more widely available. If it is true that the market is the best way to allocate resources, it must result in an improvement in the economy as a whole. The increasing competition from intermediaries has led to a decrease in the benefit margin of transactions on the market which benefits the users.

From 1980 to 1990, the number of shareholders in France has increased from 1.5 million to more than 10 million. They now have access to foreign financial products, and also, privatisation has played an important role in this increase.

THE ORGANIZATION OF THE MARKET

Several texts have reformed the market in stocks and shares. The law of 22 January 1988 set up new structures with clearly defined powers. These were:

- the Stock Exchange Commission (CBV);
- the Company of French Stock Exchanges (SBF); and
- Stock Exchange member firms.

Also, the operating rules for the markets have been reviewed with the aim of strengthening security, improving liquidity and producing greater efficiency. The role of French financial intermediaries has changed considerably, with some regroupments taking place from as early as 1988.

Since 1 January 1992, the monopoly of brokers has been abolished. Most of the French Stock Exchange member firms have allowed access to their capital to French or foreign banks. Professionals with new expertise have appeared: the market-makers or dealers who allow anyone to find a partner or a customer for buying or selling. This activity demands an excellent knowledge of the market as well as a competent knowledge of management techniques. The Stock Exchange member firms will be able to deploy their skills in the negotiation of stocks and shares within the whole European area. However, competition will increase.

THE CREATION OF NEW MARKETS AND NEW PRODUCTS

Some new markets have been created: for example, the French International Futures Market (MATIF) in 1986; and the Paris Market in Negotiable Stock Options (MONEP) in 1987. On these financial markets, a new range of products are on offer.

The MATIF is an exchange for derivative financial instruments: fixed-term contracts or 'futures' and stock options. It allows investors to protect themselves against the risks of interest rates and against variations in share prices. It also allows people to speculate. The MATIF deals with products from interest rates: contracts on notional loans, contracts on three-month Treasury Bonds, three-month PIBOR contracts,

contracts on options on notional transactions, a contract on ECU, and two contracts on the Exchange index (CAC40).

The MONEP is an options market where the buyer has the right to buy (purchase option) or to sell (selling option) a fixed amount of shares at an agreed price in return for paying the person selling the option a sum of money called the price or the option premium. On the MONEP, share options and index options can be negotiated.

Electronic trading, which has developed over the last few years, assures the most efficient spread of information possible among the different participants in the market. Electronic trading methods not only add to a clearer development of transactions thanks to better information; but also add to liquidity, as the electronic system of price quotation extends operating time, to efficiency due to lower transaction charges and narrower margins, and to security.

From 1980 to 1991 there has been a rapid rise in the French market, with the amount of capital held by national Stock Exchanges having increased considerably. The figures in 1991 were 240,597 billion ECU in France, 274,836 billion ECU in Germany on the main market and 609,150 billion ECU in the United Kingdom. The volume of transactions in bonds has also increased considerably, rising tenfold in 10 years. In 1991, it was of the order of 432,302 billion ECU in France, 441,867 billion ECU in Germany on the one main market, and 746,443 ECU in the United Kingdom. The expansion of the market in derivative instruments has been just as fast.

The consequences of the European market

Changes in the financial system have had a favourable effect on markets but at the same time raise a few problems. Deregulation has had an effect on all elements of the financial market.

Beneficial consequences

MODERNIZATION OF THE STOCK EXCHANGES

This modernization process has had a favourable impact for users, for the markets and financial instruments and for intermediaries.

European financial integration is an essential dimension in the enlarged single market. It is important not only for the financial professions but also for all businesses and investors. In view of the forthcoming common currency, the ECU, European financial markets will once again have to develop. The complete freedom of movement for capital, the free availability of services in every country of the Community creates an outstandingly favourable situation, in the medium and long term.

The growth of liquidity in European exchanges attracts new investors and managers of foreign portfolios, and also encourages a larger number of foreign firms to be quoted on these markets, in the same way as multinational European firms are quoted on the American market. But the market is still too segmented and one can expect new groupings in different places.

Increased competition in the markets will very probably lead to a regrouping of exchanges.

THE PLAN TO PRODUCE A EUROPEAN SHARES LISTING

This listing of European companies would consist of 250 to 300 multi-national companies which would be among the most active in the national financial market. These companies would be quoted on the various European exchanges and the quotations would be made simultaneously on several markets. This listing would strengthen co-operation between the different European exchanges.

The advantages of this European listing will be numerous and will include:

- the large European companies having an enlarged market available; and
- the exchange intermediaries having greater possibilities for arbitrage.

The limits of the European financial market

If the circulation of savings is too easy, this can have disagreeable conse-quences in certain cases. This can clearly be seen in the following list of risks associated with the European financial market.

THE RISK OF LOSING LOCAL CONTROL OF SAVINGS

Free movement of capital can lead, if the authorities in charge of monetary affairs do not take care, to a certain amount of imbalance in the location of savings. There is, however, no need to exaggerate this risk because, on the one hand, capital moves in a fairly sluggish way and on the other the risks can be softened by appropriate fiscal measures.

THE RISK OF MORE SEVERE COMPETITION BETWEEN BANKS

In a single European financial market, French banks have been obliged to rethink their strategy and the nature of their trade. As a consequence of the objectives pursued, they have to adopt a position in this market.

THE RISK OF GREATER VOLATILITY IN MARKETS

It is noticeable that the room taken in the financial market by institutional investors is larger. Their behaviour pattern is more uniform and the effect of that is to accentuate market movements. The markets then have a tendency to become overheated. A larger number of transactions are carried out for a purely financial purpose, without any economic consideration. The technical aspect of markets makes them more sensitive to a breakdown in the listings, which might have significant consequences for the market.

THE RISK OF IRREGULARITIES

Supervision of the markets has always played an important role. Having accepted the more and more international character of financial markets, close alliances between the different institutions must be woven. Since the 1980s, we have witnessed a development of international co-operation.

The objectives of the French Securities and Exchange Commission (COB) have been increased. They include:

- overseeing the 'protection of savings invested in stocks and shares or in any other way, achieved by appealing to the general public for savings and by providing information for investors'; and
- the correct functioning of the Stock Exchange markets, of financial instruments quoted or of negotiable contracts.

The law of 2 August 1989 foresaw the need for a framework of international co-operation. The Commission can conduct enquiries at the request of foreign authorities exercising similar functions and under the same obligations of professional secrecy with, however, two reservations. These are an insistence on reciprocity and the guarantee of total confidentiality on the part of the foreign authority.

As a result of the reforms carried out on the markets, we are witnessing a certain degree of convergence between the different financial systems of the industrialized countries, whether they be European, American or Asian. Circuits have been modified, products have been diversified. However, these reforms which have encouraged the development of competition have not yet been completed. There still exist, nevertheless, disparities in the fiscal rating of financial instruments which are liable to produce bad effects. Moreover, the treaty of Maastricht with its vision of a single currency will introduce some fine tuning. The creation of a single European exchange market or of a network of exchange markets remains a problem to be solved and the response which it will arouse will depend on the relative competitiveness of the different European financial systems.

Chapter 10

The European monetary system and French monetary policy

François Bilger

Since March 1979 the European monetary system (EMS) has governed the monetary relations of the EEC member countries. France has not only joined the EMS, it also played a leading part in its creation and development. To gauge the advantages and costs of the EMS for France, it therefore seems appropriate to distinguish between its global results in regard to France's European monetary integration policy and its specific effects in regard to France's policy of national monetary stabilization.

France and the monetary organization of Europe

France is probably the country which has been the most active in campaigning for an international monetary system that is both orderly (stability of exchange rates) and balanced (absence of hegemony). It did so first of all in international institutions where it even proposed, in the 1960s, a return to the gold standard; then, and above all, it did so in the European framework, constantly advocating the realization of monetary union as quickly as possible. Compared with Germany, which stressed the need for a preliminary convergence of economic policies and performances ('economist approach to economic and monetary Union'), France consistently recommended the prior stabilization of exchange rates as a stimulus to economic co-operation and convergence ('monetarist approach'). It was this conception that prevailed in the end.

We can distinguish three periods in the monetary history of the Community (Maillet and Rollet, 1988).

From 1958 to 1971 Europe of the Six was set up and operated under the international monetary system of Bretton Woods, which did not give it a monetary identity but did provide it with real exchange stability (±1 per cent margin of variation around the central rates as defined in relation to the dollar) and, indirectly, automatic co-ordination of monetary policies, further reinforced by a few simple consultation and mutual assistance arrangements established by Articles 103 to 108 of the Treaty of Rome at the request of France (Genière, 1975). In 13 years, there were only four monetary readjustments, and the biggest of them, the devaluation of the franc on the 8 August 1969, after 11 years of stability, was not even due to an actual economic disequilibrium, but to the social-political events of May 1968. Be that as it may, this first period of great external and internal monetary stability was characterized by both the rapid progression of Community integration and the achievement of remarkable macro-economic performances. However, the domination of the IMS by the dollar, the increasingly frequent crises of this gold exchange standard system and, finally, the difficulties created for the Common Agricultural Policy by the monetary transformations of 1969 caused the EEC member-states, in particular France, to contemplate, in the light of experience, the establishment of a genuine European monetary union within the framework of the IMS. In December 1969, the Hague meeting of Heads of State and Government launched this project, which took shape the following year in the Werner Report. But scarcely had the first measures been taken than the dollar crisis led to the collapse of the IMS in 1971–72 and the sudden interruption of the envisaged process of monetary unification.

The second period, extending from 1972 to 1978, was therefore marked by the absence of a real international monetary system and a search for a practicable regional system, whose initial form was the European monetary snake (±2.25 per cent margin of variation between currencies), at first linked to the dollar, then floating. Initially established between 10 European countries in April 1972, it was rapidly reduced, under the effect of the enormous disequilibria resulting from the first oil shock of 1973 and the world economic crisis of 1975, to four members grouped around West Germany (FRG, Denmark and Benelux). France tried in vain to stay in the group: it left it for the first time in January 1974, returned to it in July 1975 and abandoned it permanently in March 1976. The French franc was, at the time, like the British pound and the Italian lira, a floating currency in relation to this 'mark zone' as well as the other major world currencies. However, an embryonic European currency appeared in 1975 with the EUA (European Unit of Account), a basket of currencies similar to that of the IMF's SDR (Special Drawing Rights). Mutual assistance between the European central banks was also increased. The elements of a new European system were thus put in place, but in a disparate way. Throughout this period of instability, economic performances as well as the process of integration deteriorated considerably. The Community therefore set out to find a more satisfactory form of monetary organization, one that reduced the transaction costs due to exchange risks and the errors of allocation due to the uncertainty of exchange rates and included all member-states. Thus in 1978, following a proposal of the Commission and a joint initiative by France and Germany, the European monetary system was adopted in order to make the Community a zone of exchange stability again within a world increasingly disrupted by the economic and monetary crisis, while also asserting the monetary identity of Europe and resuming the progress towards monetary union.

The third period was, therefore, the one which started in March 1979, with the implementation of the EMS (CEC, 1979; Ypersele and Koeune, 1988). This system is, like the old IMS, a system of rates that are stable in the short term but revisable in the medium term together, of course, with rates floating in concert against other world currencies. The instantaneous stability is, as in the Snake, less constraining (±2.25 per cent instead of ±1 per cent), but the adjustment of central rates is more so, requiring, even for slight variations, a collective negotiation and a general agreement, which practically speaking excludes competitive devaluations or revaluations by its very nature. On the other hand, interventions on the market and acts of mutual assistance between central banks are more extensive and, to some extent, more automatic. Another novelty is the creation of a divergence indicator. The burden of the adjustment is therefore better defined, more organized and, in principle, more equitably distributed between surplus and deficit countries. Finally this set of measures (relatively large margin and relatively slight readjustment), which allows a slow shift of currencies, has much greater anti-speculative effectiveness. The principal distinctive feature of the EMS compared with the old Snake is the creation of the ECU, a basket of domestic currencies (Table 10.1) and the basis of the central rates which serve to determine the grid of bilateral parities. It is also the embryo of a European currency by the creation of the ECU instead of national currencies through its function as a reserve instrument and means of payment between central banks and finally, outside the official sphere, through its function as an instrument of accounting and private financial transactions.

Table 10.1 Composition of the ECU[1] (in per cent)

DEM 30.1%	NLG 9.4%	IRP 1.1%
FRF 19.0%	BEF 7.6%	GRD 0.8%
GBP 13.0%	ESP 5.3%	PTE 0.8%
ITL 10.15%	DKK 2.45%	LUF 0.3%

1. September 1989 revision

Source: Commission of the European Community

The EMS does not constitute, it should be noted, a system of fixed, immutable rates radically opposed to the system of floating rates, but rather an intermediate system of limited flexibility in the short run and of concerted, progressive stabilization in the medium term, with the constant possibility of withdrawing from it. The constraint of rates' stability is therefore only relative. On the other hand, the EMS is clearly opposed to the system of floating rates in that it is a co-operative system of organized interdependence through multilateral supervision and bilateral co-operation. This implies, of course, a certain loss of economic sovereignty, i.e. a certain restriction of exchange and monetary policy as well as, indirectly, of domestic economic policy as a whole, which is made more flexible, it is true, by the margin of variation, the possibility of adjusting the central rate, and even the freedom of withdrawal. Such a system also affords, however, a certain control over the exchange policy, the monetary policy and, indirectly, over the economic policy of partner countries. This interdependence between partner countries is formalized in the various procedures of consultation, co-operation and co-ordination between domestic authorities in the committees established within the framework of the Community: Economic Policy Committee, Monetary Committee and above all Committee of Governors of Central Banks.

The EMS was originally designed as a mere transitional stage towards an 'institutional phase', scheduled two years after its implementation, involving the creation of a 'European Monetary Fund' and the full use of the ECU as a reserve asset and an instrument of intervention and payment, i.e. a common European currency. For a long time the second oil shock and other major causes of disequilibrium did not allow this evolution. In the absence of these institutional advances, the system is itself gradually being transformed into a 'mark zone', for reasons which are both economic (differing economic and commercial importance and uneven monetary credibility of the participating countries) and technical (need for a currency playing the role of n-I currency). The mark is becoming the central currency and anchorage point of the system as well as the European partner of the dollar in world monetary affairs (see Table 10.2); the Bundesbank is acting as the quasi-central Bank of Europe; and German monetary policy is imposing its inflation rate, interest rate and external exchange rate orientations on every other country. Theoretically of a co-operative type, the system is therefore reverting to a hierarchical type, characterized by adjustment asymmetry and unequal interdependence between Germany and its partners.

This evolution is having some positive effects: the German virtues are progressively becoming European, notably in the field of price stability, and the EMS is protected from the crises and collapse of the old IMS, due to the lax policy of the leading country; moreover the countries belonging to the narrow-band exchange mechanism are together producing an increasing foreign surplus *vis-à-vis* the other countries, which represents a sound basis for their growth; and finally the general alignment of European currencies on the mark and their disconnection from the dollar are ensuring Europe's monetary identity in international monetary relations. The EMS could be regarded as a machine for

Table 10.2   Intervention currencies[1] in the EMS and the USA (in per cent)

	1979–82[2]	SME 1983–85	1986–87[3]
US dollars	71.5	53.7	26.3
EMS currencies	27.2	43.5	71.7
of which: mark	(23.7)	(39.4)	(59.0)
Others[4]	1.3	2.8	2.0
		United States	
Mark	89.7	67.9	57.5
Yen	12.3	22.1	42.5

1. The total interventions comprise purchases and sales
2. Since March 1979
3. Up to June 1987
4. Since 1985 the interventions have included interventions in the private European monetary units.

Source: IMF Finances and development September 1990.

bringing the European economies closer together, thus constituting a good preparation for the future monetary union. But subordination to a leader country imposes economic and political costs on the other countries in so far as, barring an ever difficult readjustment of exchange rates, it can lead to a systematic overvaluation of their currencies and a forced alignment of their economic policy objectives with those of Germany. Such a subordination is of course opposite to the partnership inherent in the EEC. France tried in 1988 to correct this hegemonic situation somewhat through the creation of a Franco-German Economic and Monetary Council, to regain in influence what it had lost in autonomy, but such an institution cannot by itself modify a reality based on the superior economic power of Germany and above all on the great credibility of its central bank.

Despite, or because of, this unforeseen development, the EMS proved surprisingly robust: it managed first of all to survive the upheavals of the 1980s (second oil shock, advent of a socialist-communist government in France and a massive increase and decrease in the dollar), then to consolidate itself progressively. After intense controversies during the early years, based on econometric studies whose methodological rigour sometimes masked their analytical shallowness, it is commonly accepted today (Gleske et al., 1989; Gros and Thygesen, 1988; Ypersele and Koeune, 1988; Maillet and Rollet, 1988) that the EMS has indeed created an island of growing exchange-rate stability and even, today, quasi-solidity. This is reflected in the progressive reduction in the variability of rates and the frequency and scale of monetary readjustments (Table 10.3);

Table 10.3 Realignments of central parities within the EMS (percentage variations)

	DEM	FRF	ITL	DKK	BEF	NLG	IRP
24 September 1979	+ 2.0			− 2.9			
30 November 1979				− 4.8			
23 March 1979			− 6.0				
5 October 1981	+ 5.5	− 3.0	− 3.0			+ 5.5	
22 February 1982				− 3.0	− 8.5		
14 June 1982	+ 4.25	− 5.75	− 2.75			+ 4.25	
21 March 1983	+ 5.5	− 2.5	− 2.5	+ 2.5	+ 1.5	+ 3.5	− 3.5
22 July 1985	+ 2.0	+ 2.0	− 6.0	+ 2.0	+ 2.0	+ 2.0	+ 2.0
7 April 1986	+ 3.0	− 3.0		+ 1.0	+ 1.0	+ 3.0	
4 August 1986							− 8.0
12 January 1987	+ 3.0				+ 2.0	+ 3.0	
5 January 1990			− 3.7				

Source: Commission of the European Community

that it has moreover greatly contributed, under the impetus of the leader country, to disinflation and later to a pick-up in activity and employment; and finally that it has, by reducing the exchange risk, and fostering the increasing convergence of economic policies under the effect of the exchange-rate constraint, promoted the revival of the commercial, economic and financial integration process within the Community. Significantly, this progress was not obtained by a reinforcement of exchange controls or any other restrictive measures but, on the contrary, was accompanied by the progressive abolition of all such controls and by the establishment of free movement of capital. Finally, the increasing convergence of member countries' macroeconomic performances, as well as the increasing autonomy and specificity of the Community economy in the world-wide economy, have made the reactions of national economies less sensitive and more symmetrical to external shocks, which has constantly consolidated the system. It is true that any satisfaction France could draw from this success has long been tempered by the absence of the institutional progress and hence by the progressive transformation of the EMS into a 'mark zone'. The economic advantage was thus paid for, as we have seen, by a political cost.

This situation has recently been changing, however, and the system is now evolving towards a less hierarchical and more co-operative functioning (Mathes, 1990). The technical agreements of Basle and Nyborg between central banks — as well as the reduction of the German lead in the field of price stability, the increasing credibility of the exchange stability of all currencies and the free circulation of capital — have progressively reduced the system's asymmetry since 1987. Even if the big fall in US interest rates and the steep rise in German interest rates created temporary tensions, the substitutability of the participating currencies increased. The entry of the pound into the exchange mechanism and, for some time, the rebalancing effects of the German reunification process, will also help to increase this substitutability. Above all, the revival of the monetary unification project in 1988, the coming into force of its first phase on 1 July 1990, and the adoption of the Maastricht project in December 1991 are substantially altering the system's prospects. With a considerably delay, it is true, but in an apparently unstoppable way, the initial strategy is thus progressively being implemented.

The recent widening of the EMS fully reflects this dynamic. Although all the Community member-states are automatically part of the EMS, only eight joined the exchange mechanism at the outset, with Italy being allowed, moreover, a bigger fluctuation margin (6 per cent instead of 2.25 per cent). Great Britain and then (after their accession) Greece, Spain and Portugal let their currencies float to begin with, but on 5 January 1990 Italy joined the group of countries with a reduced fluctuation margin. Following this, Spain, on 19 June 1989 and Great Britain itself on 8 October 1990 (after long remaining aloof) acceded to the exchange mechanism with a large margin of fluctuation, in order to take advantage of the disinflationary effects and stabilizing disciplines of the system. Therefore, only the Greek drachma and the Portuguese escudo are still floating, but are following fairly closely the fluctuations of the ECU. The other Western European currencies are also managed in relation to either the mark (Swiss franc and Austrian schilling) or the ECU (Norway crown and Sweden crown). Just as the EEC has progressively absorbed the EFTA countries or attracted them into its orbit, so the EMS is progressively imposing its co-operation method and exchange discipline on all European countries.

Although received with scepticism at the start, the EMS now enjoys a broad consensus. It is functioning more and more satisfactorily from the technical standpoint and even the causes of the system's asymmetry and fragility are, as we have seen, being attenuated or eliminated. At the same time, its economic and even political results, which were long divergent to the advantage of Germany because of its structural superiority and of its institutional domination, are now being redistributed over all the partner countries. The net balance of the system's advantages and global costs, which was fairly slight or even negative at the start, is now growing and becoming more evenly distributed. France has, of course, every reason to welcome this trend, which shows, no doubt belatedly but nevertheless convincingly, the effectiveness of its monetarist strategy of economic convergence and is making it possible to envisage the achievement of monetary union, in order to 'communitise' monetary power and thus complete the monetary integration of Europe.

The EMS and monetary stabilization in France

There is a certain paradox in French monetary policy. Whereas, as just mentioned, no other country has campaigned so strongly for European and even international monetary stability, this stability does not necessarily have a pre-eminent place at domestic level. As the central bank is not independent of the government and does not, as in Germany, have a prior mission of ensuring the currency's stability, monetary policy is subordinated to the government's global economic policy and hence to the hierarchy of its macro-economic objectives. As a result, the objectives of the central bank can vary with the government's policies, and the advantages or disadvantages of the EMS for domestic monetary policy can be assessed in differing ways, depending on current governmental strategy.

In a long-term context, however, there is a certain constancy in the strategic options linked to the country's fundamental interests and especially to its degree of international openness (Pébereau, 1987). Thus from the end of the Second World War to the creation of the Community, French economic policy, in an economy in need of rebuilding and still largely closed, usually gave priority to growth and full employment, to the detriment if necessary of the internal and external stability of the currency. In the second stage, from the beginning of the Community in 1958 to the world-wide economic crisis of 1975, it generally tried to achieve simultaneously, in an opening economy, the twin objectives of real growth and monetary stability. This it managed to do without too much difficulty within the framework of the then IMS — except for the monetary transformation imposed by the exceptional events of May 1968 — as long as the international and European environment was both expansive and stable, but which it ceased to be able to do when the IMS collapsed and the international environment became recessive and inflationary. The oil crisis at the end of 1973 and the expansionary policy of late 1975 led a sharp acceleration of inflation and, as already mentioned, the franc's withdrawal from the Snake and its substantial devaluation.

This marked the beginning of a third period, when French economic policy, drawing lessons from this failure and making a virtue of necessity, finally gave priority to internal and especially external monetary stability. This was regarded as the very condition of sound and sustainable growth in an open economy and as the basis of a virtuous circle of macro-economic performances which led from stabilization of exchange rates to contribution to the stabilization of prices to equilibrium and even foreign surplus and to acceleration of growth and improvement of employment. This new strategic approach, adopted and applied by the French government from 1976 and especially from 1978 to 1981, was temporarily abandoned by the new political authorities from 1981 to 1982 in the name of 'another economic logic' and for the sake of a very audacious return to post-war policy; but it was then permanently confirmed, after the resounding failure of that policy, by the successive governments, both right- and left-wing, from 1983 to the present time.

It was in the third stage that the creation of the EMS very logically occurred in 1979. While this creation was to serve, as we have seen, the objectives of France's European monetary policy, it also responded to the new priorities of the domestic economic policy of competitive disinflation. In the minds of the political leaders at that time and of most of those who followed them, the EMS represented the logical complement to and main support of the adopted new economic strategy. It appeared as a sort of self-discipline all the more freely accepted as it corresponded to the new priority assigned to monetary stability and at the same time the means of more easily achieving such stability by the symmetrical and concerted intervention of the surplus and deficit countries and by mutual assistance between the central banks of the system. The EMS also represented the means of progressively 'buying' the credibility of the Bundesbank and the reputation of the German currency and hence of eventually rebalancing the Franco-German tandem or even sharing Germany's leadership over monetary Europe.

Logically, then, the French government should have supplemented its accession to the EMS by giving French monetary policy real autonomy (independence of the central bank and obligation for it to defend the value of the national currency as a matter of priority). This was not the case, probably because at the time there was neither a sufficiently broad political consensus nor an absolute resolve in favour of the new economic strategy — as the events of 1981—82 were, incidentally, rapidly to prove. It was not until the monetary union project was adopted that the need for this reform became accepted.

The question arises how far have the objectives linked to accession to the EMS been attained? By voluntarily submitting to the discipline of the EMS, France has, of course, obtained by definition a distinct stabilization of the franc's exchange rates in the short run in accordance with the very principle of the system's functioning. Through the restriction of the variation margin to ±2.25 per cent the volatility of the exchange rate was considerably reduced during the period 1979—91 compared with that of the years 1972—78. This difference was not without significance for private operators, in so far as it reduced the exchange risk. It also partly explains the reorientation of France's foreign relations towards the European market (from 57 per cent of exports in 1979 to 63 per cent in 1990).

But the stabilization of the central rate was much more laborious. To begin with, the franc was a fairly unstable and even depreciating currency (see Table 10.3 above). To correct inflation differentials, the central rate in relation to the ECU was devalued three times from October 1981 to March 1983. Thereafter, it registered only slight modifications that offset only about a half of the cumulative price differentials, which reflects the will of the authorities to ensure not only the franc's stability but also its strength, in spite of unfavourable price-elasticities, with a view to accelerating disinflation and at the risk of delaying the restoration of external equilibrium. Altogether, the franc fell from 5.7981 ECUs in March 1979 to 6.90403 ECUs on 12 January 1987, a devaluation of more than 19 per cent. Compared with the repeatedly revalued mark, the devaluation amounted to 37 per cent. It was therefore only after eight years that the exchange rate of the franc became fully stabilized in relation to the ECU, and it was only in 1989 that the French government clearly indicated its intention of firmly maintaining the franc/mark parity in future and that political and industrial circles seemed to give their support to this objective, after some of them had long recommended devaluation or even withdrawal from the exchange mechanism.

The slowness of this process was due to various factors. First was the unbalancing effect of the second oil shock which also affected other members of the EMS. Second and above all, was the single-handed resumption in 1981–82 of the old strategy of priority growth, i.e. an economic policy of budgetary deficit, wage increases, monetary expansion and industrial conservation, at complete variance with the requirement of external equilibrium and exchange stability and hence with the EMS's logic. The final factor was the increasing trade deficit, linked to the growing overvaluation of the franc within the EMS up to 1987 and, with respect to Germany, up to the present time. This was, especially, the trade deficit resulting from the substantial fall in the dollar from 1985, which once more disrupted exchange relations within the EMS and reduced the international competitiveness of French firms in spite of the progressive reorientation of foreign trade towards the Community.

The stabilization of a relatively high nominal exchange rate required, from March 1983 onwards, a particularly rigorous policy of deceleration of the money supply sustained by the reduction of the budgetary deficit

Table 10.4 Economic policy indicators

	1983	1984	1985	1986	1987	1988	1989	1990[1]
M2 money supply ann. var. as %	13.7	9.8	6.0	4.0	4.4	3.7	4.5	0.7
Nominal remun. of employees per capita ann. var. as %	10.1	8.2	6.6	4.1	3.7	3.8	4.0	4.0
Funding balance of public admin. as % of GDP	− 3.2	− 2.8	− 2.9	− 2.7	− 2.0	− 1.4	− 1.2	− 1.1

1. Forecasts

Source: Eurostat

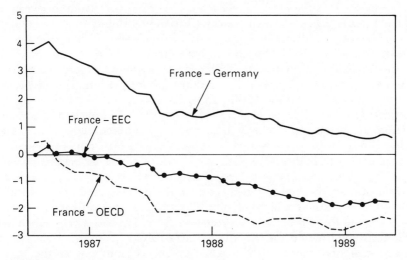

Figure 10.1 France's inflation differentials[1]

1 Differentials calculated on basis % variations (in annual mal shifts) of the consumer price index

Source: OECD

and the disindexation of nominal wages (see Table 10.4), as well as a policy for the structural adaptation of supply. It resulted in sharp disinflation (see Figure 10.1) but because of its failure to produce an increasing foreign surplus rapidly, its cost in terms of growth and employment was high: from 1983 to 1987, French growth was, for the first time since the Second World War, inferior on a long-term basis to the average rate of industrialized countries, and the unemployment rate continued to rise.

It was, of course, the slowness and cost of this exchange rate stabilization policy that repeatedly provoked a debate on France's membership of the EMS, notably in 1982—83 and again in 1987—88 (Le Cacheux and Leconte, 1987). Some thought that in order to align its nominal performances on those of Germany, France would be compelled to sacrifice growth and full employment on a long-term basis. It is true that, taking into account the initial geographical and sectorial structure of France's external relations and the similarity of collective preferences between the United States and France, a worldwide monetary system geared to the dollar would have been less constraining for France than a regional system based on the mark, as shown by the close correlation between the French trade balance and the dollar's variations. But as France could not take the risk of disorganizing intra-EEC relations, a choice had to be made, between the EMS and a quite limited type of floating. The criticism of the EMS was thus in reality a criticism of the stabilization strategy and, even more deeply, of European integration. The advocating of the franc's withdrawal was an elegant way of recommending the return to the illusory facilities of chronic inflation and systematic devaluation, whereas external adjustment constitutes, in fact, a vicious circle for an open country whose exports have a high import content, as is the case with France. The EMS could not of course be held responsible for the French economy's loss of competitiveness between 1979 and 1985, nor for the high interest rates prevailing throughout the world at the time — without which inflation would have been difficult to control — let alone for the dollar's depreciation from 1985 to 1991, which was the main explanation for the loss of extra-EEC market shares. It did not even entail the choice of an exchange rate as ambitious as the franc's from 1983. The provisional interruption of the 'virtuous circle' between 1986 and 1991 can be explained in fact by this option of French governments in favour of an artificially over-valued exchange rate, worsened by the unfavourable circumstance of the dollar's fall. The only fault of the EMS was to serve as an indicator of the monetary consequences of external shocks and economic policy errors as well as profound economic disparities. But in so far as it contributed to the reorientation of economic policy from 1983 — an influence that is historically established — it is clear today that the EMS has had a favourable effect on the French economy. As its initiators had hoped, it has indeed had the advantage for France of constituting a permanent factor of self-discipline and rationalization of economic policy, a useful indicator and safeguard for disciplining the action of public authorities and the behaviour of economic forces as well as ensuring really satisfactory performances in the long run.

It was thanks to the maintenance of this new policy of medium-term rigour and structural adaptation, that from 1987, i.e. from the international fall of interest rates and import prices, then of the world-wide and especially German revival, the virtuous circle of disinflation and growth started to emerge (see Figure 10.2) and that, for the first time since 1970, growth again overtook the increase in prices. The situation deteriorated again in late 1990 under the influence of the world recession, but the latter affected France less than most of the other developed countries and in 1991 the French inflation rate was lower than Germany's. It is also thanks to this strategy of a stable and strong currency and thanks to the liberal institutional reforms it induced or allowed that France can today satisfactorily internationalize its productive system and indeed soon catch up Germany and Japan. It is, finally, thanks to this stabilization and modernization strategy that France can hope to progressively improve its

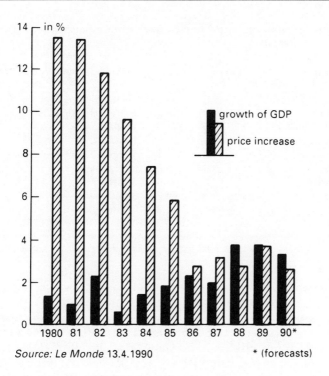

Source: Le Monde 13.4.1990   * (forecasts)

Figure 10.2   The virtuous circle of growth and disinflation

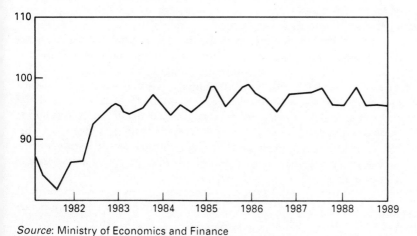

Source: Ministry of Economics and Finance

Figure 10.3   Cover ratio fob/fob (as a %), seasonally adjusted

Table 10.5   France's principal foreign trade balances in 1989 (in billions of francs)

Principal negative balances		Principal positive balances	
1. FRG	− 59.6	1. United Kingdom	18.4
2. Japan	− 29.2	2. Switzerland	15.4
3. United States	− 21.3	3. Spain	9.2
4. Belgo-Lux. Econ. Union	− 14.0	4. India	4.2
5. Norway	− 13.1	5. Egypt	3.6
6. Italy	− 6.8	6. Algeria	3.3
7. Brazil	− 6.4	7. Greece	3.2
8. Ireland	− 6.2	8. Tunisia	2.7
9. USSR	− 5.8	9. Portugal	2.3
10. Sweden	− 5.3	10. Hong Kong	2.3

place in the international division of labour, which an ill-advised economic interventionism and a certain protectionism have long allowed to deteriorate (INSEE, 1989). Although France remains the fourth world exporter, its persistent trade deficit (see Figure 10.3) reveals a certain lack of off-price competitiveness and shows that the effort to modernize and adapt productive structures is not yet finished. At present, therefore, France's market shares are still very sensitive to relative prices (INSEE, 1990): it has surpluses only with countries outside the exchange mechanism (see Table 10.5), and the recent accession of Spain and Great Britain to this mechanism, which will lead them to make a bigger stabilization effort, will not improve the situation in this respect. Of course, German reunification, which is equivalent to a vast economic reactivation policy for Europe, will on the other hand reduce the trade deficit for some time, but this reduction is liable to be only temporary.

The slow rise in the dollar is more encouraging in the longer term, but as long as a cumulative inflation differential with Germany − the principle trading partner (it was still 15 per cent in 1991 in relation to 1979) − and a structural inferiority exist, it is essential that France continue to systematically improve its price-competitiveness (Bilger, 1985). Not until it succeeds in securing a permanent foreign surplus will it lastingly enter this virtuous circle of macro-economic performances, the characteristic of the strongest economies.

While the durable stabilization of the franc now seems more fully secured, it has not yet attained the other objective of French monetary policy, which is to provide France's central bank with a credibility comparable to the German central bank's and endow the franc with an international status comparable to the mark's. France is still obliged, despite disinflation, to maintain an interest rate differential of around one point with Germany, which of course represents a considerable cost for

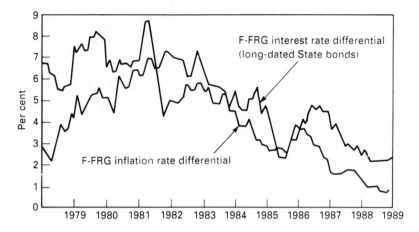

Source: Ministry of Economics and Finance

Figure 10.4   France–FRG differentials in interest rate and inflation rate

French companies and public borrowers (see Figure 10.4). It is possible that the financing needs resulting from German reunification will enable this gap to be further reduced, but the respite would be of short duration if its underlying causes were not eliminated.

This gap results from several factors. First of all, as we have seen, the stability of the franc in relation to the mark is still too recent to be taken for granted by international operators, just as the total liberalization of capital movements started only in January 1990. A bad reputation takes a long time to eliminate. Not until 10 years after tying the florin to the mark did the Netherlands cease to have to bear a risk premium in their interest rates. Besides, the persistent trade balance deficit, due to the franc's overvaluation and to a lack of investment, industrial moderniza- tion and commercial dynamism still casts doubt on France's ability to maintain this stability; while unified Germany continues to have surpluses, albeit reduced, but still comfortable. France must therefore continue to incur international debts, which perpetuates the deficit of current transactions, continues to make attractive interest rates necessary and maintains an exchange risk for holders of francs. It may be said that the franc is stable and even firm, despite the removal of exchange controls, but not really strong yet. To be strong, a currency must not only be stable on a long-term basis, it must be systematically under- valued and hence appear a permanent candidate for revaluation. Last but not least, France has not yet carried out the institutional consolidation of its declared resolve to give priority to monetary stability, which also casts doubt on that resolve, whereas in practical terms the dependence of the Banque de France in relation to the Bundesbank is already resulting in its independence in relation to French government. Even the French insistence on the accelerated implementation of monetary union gives rise to suspicion concerning long-term intentions: is France definitely aiming at exemplary monetary stability or is it still only aspiring to the sharing of the stabilization burden or even to a relaxation of its standards?

It is not surprising, therefore, in the face of persistent questions, that the franc is still neither regarded by international operators as a strong currency in comparison with the mark, and nor is it perfectly substitutable for the latter; thus a differential of credibility between the French and German central banks still remains. The persistent gap between German and French interest rates and the necessary alignment of French monetary policy on that of Germany cannot therefore be regarded as costs of the EMS but rather as the costs of a still inadequate economic competitiveness and a still uncertain monetary determination.

All in all, the EMS does seem to have offered France the advantages it could have expected. These would be the reduction of short-term exchange rate volatility, stabilization of mid-term rates, incentive to rationalize and 'discipline' the economic policy, and improvement of macro-economic performances. If membership of the EMS seemed to have resulted in certain costs, these are not in fact attributable to the EMS, but to errors of economic policy or to structural defects whose harmful consequences would have been equally, if not more, apparent in a wide-open economy with a floating franc.

The clearest evidence of the truth of this assertion is to be found in a comparative study of performances achieved during the last few years in France, Germany and Great Britain (see Table 10.6). It cannot readily be seen that France occupies an intermediate position. Germany progressively obtained — up to reunification — the best results overall, which was not always the case before the entry into force of the EMS and especially before the collapse of the Bretton Woods IMS. So far, therefore, this country has succeeded in deriving net gains superior to France's from the EMS, thanks to its structural lead and dominant position as well as the duration and vigour of its stabilization policy. But France has been progressively catching up, except in respect of its foreign balance, whereas Great Britain, which made the opposite choice of a floating exchange rate and monetary independence and was thus able to secure a stronger growth rate for a while, is today seeing the gap increasing, except with regard to unemployment rate. It is therefore evident that the ultimate price of Great Britain's option in favour of freedom rather than exchange stability is monetary depreciation and a loss of international competitiveness, hence increasing foreign indebtedness. The British deficit *vis-à-vis* France (see Table 10.5 above) is significant in this respect and the international dependence of the British economy is also apparent in interest rates markedly higher than those in France.

Of course, there are not only the strictly economic performances to be

Table 10.6   Macro-economic performances of Great Britain, France and Germany

	GB	F	FRG
Growth rate[1]			
1985	3.6	1.7	2.0
1986	3.1	2.1	2.3
1987	3.8	2.2	1.9
1988	4.2	3.4	3.7
1989	2.2	3.3	3.8
1990[5]	2.1	3.2	3.5
Unemployment rate[2]			
1985	11.5	10.3	7.3
1986	11.5	10.4	6.5
1987	10.6	10.5	6.4
1988	8.7	10.2	6.4
1989	6.8	9.5	5.6
1990[5]	6.5	9.1	5.4
Inflation rate[3]			
1985	5.3	5.8	2.1
1986	4.4	2.7	− 0.2
1987	3.9	3.1	0.7
1988	5.0	2.7	1.1
1989	5.3	3.5	3.1
1990[5]	5.5	2.7	2.7
Foreign balance[4]			
1985	0.7	0.1	2.6
1986	− 0.9	0.5	4.4
1987	− 1.6	− 0.4	3.9
1988	− 3.2	0.4	4.1
1989	− 4.1	0.5	5.3
1990[5]	− 3.3	− 0.5	5.8

1. GDP at constant prices, annual variation as %
2. as % of civilian active population
3. implicit index of private consumer price, annual variation as %
4. current transactions balance, as % of GDP
5. forecasts prior to German reunification and the new oil shock.

Source: Eurostat

taken into account, but also the political costs. The franc is now *de facto* in the mark zone, and Germany has clearly reinforced, thanks to the EMS, its leading role in world-wide and especially European monetary affairs. But this leadership has been detrimental to Great Britain and possibly more so to France. British independence during the last 10 years has therefore proved more superficial than real, and Great Britain's recent joining of the European monetary bloc clearly denotes acknowledgement of this fact. Monetary independence cannot be decreed, it has to be built up.

By voluntarily submitting to the fairly flexible collective constraints of the EMS, but by also benefiting from its occasional collective support, France therefore seems to have made the right choice, even if the tangible results have not always been optimum. For five years it has been reaping the initial benefits of the virtuous circle of internal and external monetary stability. It should now, by intensifying its economic effort and showing monetary courage, ensure that all the other advantages accrue so as to be able to approach in the best possible manner the monetary union planned for the end of this century.

June 1991

References

Bilger, F. (1985) L'expansion dans la stabilité, Economica, Paris.
Commission of the European Community (1979) The European Monetary System, European Economy, no. 3, July.
Genière, R. de la (1975) Vingt-cinq ans de coopération monétaire, Eurépargne, no. 10/75.
Giavazzi, F., Micossi, S. and Miller, M. (1988) The European Monetary System, Cambridge University Press, Cambridge.
Gleske, L., Granet, R. and Scharrer, H.E. (1989) Zehn Jahre EMS, eine Bilanz, Wirtschaftsdienst, Hamburg, no. 2, February 1989.
Gros, D. and Thygesen, N. (1988) Le SME: Performances et perspectives, Revue de l'OFCE, no. 24, juillet.
INSEE (1989) La France dans la perspective du grand marché européen, Economie et Statistique, no. 217–18, janvier–février.
INSEE (1990) Rapport sur les comptes de la Nation 1989, INSEE Etudes, Paris.
Le Cacheux, J. and Leconte, F. (1987) Les contradictions du SME, Lettre de l'OFCE, no. 50, 16.12.
Maillet, P. and Rollet, P. (1988) Intégration économique européenne, théorie et pratique, Nathan, Paris.
Mathes, H. (1990) Aufweichung des EG-Stabilitatsstandards? Wirtschaftsdienst, Hamburg, no. 8, August.
Pébereau, M. (1987) La politique économique de la France. Les objectifs, Coll. U. Armand Colin, Paris.
Ungerer, H., Evans, O., Mayer, T and Young, P. (1986) The European Monetary System. Recent Developments, IMF Occasional Paper no. 48, Washington DC.
Ypersele, J. and van Koeune, J.C. (1988) Le système monétaire européen, origines, fonctionnement et perspectives, 3 edn., Perspectives européennes, Commission des Communautés européennes, Bruxelles.

PART II: FOREIGN POLICY

Chapter 11

Has the European Community been a benefit to France's foreign trade?

Jacques Mallet

Nothing is more hazardous than evaluating costs and benefits in such a complex undertaking as the European Community because it is not just a commercial treaty, nor even an economic organization, which has as its aim the complete integration of economies. Its purposes are of a political nature. The fundamental change of relations with Germany, which for all French Governments since 1950 has been the objective as well as the basis of the European Community, is incalculable. The same goes for the political weight of Europe, which has been greatly reinforced by the development of the Community.

Is such a calculation possible for foreign trade? There are, of course, statistical difficulties because since 1957 — the date of the signing of the Treaty of Rome — the Community has grown from six to nine member-states in 1973, to 10 in 1981, and 12 in 1986.

The Community has also increasingly opened itself to foreign countries after several GATT negotiations,[1] the finalizing of association treaties and various trade agreements. It is becoming difficult to isolate the effects of European integration from the consequences of the decrease in European protection and the growing volume of trade with the rest of the world.

One must also say that foreign trade should, from now on, be analysed in a wider sense. Beyond trade of goods and services one has to take into account movements of capital and technology transfers (international investments, patents).

Finally, foreign trade is only a result of many factors in which Community measures often have less effect than external events, for example the fluctuations of the dollar or of the oil price, the situation of the world economy, and fear over the results of international conflicts. Home macro-economical policies and company strategies also intervene for a large part but on the other hand, it is true that the Community, with its own dynamic, has had much influence on foreign environment, home policies and the strategy of companies.

The balance between these different factors varies depending on the periods of time and the sectors involved. All one can say is that the development of the European Community and its commercial policy have reinforced the Community's impact on the evolution and structure of exchanges, as much between members as with other countries.

The global results

Having made these few preliminary remarks, one can nevertheless try to measure the impact on France's foreign trade by first making a brief report on global results to which being a member of the Community contributed. The Community has opened to foreign markets an economy which, for a long period of time, had essentially been looking towards a domestic market and the 'Franc zone'. (This is in spite of its participation in the liberalization efforts of OEEC as far as quantitative restrictions are concerned.) Its purchases from and its sales to foreign countries, which formed in 1959 roughly 10 per cent of its GNP, are today more than 20 per cent. They have been more than doubled compared to total production. France has become the fourth exporter in the world. At present, two workers out of five are working for foreign trade, versus one out of ten in 1959.

Over the same period, one can see an acceleration of intercommunity trade which has developed faster than trade with other countries (twice as fast between 1959 and 1972). The share of the EEC in French foreign trade which was of 28.6 per cent in 1958 was over 60 per cent in 1989.[2] Trade with western Germany has been greatly developed: the Federal Republic has become France's main supplier and main client with 16 per cent of exports and 19.3 per cent of imports in 1989 (16.2 per cent and 22.7 per cent respectively for our manufactured goods).[3]

These are important results, but since the first two oil crises, at the beginning of the 1980s, the situation has worsened. France has lost some market shares in the Community as well as in the other countries; its imports have increased faster than its exports; and its foreign balance was in deficit,[4] whereas that of the Community as a whole tended to right itself. Despite a certain improvement since 1986, the deficit has remained till recently and was particularly noticeable for industrial balance — since 1987 — and Franco-German trade. West Germany, which was France's main partner was also the main deficit: FRF 60 billion in 1989 and 75 billion for manufactured goods alone (out of a total deficit of 84 billion with its European partners).[5] One must, however, notice the increase of French exports to Spain, with which it has had a surplus of FRF 8.801 billion and to Great Britain, with which the surplus reached FRF 18.471

billion. In both cases, the favourable commercial effects of the widening of the Community are noticeable.[6]

In this contrasted record there is a strong point: foodstuffs. It is the only important sector where French trade has been in surplus, and also the only one where the single market is already in existence. In 1989 the surplus reached FRF 50.9 billion. The major part of the sales — mainly gross products or first transformation goods — are sent to the Community. Trade with countries outside the Community in profit and then in deficit in 1986 and 1987, straightened out in 1988 and made a surplus of FRF 8.7 billion in 1989 — an increase of 23 per cent compared to the previous year, due to an important increase in sales for cereals, sugar, drinks and alcohol.[7] The main customers were Italy, West Germany, then Holland, Belgium and Luxembourg. Great Britain came in fifth place. Sales to Spain have increased a lot since it has become a member of the Community, from FRF 1.9 to 5.8 billion between 1985 and 1988. They reached FRF 7.7 billion in 1989 and equalled importations, proving many pessimistic predictions wrong.[8]

These few figures must be complemented by a more precise study of the evolution of France's foreign trade and of the Community. The growing interdependence between European economies has indeed led to a synchronization between good periods for the Community and for France. The rapid implementation of the customs union — achieved as early as 1968 — and of the Common Agricultural Policy have contributed, from 1958 to 1972, to a strong expansion of trade and growth of the economy (there is between these two 'variables' a high correlation). All the six countries have benefited from it: the Community is not 'a game of nil sum'. France has been one of the main beneficiaries, with an average annual growth of 5.5 per cent.

The two oil crises of 1973/74 and of 1979 opened a difficult period for Europe and for France. It signified the end of the '30 glorious years'. The third industrial revolution coming the Pacific coast, the stunning expansion of Japan and of the 'little dragons' of South East Asia, the industrialization of some Third World countries, the imbalance in world trade and the disorder of the international monetary system, hit Europe headlong; and more particularly France. This is because of its deficit in energy (even reduced by its nuclear energy programme); the fragility of its economy; and the structural weaknesses of its foreign trade which, in the long run, constantly tended towards a deficit. Having partially compensated for its losses by sales, by 'big contracts' in oil producing countries and in the Third World, France then took time to return to the European market, in which Germany had grown very powerful, and the decrease in oil revenue and the debts of developing countries had reduced those outlets. Moreover, France was badly placed with leading South East Asian markets and hardly present on the American market which was in rapid development. France, therefore, lost on all counts but the decline of its foreign trade corresponds with a decrease in the European economy — where growth slowed down, inflation and unemployment were growing and market shares getting smaller.[9]

After the signing of the Single Act and the speedy realization of a great economic space without internal frontiers, available to services and capital, a new period of expansion began. Investments are waking up, growth is starting again and intercommunity exchanges are heading towards an ascending path: the economy's competitiveness is improving and unemployment is reducing. Pushed by the 1992 dynamic, the French economy had a growth rate of 3.5 per cent in 1988 and 1989, and productive investments are increasing twice as fast as production. Between 1986 and 1989, 860,000 new jobs had been created, 400,000 in 1989 alone.

The optimistic world-wide economic situation and in particular the expansion of the American economy no doubt contributed to this positive evolution. But the creation of a single market has also been an important stimulus.

The slowing down of the world economy following the Gulf crisis, in particular in the United States, in Europe and at present in Japan — which adds to a gloomy climate in France — has, since then, led to a decrease of growth, a fall in investments and a rise in unemployment. The expected revival is late to come. Despite this unfavourable environment, the better competitiveness of French companies has allowed a recovery of foreign trade. Our country has gained market shares, mostly in the Community, where it has a beneficial balance (of FRF 1.8 billion in 1991). Today France's deficit comes totally from trade with the United States (FRF 48 billion), Japan (29.1 billion) and with newly industrial Asian countries.

Why was French foreign trade so good during the first period, so bad during the second, and so difficult to straighten up until now? The Community has suppressed obstacles to foreign trade, brought down protections; opened opportunities to exports and investments; imposed constraints and disciplines; and transferred at Community level most of the abilities in the field of commercial policy. The invigorating climate of competition has stimulated initiatives, but has also revealed and enlightened the weaknesses and errors of each country.

In 10 years the Common Market has contributed to breaking the yoke of protectionism, 'corporatism' and 'colbertism' which was strangling the French economy. But the latter would not have been able to bear this salutary economic shock if reforms and stabilization of currency had not been implemented at the end of 1958 — and if French company managers, hostile to the Community from the start,[10] had not actively involved themselves in taking on the European challenge.

On the contrary, at the beginning of the 1980s, France went alone with a boosting policy, through consumption and public expenses which immediately worsened inflation, increased budgetary and foreign deficit[11] and weakened the currency. At the same time, companies adopted too defensive an attitude facing the crisis. The necessary changes in the least competitive sectors — textile, steel industry, shipbuilding — were therefore delayed behind a 'ligne Maginot' of ruinous subsidies, which only managed to make inescapable 'restructurations' even more painful (though successful for the steel industry).

Since 1983, France has taken again the way of European 'convergence'. The common disciplines, in particular that of the European Monetary System, have had a major role in this return to reason. It is not too much to say that they determined the necessary change in French economic policy. But, to put the country on its feet again and enable the weakened companies to regenerate their 'margins'[12], the choice of 'rigour' had to be made. The home demand noticeably decreased during the two first years 1984—85. This late adjustment, compared to the one which had been undertaken at the time of the second oil crisis in other European countries, explains why France has taken little part in the international growth which started in 1983. This delay had a negative effect on foreign trade.

Better competitiveness

Despite an important mobilization of manufacturers, of which a majority are in favour of the common market,[13] the handicaps specific to French industry and economy, in a competition becoming world-wide and global, have been clearly noticeable. The 'price competitiveness', which remains vital, has very much improved, mainly because of the moderation in salary increases, and despite a high level of social expenses. Companies took the opportunity to improve their margins more than for gaining new market shares but, in the current phase, it seems that the major handicaps come from what we call the 'non price competitiveness', which commands the capacity of industry to adapt to the evolution of European and world-wide demand: the importance of own funds and investments of companies; the expenses in R&D programmes; the quality of products; the effectiveness of marketing and of after-sale actions; the number of plants in foreign countries; the workers' level of qualification; and so on.

Some recent studies have enabled us to calculate indicators of competitiveness and of specialization for French industry per sector. These studies are showing that France has low specialization levels in sectors which are not very dynamic (the food industry, metalwork, chemistry) of which the share in world trade has been slowing down during the last 20 years. France is unstable in some of its stronger sectors which are currently under threat, such as car manufacturing. Finally, many sectors, in which France benefits from strong positions, are exposed to the risk of deep changes resulting, for instance, from the opening of public markets, and much hinges on international negotiations: such is the case for agriculture; for services (of which France is the second exporter in the world), in particular for banks and insurances; for aeronautics; and, of course, for car manufacturers facing Japanese competition.

Today, the manufacturers' worries are not so much on the expected results of the single market, considered overall as beneficial, but more about the fact that it has no 'external section', and about the risks linked to the Uruguay Round, the opening of French markets without counterpart to foreign competitors: United States, Japan and newly industrialized countries. The farmers, as far as they are concerned, denounce both the bad management of the Common Agricultural Policy and the dangers of breaking up the support and the protection system in European agriculture, which would call to question the economic survival of many of them and cause a large part of home territory to be destined for 'desertification'.

There was, at the beginning of the Community, a sort of 'implicit contract'. France accepted the industrial common market, in which the more powerful German industry should benefit more, in exchange for an opening and organization of agricultural markets, from which France, the main producer of a Europe then in deficit, thought it would take the biggest profit. This rather simplistic scheme was rapidly outdated. France has become a great industrial power and, in turn, its industry has also benefited from the Common Market. France has, it's true, for many years, benefited a lot from the Common Agricultural Policy, but this policy also had secondary effects. In 1964 the choice of high common prices for cereals — under the pressure of our German partners — made it impossible for specialization to act in its favour. At the beginning of the 1970s, high guaranteed prices gave rise to surpluses and to unbearable budgetary costs, which obliged the Community in 1984 to reform most of the CAP's mechanisms: milk quotas, limitation of guaranteed quantities, tax of co-responsibility on cereals, then, in 1988, a ceiling on agricultural expenses.[14]

The CAP became, therefore, less advantageous to French interests and it will be even less so in the future. Overall, the CAP's evolution has been beneficial to countries in deficit: the 'monetary compensatory amounts' have helped German and Dutch exports; Germany has developed its production and its sales in the Community; and Great Britain has made surpluses with cereals. Gaps have been created in the Community 'preference' with the joining of Great Britain; the conclusion of preferential agreements — notably with the Mediterranean countries — and finally with the GATT agreements, allowing imports without levy for about 50 million tons of animal food.

It is undeniable that the CAP has helped the modernization and the expansion of French agriculture, at least up to recent years, and at the same time regulated prices for consumers. It has contributed to a smooth, progressive re-conversion (the share of the working population employed in agriculture went from 18 per cent in 1957 to 6.25 per cent in 1989), but it gave life to a 'dual agriculture', in which less than a third of the farms produce two-thirds of the crops. At the same time, small family farms face increasing hardship, surviving only at the expense of major debts or thanks to subsidies which reach, in some regions, 50 per cent of the revenue. Out of one million farmers, it is likely that, by the end of the century, 400,000 to 500,000 will have left their farms, a movement which has already started. Is it desirable or possible to speed up the process? Recent difficulties in the cattle meat and lamb markets, and the violent reactions which followed, have shown the seriousness of a crisis which is depriving hundreds of thousands of farmers of hope.

Nothing has better expressed their anxiety and will to survive than the great rally where 200,00 farmers from all over France gathered in Paris on 29 September 1991.

Everything taken into account, French agriculture would have a lot to lose by a renationalization of agricultural policies. The export refunds, in particular, remain an important element for French foreign trade — even if the biggest part of its agricultural exports are sold within the Community, and therefore without restitutions. Producing 23 per cent of the Community's crops, French agriculture clearly has an exporter vocation.

Victim of its own success, the CAP has faced, as we have seen, growing difficulties which made a fundamental reform of its mechanisms inescapable if better production control was to be ensured. This reform, proposed by the European Commission at the end of 1990 and strongly criticized by agricultural leaders, would not only have negative consequences for France, in particular for its foreign trade. Significant falls in prices — for cereals among other things — largely compensated by aid to farmers, would open new markets to French exports in the European Community. But it would be necessary at the same time to take measures at outer borders of the Community to reduce imports of cereal substitutes (soya bean, corn gluten for example), measures rejected by the United States.

At the end of this short study it is unquestionable that the participation of France in the Community has and will advantage more than inconvenience its foreign trade. But today there are still major uncertainties which prevent a definitive assessment.

The advantages are obvious, for consumers as well as for producers. For France, the European Community has been since 1958, and even since 1951 with the European Coal and Steel Community, a powerful stimulus for the growth and modernization of its economy as well as for the expansion of its foreign trade. It has made easier its integration in world trade and it has been rapidly pushing the necessary reforms for its competitiveness. There is still a lot to do, in particular the reduction of compulsory levies, the decreasing of expenses which are weighting on companies, and the improvement of the education, training and apprenticeship system.

Those advantages should even be bigger in the coming years with the completion of the single market. Evaluating the costs of 'non Europe', the Cecchini report tried to put a figure on expected gains from their elimination in terms of growth, prices, employment and foreign balance. Those gains are important. They will depend, for a large part, on common accompanying policies. But the report does not hide difficulties of the adjustment period which could have, at the beginning, negative consequences. Optimists think that the most difficult part is over. Will the future prove them right?

The prospects provided by the Single Act have already given a fresh boost to the internationalization of our important companies. Small companies, and many medium-size ones, still too often remain aloof from this movement, because of their insufficient size. As shown in a recent survey of 300 companies by the Industry Ministry (*France 300*), the anticipation of the 1992 target brought about a change in manufacturers' state of mind and attitudes. Most of them are now confidently adopting an offensive strategy for conquering foreign markets. In a new move, they now want to establish themselves abroad and first of all in Europe — though it is very difficult in Germany. They are looking for European partners to form alliances with them, set up 'joint ventures', mergers and acquisitions. In this way French industry will be able to enhance its assets more and compensate for its weaknesses. The specialization problems will be solved with the creation of European 'competitiveness poles' between complementary companies. Beyond the commercial Europe, almost completed, an industrial Europe is beginning, based on companies' initiative and synergy.

On the other hand, the Community and the European Monetary System (EMS) have led or should lead to convergence of national policies. In an open economy governments understood that they had to fight against inflation and ensure currency stability. Times of competitive devaluations are over. This is an expensive facility. Creating an imported inflation and diverting companies from necessary productivity efforts eventually ends in a deficit once again.

A large economic area, making up between 50 per cent to 60 per cent of its trade, has wider manoeuvre margins than national economies. It can gain a greater economic autonomy. The dynamic of a big market will help us to resist more easily the consequences of necessary adjustments in the American economy.

The Community has had very positive, direct or indirect, effects on co-operation for R&D programmes (Community programmes, Eureka, Airbus, Ariane). Many of those co-operations have a 'variable geometry', but their political and economical support has been the reinforcement of European integration.

Finally, as the first commercial power of the world, the Community has acquired a negotiation power, at international level, greater than that of national states. This was noticeable during the GATT negotiations, where the European Commission negotiated on behalf of the Twelve.

More generally, the European Community has had an educational role. It has made French people more attentive to international economic realities and to the importance of foreign trade. It is, in some way, responsible for the creation in 1974 of a Ministry of Foreign Trade.

Among the disadvantages, some observers think that the European Monetary System, as it is currently working, is obliging the French to slow down growth, whereas French demography would require a more rapid development; and forcing the application of a monetary policy very close to that of the Bundesbank in terms of interest rates. But in any case, in view of the high elasticity of imports in terms of growth, a policy aiming to support a very rapid development would soon be hampered by the degradation of our foreign trade. In the long run, the disciplines imposed by the EMS have proved to be beneficial.

Secondly, one must underline that the liberalization measures launched by the Single Act should normally lead to the end of the remaining national protections — quotas for cars and textiles, safety clause of 'Article 115' and various subsidies — and to an almost automatic opening of the European market to foreign countries. It will be the biggest solvent market in the world. Wealthy, homogeneous and transparent, it will become a very attractive target. In spite of recent progress in anti-dumping measures, the commercial policy of the Community has a lot of difficulties asserting itself. This is because of the divergence of views and interests between the Twelve, and because it does not have at its disposal instruments and means which can be compared to that of its great partners. An aggravating circumstance is the absence of a common policy, or even co-ordinated policies, concerning Japanese investments.

EC is not a fortress

More dependent on foreign trade than its main partners, the European Community is not, cannot be and will not be a fortress. Of all the great economic powers, the EC is, whatever may be said, the most open. Even in the relatively protected agriculture sector it remains the foremost importer in the world. The single market will be even more open than the Community is currently. It must be open but not just given. The demand for reciprocity does not express, on behalf of Europe, a protectionist attitude but the search for mutual advantages. With regard to Japan, a guarantee of access to market should be obtained, so that the concessions really counterbalance each other.

This point is still far off. An agreement has indeed been concluded, on 31 July 1991, between the EC and Japan in the problematic car sector. This agreement provides a limitation of Japanese exports during a transitional period, expiring at the end of 1999. By this time they should have reached a maximum figure of 1,230,000 cars. However, as nothing has yet been clearly decided about the Japanese plants in the Community, the effectiveness of the agreement is much reduced.

This having been said, the interest for France, as for Europe, is to contribute to the maintaining and developing of an open, multilateral system of international trade in goods and services; and to the reinforcement of GATT rules, for example for the settling of disputes, the respect of intellectual property and the fight against imitation and unfair competition. The EC has every interest in seeing the Uruguay Round succeed (despite its extraordinary complexity) in a global, balanced and realistic agreement, taking into account the difficulties of sectors which are the most affected by foreign competition, such as cars and textiles, and not endangering the European aeronautic co-operation (Airbus).

It is also very interested in putting an end to the subsidies war between Europe and the United States by means of a substantial and progressive reduction of all forms of support for agriculture. But it will not accept a brutal dismantling of the Common Agricultural Policy. This would massively reduce aid to exports and edict quantitative limitations on European agricultural exports, without touching direct aid allowed by the Americans to their farmers, or reducing imports of grain substitutes. For France, it is important that European agriculture maintains its export capacity. To a substantial degree, the future of world trade, and therefore the expansion of French foreign trade, will depend on the results of the Uruguay Round.

The divergences between Europe and the United States on agriculture are the main obstacle to success (in this conflict France stands in the front line). It is not, however, the only obstacle. From the French point of view, Japan is looking for free trade in one direction only, and as for the United States, they are clearly leading an aggressive commercial policy. By trying to create a North American Free Trade Area (NAFTA) and later a single market from Alaska to 'Terre de feu', and conducting, increasingly, a 'managed trade', they are apparently trying, in the name of free trade, to dictate their conditions to the European Community under the menace of unilateral measures which runs counter to the rules and spirit of GATT.

In Paris, economic and government circles are particularly worried about the protectionist attitude of American administrations in the services sector. They generally believed that the chances of compromise — wished for by businessmen afraid of the risks of a commercial war — would be better after the American elections because protectionist lobbies, very powerful on the other side of the Atlantic, are influential in presidential campaigning.

Many people in France think that, instead of seeking the inaccessible target of generalized free trade, it would be more realistic to look for agreements between unlocked 'regional areas' in the view of a world economy structured around three 'poles': North America, Japan and the European Community. Based on a common civilization and cultural affinities, ruled by a political will and respecting national states' identities, they can push even further the integration of open economies. Falling between an impossible world free trade and a dangerous protectionism, 'regionalization' will be the first step towards 'internationalization'.[15] Such a policy would require a modification of the GATT rules to adapt them to a new world.

New challenges

Other questions currently are arising, such as: what will be the consequences for France, in particular for its foreign trade, of the unification of Germany — our first commercial partner — and of the great changes in Eastern Europe? These events, of major importance, don't throw the existence of the European Community back into question, but, rather, will enlarge its prospects. The government of Chancellor Kohl wants to integrate German unification to the European union.

At first, the unification has reduced German commercial surpluses and increased demand in the former GDR, where France is, by far, the foremost foreign investor. It allowed a readjustment in Franco-German exchanges, to which the 'competitive deflation' policy, conducted by France since 1983, has also contributed.

The cost of unification, which has been largely underestimated, added to high salary increases in German industry, have led to a rise in inflation, which the Bundesbank had to fight with high interest rates. Growth has therefore slowed down in Western Germany, while the former GDR experienced a strong expansion. This credit policy of France's main partner in the European Monetary System made impossible a softening of interest rates in France, which would have been more than welcome in a time of weak economic activity.

Recent research by the Observatoire Français des Conjonctures Économiques (OFCE), indicates that, up to now, the French economy has benefited on the whole from German unification. It gained, in terms of foreign trade, 25 billion francs in 1990 and 30 billion francs in 1991, and in terms of growth, 0.8 points: without Germany's unification, French growth in 1991 would only have amounted to 0.4 per cent instead of the 1.4 per cent expected, and unemployment would have become even worse.

In the long run several issues are possible depending on the evolution of East Germany. Will it be a 'fifth dragon' or 'new *mezzogiorno*'? The important structural weaknesses of the former GDR's economy suggest it will stay, for at least 10 years, a burden to the Federal Republic. When the 'restructurations' are completed at the expense of enormous budgetary transfers, with probably a certain 'de-industrialization' of Eastern Germany, the latter will form about 5 per cent of western German industry. The predictable success of the unification won't result in a substantial change in the economic relationship between France and Germany. However, with Germany at the centre of all markets in the 'great Europe', it will have a leading position in 'Mittel Europa'.

The success of Europe of the Twelve has led the EFTA countries to sign a treaty which will in 1993 widen the single market to 18 countries forming, with nearly 370 million inhabitants, the greatest free trade area in the world. It is, for them, a step towards membership in the European Community for which Austria, Sweden and Finland have already applied. France is currently sending a small part of its exports (about 5 per cent to 6 per cent) to this large commercial area which will open up new opportunities for the economy.

Other prospects of enlargement, more uncertain, will open in Central Europe, a region where German businessmen have been very active, but French exporters not active enough. The association agreements, recently concluded with Poland, Hungary and Czechoslovakia, will end in the full membership strongly wished for by these countries. These agreements provide guarantees in somewhat unsteady sectors (e.g. agriculture, steel, textiles). Other countries in Central and Oriental Europe, less advanced towards reform and democracy, have the same desire to become, in the future, members of the European Community. At the end of the century there will be movement towards a great European organized area of 500 million people from Brest to Brest Litovsk. The Republics of the former USSR are, in many ways, a specific problem requiring new forms of co-operation. In the coming years, French exporters should be finding greater and greater interest in this European 'new frontier'. At present, it is impossible to evaluate the effects this evolution may have on French foreign trade.

There is one last point to be addressed: the Maastricht treaty impact. The creation of a European currency would be the natural complement to the single market, enabling the free movement of goods and capital, without controls, at the internal borders of the Community. A single currency, ruled by a collective board, would enlarge the 'margins manoeuvre' of French policy, today compelled to constantly support the franc credibility in front of DM. It would suppress for exporters the high costs resulting from the exchange between currenciers or from the covering of exchange risks and would reduce the monetary uncertainties which hamper investments. French businessmen have well understood these benefits. It would finally transfer to European level the balance of payments problem and allow member-states new possibilities for growth. The implied disciplines would ensure that this growth may be achieved in a context of stability. As the foremost currency in the world the ECU would make the European economy less dependent on fluctuations of the dollar and yen. For instance, the ECU would be used — instead of the dollar — for oil imports and Airbus exports. The global assessment of Economic and Monetary Union (EMU) would therefore be beneficial to France, in particular for foreign trade.

A necessary addition to that must be the fall-outs of the Cohesion Fund devoted to the development of the less prosperous countries of the Community, (Ireland, Greece, Portugal, Spain). For these French exports raised 60 billion francs between 1985 and 1990 (that is to say a quarter of all French commercial surplus inside Europe of the Twelve). France would obviously benefit from the aid given to their development.

Nothing rationally justifies the fears of many French people regarding 1 January 1993 and the Maastricht Treaty. It is a challenge and an opportunity. For France, whose growth increasingly depends on foreign trade, it would be suicide to enclose itself in the hexagon's borders through fear. But there are several ways to organize the necessary opening of the French economy.

With or without the European Community, France cannot escape the hard constraints of world competition if it wants to remain an important nation. In a strong and coherent community, endowed with a large organized market, a single currency, strong agriculture, with substantial R&D programmes and truly European companies, but also with a common external policy, France would be in a better position to face competition. It will have, without any doubt, the greatest interest in belonging to this Community. It would have much less in belonging to a large free trade area of 25 to 35 countries, lacking consistency and common policies, deregulated, and open to all outside winds. An ill-managed enlargement of the European Community may lead to that dangerous drift.

Formulating, in these terms, the problem of France's foreign trade is, finally, to pose that of the political union of Europe. We need to reinforce the Community by creating a political union, and be able to enlarge it without destroying it. That is the Maastricht Treaty's prospect.

Notes

1. At the end of the Kennedy Round the common external tariff was around 5 per cent. As an average of domestic customs duties it does not have 'tariff peaks' like the American tariff. New reductions will be made after the Uruguay Round, which has been widened to non tariff protections, currently the most important.
2. In 1991 this percentage is of 63 per cent for exports, of 58.1 per cent for imports.
3. In 1991 France made with Germany 18.6 per cent of its exports and 17.7 per cent of its imports (19 per cent and 20.8 per cent for manufactured goods).
4. France's trade deficit was of FRF 30.4 billion in 1991 (about 0.4 per cent of French GNP).
5. This deficit has been reduced to FRF 7.4 billion in 1991.
6. In 1991 the trade surplus with Spain has been of FRF 15.3 billion (the greatest excedent); with Great Britain of 10.6 billion. The devaluations in 1992 of the pound sterling, the peseta and the lira will noticeably affect the trade with these countries.

7. France is the second exporter in the world for cereals.
8. In 1991 this surplus has been of 44.4 billion. With countries outside the Community it has been of 2.4 billion. Our agricultural exports to Spain have amounted to 12.6 billion francs, showing a surplus of FRF 2.2 billion.
9. It is true for all EEC Countries, including Germany.
10. In particular, textile and metalwork industries.
11. France is one of the developed countries where the elasticity of imports is the highest compared to domestic demand.
12. French companies only got back in 1989 to the 'margin' level they had in 1973.
13. This positive attitude and this 'mobilization' were clearly shown in the 'White book' (*Notre enterprise, l'Europe*) published at the end of the convention of the French Confederation of Industries (CNPF) on 13 December 1988, where gathered representatives of 50 industries and of 35 employers' unions. The Single Market's prospects gave rise to many studies on every aspect of French economic competitiveness.
14. The budget of the Community Agriculture Fund went from 70 to 60 per cent of the Community budget.
15. It is one of the conclusions of the last CEPII report, *Economie mondiale 1990– 2000 – L'imperatif de croissance*, Economica, Paris, 1992.

References

Storelu, L. (1987) *L'ambition internationale* Seuil, L'histoire immédiate, Paris.
David, F. (1988) *Relations économiques internationales La politique commerciale des grandes puissances face à la crise*, STH, Paris.
Lafay, G., and Herzog, C. (1989) *La fin des avantages acquis* Centre d'études prospectives et d'informations internationales (CEPII), Economica, Paris.
La France dans la perspective du grand marché-européen, Economie et Statistiques no. 217--18, INSEE, Paris, janvier—février 1989.
Ou en est la compétitivité française? Direction des relations économiques extérieures. Ministère de l'économie et des finances. Ministère du commerce extérieur. *La Documentation Française.* Paris, juin 1989.
La compétitivité de l'economie française dans la perspective du marché unique. Ministère du commerce extérieur. *La Documentation Française.* Paris, premier trimestre 1990.
Poncet, J.F., and Barbier, B. (1989) *Les conséquences pour l'économie française de l'achèvement du marché intérieur européen en 1992.* Report of the information group appointed by the committee on economic affairs of French Senate, Paris.
Europe technologique industrielle et commerciale. Report of the committee chaired by Antoine Riboud for the nineteenth plan 1989—92. Secrétariat d'Etat auprès du Premier ministre chargé du plan. Paris, juillet 1989.
France 300, Ministère de l'industrie et de l'aménagement du territoire. Paris, juillet 1989.
Esambert, B. (1991) *La guerre économique mondiale* Olivier Orban. Paris, septembre.

Chapter 12

France, the Third World and the Community

François-Georges Dreyfus

On France's request, in particular, the Treaty of Rome in setting up the European Economic Community included provisions for support for different developing countries. The Yaoundé Convention, for 18 French-speaking African countries in 1963 and the Arusha Agreement in 1969, for English-speaking countries, gave substance to this principle, which was given its final form in the successive Lomé Agreements. However, when it came to determining how to use both the aid coming from the individual states and the aid from the Community, there was a problem.

Even though the Single Act did not set out a common policy toward the Third World in specific terms, it did succeed in consolidating Community policy, as was confirmed in the Maastricht Treaty (130 V– 130 Y). This meant that the Community and France, not to mention the states involved, had to start thinking along new lines.

When the EEC was founded, France was adamant about making provisions in the Treaty of Rome for the various Overseas Territories then under her control: Algeria, French West Africa (Mali, Senegal, Niger, Mauritania, Guinea, the Ivory Coast, Benin), Togo, French Equatorial Africa (Gabon, the Congo, Ubangui-Shari, known today as the Central African Republic, Chad), Cameroon, Madagascar and the French Coast of Somalia. Articles 131 to 136 of the Treaty served this purpose, and provided for a unilateral system of association to promote sustained relations in the two important areas of trade and aid. In 1958, the European Development Fund was established, making it possible to set up infra-structures funded through non-repayable aid. Naturally, these provisions applied to the Belgian and Dutch territories.

The implementation of institutional co-operation

Between 1960 and 1963, many of these Overseas Countries and Territories became independent, which meant that the nature of the relations they entertained with the EEC had to undergo certain changes. The African and Malagasy countries were intent on maintaining the benefits secured by their links with Europe. The EEC thus signed the first Yaoundé Convention with 18 African countries (the former French Overseas Territories, not including Algeria or the Congo, which had become Zaire by then), forming the Association of African and Malagasy states (AAMS). This convention was concluded for a five-year period (1964—69) and covered preferential trade agreements, and technical and financial assistance within the framework of the European Development Fund (EDF).

From 1966, the prospect of the inclusion of Great Britain into the Common Market posed the problem of integrating the African states belonging to the Commonwealth into the Yaoundé association. The Arusha Agreements, between the EEC and three English-speaking African states, Kenya, Tanzania and Uganda, were thus signed in 1969 for this reason. On 29 July 1969, the second Yaoundé Convention was signed.

With Great Britain's entry into the Community in 1973 the problem of the other African countries arose. They had to choose between three possible solutions:

- taking part in renegotiating an agreement along the lines of the Yaoundé Convention;
- negotiating preferential trade agreements, along the lines of the Arusha agreements; and
- negotiating ordinary trade agreements.

In the end, the English- and French-speaking Afro—Caribbean—Pacific (ACP) countries decided to work out a common stance, basing co-operation on the principles of the Yaoundé Convention, hence the Lomé Conventions.

Forty-six ACP countries were included in the first Lomé Convention of 1975 and implemented the system of stabilization of export earnings, or STABEX, with a view to maintaining a certain level of income for exporters of basic products. At the same time, a number of institutions were being set up: the Council of Ministers, the Council of Ambassadors, the Consultative Committee.

The second Lomé Convention, signed between the EEC and 57 of the ACP countries on 31 October 1979 introduced another scheme, or SYSMIN (MINEX), designed to maintain the viability of the mining sector in the ACP countries. Finally, on 8 December 1984, a third convention was signed with 65 ACP countries, and then signed by Angola in 1985.

The third Lomé Convention focused on a more independent approach to development for ACP countries and aimed to make Community aid more effective. In addition to this, aid in very specific areas was provided for: i.e. for combating drought and desertification, to assist the fishing industry etc.

The volume of European aid

The EDF and the European Investment Bank (EIB) invested relatively small amounts in terms of aid to the ACP countries, as illustrated in Table 12.1. However, under Lomé II, the payments made on 31 December 1988 only covered 74 per cent of the funding commitment and, under Lomé III, they only covered 27.2 per cent of the funding commitment. Since 1960, the European Community member-states have given more than 140 billion dollars in aid to the Third World, or nearly six times what was given as Community aid.

Table 12.1 Aid to ACP countries (in million ECUs)

	Treaty of Rome	Yaoundé I	Yaoundé II	Lomé I	Lomé II	Lomé III	Lomé IV
EDF	581	666	828	3,000	4,823	7,855	7,995
EIB	–	64	90	390	685	1,100	1,300
Total	581	730	918	3,390	5,508	8,955	9,295

Note: a total of 29,377 million ECUs from 1960 to 1990, the equivalent of approximately 35 billion dollars.

This aid can be broken down as follows, by donor country:

West Germany	30 billion
France	50 billion
Great Britain	30 billion
Other states in the Community	30 billion

These figures only cover subsidies and direct aids, and do not include loans from various European governments which together come to a total which is just slightly under that quoted above. This includes neither private aid nor loans granted by financial establishments. For France and Germany, the only governments for which specific data are available, the figures in Table 12.2 have been compiled.

The total amounts donated or loaned to the Third World from the countries of Western Europe come to some 400 billion dollars, more than two-thirds of which went to Africa. But however sizeable this aid was,

Table 12.2 Aid figures for France and Germany (in millions of dollars)

	West Germany	France
Public subsidies	30,000	50,000
Public loans	60,000	50,000
Private Aid (NGOs)	6,000	2,000
Loans from financial establishments	55,000	40,000
Total	151,000	142,000

Sources: for France, *Panorama de l'action du ministère de la Co-operation*. For West Germany, *Entwicklungspolitik Jahresbericht*, 1991. For the other European countries, *Lexikon Dritte Welt*, Rororo, 1988.

Table 12.3 GNP per capita in ACP countries (1986 dollars)

	1960	1970	1986	1990
Benin	70	308	334	380
Cameroon	107	360	939	990
Ivory Coast	179	794	1,071	790
Ghana	198	514	395	380
Guinea	175	164	322	430
Kenya	84	286	376	380
Madagascar	101	266	259	230
Nigeria	78	290	807	270
Uganda	72	270	187	250
Central African Republic	90	447	321	390
Senegal	207	472	430	719
Tanzania	55	200	240	120
Zaire	92	162	170	260

Sources: for 1960, *United Nations Yearbook*; for 1970, *The LDCs, 1988 Report*, 1989, Table A3; for 1990, *Etat du Monde*, 1991 (in 1990 $)

it did not keep the situation in most of the ACP from getting worse, as illustrated in Table 12.3.

For the non-African states, the situation developed in a totally different way, not only in the Far East, but also in Southeast Asia and Latin America, as is clear in Table 12.4. The Community, suffering from guilt pangs over the colonial past, has not really taken this difficult problem into consideration within the past 25 years.

A European commission, whose development policy had Socialist leanings, was set up to deal with the problems of international development on the initiative of Willy Brandt, who chaired the commission. The *North–South* report, published in 1980, underlined the volume of

Table 12.4 GNP per capita, non-African states (1986 dollars)

	1960	1970	1980	1990
France	1,336	2,020	12,000	19,650
United States (for reference)	2,804	3,540	12,000	21,925
Argentina	606	954	1,960	2,260
Brazil	206	220	2,080	2,550
Peru	208	366	–	1,090
The Philippines	164	150	680	760
Indonesia	73	85	490	550
South Korea	67	120	1,630	5,440
Taiwan	117	133	–	7,846
Japan	451	900	9,870	25,260

Source: Etat du Monde 1991/92

Community exports to developing countries in the light of the changes in overall economic growth. This report was based on one of the commission's reports and, according to Eurostat, the Community exports only a minute share of its total exports to the ACP countries. In 1985, the volume of Europe of the Ten's exports were at their maximum level at 19,336 million ECUs, or just under 2 per cent of the Community's total exports. It seems that the Community was reluctant about tackling a problem on that scale, wanting to spare the ACP countries even the slightest disappointment.

The Community's co-operation policy

By 1960, it was decided that the major objective of the EEC was to be that of lining up with world prices. As this process resulted in a 25 per cent shortfall, there had to be some compensation for prices, which would be made possible by increasing yield by 25 per cent, to be provided through production aids. However, to be on the safe side, the Community Council of Ministers maintained an overpricing scheme. They introduced a system for the 'stabilization of export earnings' (STABEX), concluded a 'Sugar' protocol, and developed special schemes for certain types of products such as bananas, rum and beef. This was supplemented by a parallel arrangement for mineral products, known as SYSMIN, covering copper, manganese, phosphates, bauxite and aluminium, tin and iron ore.[1]

As it stands at the present time, there are a number of disadvantages involved in the provisions set out pursuant to the Yaoundé Convention and in the Lomé I, II, III and IV Conventions. The institutional system is heavy and in addition to the Council of Ministers and the Technical Committees (for agricultural products, industrial co-operation and customs co-operation), working groups on bananas and rum, not to mention the five sub-committees of the *ad hoc* groups, it also includes two technical centres for agricultural co-operation and industrial development, and a Trust Fund 'to regulate cultural co-operation' as well. Not only is all of this very costly, as is to be expected, but the system also functions poorly.

The first reason for this is very simple: from 1983 to 1987, Community aid represented 7.39 per cent of public development aid to the ACP countries, the aid of the member-states coming to five times this figure (35.19 per cent). Out of a total aid figure of US $49,865 million, the Community provides US $3,683 million and the member-states US $46,182 billion.[2]

The second reason is because the procedure is too heavy. The following figures (in million ECUs), taken from the Court of Auditors Report,[3] gives us some idea of this problem. The report also underlined the distortions there were between the funding commitments and the actual sums disbursed.[4]

	5th EDF	6th EDF
	(Position on 31 December 1988)	
Reserves	4,823	7,855
Funding commitment	4,600 (95.4%)	4,662 (59.3%)
Payments	3,422 (71.0%)	1,277 (16.3%)

A sum of 9,885 million ECUs were paid over the six EDFs from 1960 to 1988, as well as the funds provided by the European Investment Bank (EIB).

The final reason is that this money was not used wisely. The report is clear on this problem:

Over the 1982–87 period, the volume of funds used for actual agricultural development operations for recipient countries is very limited in comparison with the initial value of the products supplied by the Community . . . .
Either the funds were not used, or they were used to fund projects the Court had already warned the Commission against, and what they have basically ended up by doing is funding deficits of all kinds.[5]

The heart of the problem is in using the aid. Aid from the Community is basically public aid which means that it has to transit through the states. The problem with this is that these states have done a very poor job of managing aid funds. The *Official Journal of the European Community* and the Reports of the Court of Auditors on Community aid to development countries[6] are clear on this, as is the following statement: 'Some states seem to be incapable of knowing which of their needs should have priority'.

The limits of public aid

According to the 1986 report, the fourth EDF funded primarily industrial investments and the purchase of agricultural equipment for Guinea, one of the least developed (in the terms of the Lomé Convention) of the ACP countries, even though the basic infrastructures (electricity, roads, trails, etc.), which are absolutely necessary for them to operate, were non-existent. Supplying electrical power which can be such a problem in such countries, is largely responsible not only for the delay of nearly three years in renovating the Sanoyah textile plant, but also for making the Community raise its commitment in this operation from 30 to 43.2 million ECUs. The one-year delay in starting up the Sogulplast plastics materials plant and the additional 0.5 million ECUs the EDF had to provide to fund the project are also attributable to the poor quality of the electrical facilities. If this situation continues, the operating of both of these plants will be jeopardized. As to the cotton production development project in upper Guinea, part of the reason the project was unsuccessful is that it was virtually impossible to get the right information to farmers or to get inputs through the trails and over the bridges in this area. This stalemate situation stands as proof that an important stage of planning had been left out — that of closely taking stock of the priorities of the national economy before deciding what actions could reasonably be encouraged.

Behind African and South American underdevelopment[7] were the ill-effects of capitalism and colonialism. Behind the successful take-off of Japan, Taiwan, South Korea, Singapore and Hong Kong lay technological development. How many watches, calculators, cameras or cars are made in Africa or South America? This is the heart of the problem, and the case of the Philippines is a prime example. In 1940 the Philippines, then a U.S. colony, was considered to be the most developed of all the colonies in the Far East, in comparison to the Dutch East Indies and French Indochina, with Korea and Taiwan lying further behind. In 1965, recovering from war, the GDPs of all these countries remained relatively weak and close to one another. But what is the situation today? One only needs to look at Table 12.4 to ask oneself questions that unfortunately the Community authorities did not ask.

France and co-operation

In these circumstances, what should French policy be towards the developing world when the Community is politically and economically strong? Should it defer to Community authorities and transfer budgetary resources to them, or should it, on the other hand, pursue its own policy in this area?

At the beginning of the twentieth century France's colonial empire was both widespread and fragmented. From Morocco to Tunisia the whole Maghreb (except Rif, a Spanish colony) was under French administration, as well as most of Saharan Africa and a good part of West Africa from Green Cape to the Congo — the main exceptions being Gambia, Sierra Leone, the Gold Coast (now Ghana) and Nigeria which were British territories, and two German colonies, Togo and Cameroon, the larger part of which came under French mandate after 1918. To these can be added Madagascar, Réunion, Indochina (with a colony, the Cochinchina, and four protectorates, Annam, Cambodia, Laos and Tonkin), New Caledonia, Tahiti, and in the West Indies, Martinique, Guadeloupe and Guyana. Altogether, these territories represent 12 million sq. kms of land. But beside the Maghreb and Indochina, the 'French Empire', as it was called in the thirties, fell into decay. One may judge for oneself from the following: in 1939, for 2,500,000 sq. kms of useful land (excluding the Saharan areas) French West Africa had 3,900 kms of railway lines, 35,000 kms of telegraph lines and 5,000 kms of telephone lines, while Nigeria alone (having an area of 985,000 sq. kms) had 5,000 kms of railway lines, 25,000 kms of telegraph lines and 11,300 kms of telephone lines. Clearly, in 1940 the French Empire in Africa was underdeveloped.

It was at this time that it was decided that the Empire's economy had to be modernized and the projects drawn up by the Vichy government were adopted by the Fourth republic, where they were developed by ministers as dynamic as Coste-Floret, Pflimlin, Mitterrand and Defferre. By 1946, a 'Ten Year Development Plan for the Overseas Territories' was ratified, which was the direct descendant of the 'Ten-Year Infrastructures Plan' of 1942. In actual fact, it was not until 1950 that work on the infrastructures (roads, telecommunications, ports, airports, schooling and health policy) had actually begun. The results were dramatic: the Niger Office, the Richard Toll complexes, the Port of Abidjan, the prolongation of the railway from Bobo Dioulasso to Ouagadougou and the big international airports in Dakar, Abidjan and Brazzaville. At the same time, production figures rose incredibly, particularly for French West Africa. Examples are given in the following figures which are in millions of tonnes or for cattle in thousands of heads:

Year	Peanuts	Palm oil	Cocoa	Coffee	Banana	Cattle	Iron	ˈ ʼuxite
1938	781	21	47	8	–	3,7ʳ⁻		
1942	643	?	55	32	?			
1950	704	11	62	64	?			9
1957	1,250	18	72	112	1 ı			366

Sources: for 1938, 1950 and 1957 Beaujeu-Garnier, J. ⎾ın, A. *Images du Monde*, 1958; for 1942, Dreyfus, F.G. *Histoire de Vich*⟩

This policy was actually initiated with what was known as the Sarraut Plan in 1920, but was not implemented until many years later. The Franco-colonial block was founded on production subsidies. According to A. Van Haervebecke, (in *Rémunération du Travail et commerce extérieur*, Louvain, 1970) the effect the 'private hunting ground' had was that it artificially increased the level of prices within the franc zone. The over-payment for Senegalese peanuts came to FRF 27.2 billion CIF over the 1952 to 1959 period, despite the fact that these overprices were evaluated at 13 billion for imports over the same period, involving a net benefit of 14.2 billion for Senegal. Not only did this keep the territories' economy from deteriorating, but it made it possible to expand. Over the 1950—57 period, cassava production doubled and the volume of exports rose by six times the amount. Madame Beaujeu Garnier wrote, on the eve of independence:

the richest territory from the economic standpoint at the present time is the Ivory Coast, it is also the only country which is against the overall unification of French West Africa. Guinea is the country which most probably has an industrial future ahead of it, thanks to its mineral resources and to the big internationally-owned companies which have set up office there. (*Images du Monde*, 1958, p. 82)

Independence did nothing to change the situation, despite General de Gaulle's claim that he was 'determined to free France from the constraints her empire had laid on her', recorded in *Mémoires d'Espoir*. Even though the names had changed, the system had not: FIDES became the FAC (Fonds d'Aide et de Co-operation) (Fund for Aid and Co-operation) and the CCFOM became the Caisse Centrale de Coopération Economique (CCCE), (Cultural and Economic Co-operation Fund). The change was brought about with the Yaoundé Agreements, the ex-colonies becoming the ACP countries (Africa, the Caribbean, Pacific). The overprices paid by France were on most of the products from the colonies and were to be maintained in another form.

What characterized French aid as opposed to the aid of other member-states was its mostly being given to Africa and the following figures illustrate this very clearly:

	1976	1986
Total Mediterranean countries	25.8	23.6
the Maghreb's share	23	18.1
Black Africa	57.1	62
Middle East	9.6	4.6
Southeast Asia	4.5	5.9
Latin America	3.0	2.9

The British and the Germans were far more equitable in distributing their aid. Western Black Africa received 20 per cent (Ghana and Nigeria mostly from the British, the Ivory Coast and Cameroon from the Germans), Eastern Africa received 25 per cent, Southeast Asia received 30 per cent from British aid and 20 per cent from the Germans, and Latin America received nearly 20 per cent of British aid and more than 30 per cent of German aid.

Both of these countries were generous in terms of aid. West Germany's amounted to approximately $45 billion-worth of public aid from 1960 to 1988 and $65 billion-worth in private investments (especially in Latin America and Southeast Asia) and British public aid came to some $30 billion. Aid from the other member-states in 1986 can be broken down as in Table 12.5. If Belgian and Italian aid went first to Africa and then to the Middle East, this was not the case with Denmark and the Netherlands who were far more universalist in distributing their aid.

Table 12.5 Aid from member-states in 1986 (in millions of current dollars)

	Belgium	Denmark	Italy	Holland
Public aid	8,400	7,500	13,500	31,200
% of GDP	0.5%	0.6%	0.18%	0.81%

For Africa, allowing the Community to determine the co-operation policy would bring catastrophe, as Great Britain, Germany, Denmark and the Netherlands would probably be pushing for aid to be distributed differently. In any case, under the present conditions, and because it only deals with governments of the ACP countries, the Community's co-operation policy is subject to much controversy. The same criticism can be made about French aid.[8] The situation thus called for a reinforcement of both the role and share of non-governmental organizations (NGOs). However, this involved other problems which have not yet been solved.

The role of non-governmental organizations (NGOs)

Development aid could be handled far more easily by non-governmental organizations which, not being state organizations, do not have to go through any governments. These mini-projects, which are all sub-Saharan Africa needs to regain food self-sufficiency (which they lost with independence), are obviously of no interest to the governments. Armament is more important for them, as is equipping themselves with elaborate and costly civil services, hospitals and prestigious-looking institutions which run them into debt and are often inoperative. Another problem is that public money often disappears into the pockets of government officials at all levels, corruption in Africa and in all the other developing countries having reached drastic proportions.

Just one example to illustrate this point is as follows: between former French West Africa, French Equatorial Africa states, Togo and Cameroon together, 100,000 men were employed in the regular armed forces and more than 75,000 in the paramilitary forces in 1989. Fifty years ago, in 1939, to cover exactly the same territory, France had 26,069 men in the regular armed forces (including infantrymen) and 7,000 men in the police force, and that was a volatile time on the verge of war. Our sympathy goes to those in Burkina-Faso and in Mali suffering from poverty and famine, but the irony is that in 1984, the former spent 34 million dollars on defence and that the latter's defence budget was 36 million dollars. These two governments, who are at war with one another at regular intervals, have more cannons than the French artillery had for the whole of French West Africa and French Equatorial Africa put together in 1939.

What these countries need is encouragement to use their soil, to improve it, to reafforest, to make the best use of their herds. Can this be done? To do so, a different policy would have to be implemented: rather than sending overseas volunteers who are teachers or administrators, it would be far more intelligent to send farmers to every village and bush as agricultural instructors; instead of sending university graduates, 3rd and 4th year medical students could be sent (keeping in mind the praiseworthy testimony of François Jacob with his action in Mao in Chad from February to November 1942, in *Statue intérieure*, at the age of just 22 years). As to the shortage of elementary school teachers, would it be possible for the thousands of African students who study at French universities to pay for their education by spending a year or two in the bush, under the supervision of school inspectors? Such schemes could be put into the hands of the NGOs provided they are trustworthy — but has this always been the case?

There are the cases falling under the condemnation of the Communities' Court of Auditors, for example. In 1986, a first NGO applied for co-funding under dubious conditions. Out of the 10 projects examined, two of them were not eligible because they were nearly finished. One of the projects had been submitted to several different money-backers, so that the funds raised exceeded the cost involved. However, the commission maintained its subsidy after repayment by the NGO of one of the other money-backer's contribution. The following is an extract from the report on the cases:

10.29 There were initial errors in technical and financial planning in five of the ten projects examined which were being managed by the NGO in question, meaning that they overran their costs. The most obvious example of this was a road project which had to be dropped because the major feature, a 60 meter-long bridge, had to be totally redesigned from the technical standpoint and also because it turned out that the cement was going to cost twice the estimated cost.

10.34 Even though the NGO's remunerations were quite high, it was not capable of following up operations properly. Out of the 12 draft projects examined, only two of them showed no signs of major discrepancies between the amount applied for in the subsidy and the final cost, no inaccurate calculations, no incomplete reports or a combination of the above.

The 1989 report on 1988 is just as critical with regard to those NGOs which do not provide very detailed reports on their activities.

The example of Madagascar

Madagascar is a typical example. In 1987, the Protestant organizations voiced their desperate concern:

The island has become one of the poorest countries of the world. The ground is eroded and has been degraded by torrential storms. The population is growing at an uncontrollable rate. There is less and less food to go around. The current situation is hopeless but the future looks even dimmer.

It is true that Madagascar must be helped, but sending money, provisions and medicine will not solve the problem of its poverty. What the Protestant churches left unsaid was that the authors of this drastic situation are the Malagasy governme it and its incompetence.

When Madagascar became independent in 1960, the island was definitely not rich, but it was not poor either. It exported agricultural products (rice and cattle, in particular) and mineral products. Its GDP per capita was 13 times lower than France's — but it had now dropped to 36 times lower. When the statistics compiled in *Images économiques du monde*, (Economic Pictures of the World) 1962 are compared with those in *Chiffres du monde* (Figures for the World), 1988, just published by the Encyclopédie Universalis, some alarming conclusions can be drawn. From 1960 to 1985, output increased only slightly but the population doubled, as illustrated in the following table:

	1960	1985
Cassava (in millions of tonnes)	1,827	2,2
Rice	1,300	2,178
Coffee	57	82
Sisal (in tonnes)	11	20
Vanilla	585	628
Cattle (in millions of heads)	6,387	10,400
Graphite (in tonnes)	14,890	14,718
Mica	1,232	734

According to Madame Beaujeu Garnier in her 1962 report, 'in 1960, the national revenue had been increasing on an average of 4 per cent per year for 10 years (from 1950); the margin is small, but must be maintained to improve the standard of living'. *L'Etat du Monde 1987–1988* said that 'in 1985, GDP growth (2.4 per cent) was lower than population growth and the per capita consumption level has dropped again (by 20 per cent between 1982 and 1984). Over the 1979—1986 period, Madagascar's GDP dropped at a rate of 0.3 per cent per year'. This is all cause for concern, as with a GDP per capita of less than 101 dollars per annum, Madagascar was one of the 10 least poor nations of Africa in 1960. Today, it is one of the five poorest countries.

This should all serve as a lesson to the Community who should take heed of what was said by Edgard Pisani and is written in his book *Pour l'Afrique* (A Plea for Africa). On the basis of his experience as Co-operation Commissioner at the European Commission, he makes a number of proposals which are down-to-earth and full of common sense: 'If farmers themselves are not the ones who request roads, wells and schools, they do not feel that these things belong to them or that they are to have anything to do with them'. Edgard Pisani also had the courage to go on and say: 'ethnic groups are what counts for Africa'. He underlines the importance of the family and defines the prerequisites needed for implementing a development policy. The chapter on B. Morse and M. Strong's undertakings in 1984 to combat famine is also worth reading. As their situation placed them above local institutions, they could do whatever they wanted and it turned out they were successful. But now that the emergency situation is over, we are back to square one. Edgard Pisani adamantly stressed that Africa's main priority has to be agriculture.

The Community and North–South relations

Ever since it was instituted (Articles 131 to 136 of the Treaty of Rome), the Community considered, and rightly so, that one of its purposes was to help developing countries. This was made possible through systems of aid to the ACP countries within such frameworks as that of Lomé. However, the situation in these countries grew increasingly bad from 1970 to 1990, as their share in world trade shifted from 4 per cent to less than 3 per cent. Furthermore, the ACP share represents only a very small part of the Community's trade. More than half of this trade is conducted with just four of the countries: Nigeria, the Ivory Coast, Zaire and Cameroon. This is because of the inadequacy of the productive system and the lack of competitiveness on the part of the ACP countries. The cocoa yield alone, in kg per hectare, illustrates this point:

Average for Africa	314
for Ivory Coast	650
Nigeria	250
Ghana	180
for Latin America	481
for Asia	613
i.e. nearly twice Africa's yield, with the exception of the Ivory Coast	

Community aid for development has involved more than 20 billion ECUs since 1958, 111 billion of which was payable in subsidies. This aid was first spent on industry and transport, but this was not necessarily the most fruitful investment that could have been made. Instead of aiding industrialization, an agricultural development policy should have been followed. As M.P. Roy so accurately pointed out in *La CEE et le tiers monde* (The EEC and the Third World): 'the prestige of industry is so great that many nations look upon it as their only hope of survival'. The developing countries thus demand 'the transfer of the industrialized countries manufacturing facilities to the Third World (including the setup of basic industries: iron and steel, chemical, petrochemical, mechanical construction) and technologies'.[9] For the ACP countries, industrial co-operation has become a priority. At the present stage, they are unable to deal with this from the financial, human and technical standpoints. The mini-projects, which are an absolute necessity, on the other hand, have only benefited from 40 million ECUs and fishing aid has involved just under 62 million ECUs in aid.

When all is said and done, it was to avoid disappointing developing countries in general and ACP countries in particular that we helped them to set up 'projects which had been designed on far too large a scale for them, especially as such projects required a high level of technical skills'

(P. Roy). In actual fact, the Community has no control over these undertakings.

These considerations should serve as a basis for thought for those in the Community who are intent on helping the developing countries overcome their underdevelopment. To do so, there must be a change in the way problems are addressed, in the way people think and in the way policies are developed although this will more than likely stir up some heated reactions.

This should perhaps have been discussed during the negotiations for Lomé IV but this was not the case. The same events were maintained. Under these circumstances, as long as the Community's policy does not change (and it does not look like the Maastricht Treaty is proposing any changes), France has no reason to relinquish her own national jurisdiction over co-operation in favour of the Community.

N.B.

(1) We have not considered the Overseas Departments or Overseas Territories in this context as they are an integral part of the French Republic.

(2) Other than the Community reports, reference has been made on a number of occasions to the United Nations 1988 *Report on LDCs*; the *World Bank Development Report, Poverty*, Washington, 1990, and the OECD report: *The Sahel facing the Future*, 1988.

Notes

1. See Maganza, G. (1990) *La Convention de Lomé*, Vol. XIII of European Economic Community Law, Brussels, on all of these topics. This book covers quite a bit of information but it is unfortunately very disorganized.
2. 'The Communities' Court of Auditors Report on the 1988 Fiscal Year', in the 12 December 1989 issue of the *OJEC*, p. 191.
3. *Ibid*, p. 190.
4. *Ibid*, p. 236.
5. *Ibid*, p. 145.
6. i.e. the 1985 report published on 15 December 1986 and the 1988 report published on 12 December 1989.
7. Let us bear in mind the countless pieces of literature on the ill-effects of capitalism on the South American continent and the religious consequences thereof (liberation theology) *Contra*: Nowak, M. *The Spirit of Democratic Capitalism*, French translation, 1982: *Une éthique économique*, Le Cerf, 1988.
8. On the bases for Community policy, see the Maganza volume, op. cit. especially pp. 154 to 188.
9. This has in fact been largely confirmed in a report which has come under quite a bit of criticism with regard to France: Claude Freud, *Quelle coopération?*, Paris, Karthala, 1988.

Chapter 13

French attitudes to the foreign policy and defence of Europe

Pierre Gerbet

The Community way towards unifying Europe was defined by Jean Monnet and Robert Schuman in their historic declaration of 9 May 1950. What they proposed was both realistic and progressive: 'Europe will not be made all at once or according to a single, general plan. It will be built through concrete achievements, which first create a *de facto* solidarity'. Since it was impossible to set up a federal European power because states refused to renounce their exclusiveness in essential areas such as monetary policy, foreign policy and defence, it was decided to proceed by bringing together activities where the control of national capacities could be more easily managed by independent European institutions.

This led to the establishment of the European Coal and Steel Community (Treaty of Paris, 18 April 1951), then the European Atomic Energy Community and the European Economic Community (Treaty of Rome, 25 March 1957). As a result, the progressive integration of the economies of the member-states made it both possible and necessary to have encompassing authorities and thus it would be possible for Europe to become an entity in the field of foreign policy and defence.

It was a long-term process. An attempt to speed it up, through the European Defence Community which was proposed by France as a solution to the problem of rearming Germany, and which required a European Political Community to tie together the foreign policies of the member-states, failed in 1954. As it turned out, it was the French National Assembly which rejected the treaty for a European army, thus negating the project for a political community. After that, integration could only be economic.

The ideas of General de Gaulle

On the return of General de Gaulle to power in 1958, the question of European integration was again raised. For de Gaulle, the economic integration of the Six, very desirable from the point of view of French interests, should not be permitted to lead to political integration. He wanted to construct a Europe of States (*Europe des Etats*) which would stay sovereign, and a European Europe playing its due part in international relations — hence his idea in 1961—62 for a Union of States, whose task would be to work out common policies in foreign affairs and defence. Chancellor Adenauer personally supported de Gaulle's ideas but among France's partners and even in Germany there was strong opposition.

At the start, the institutional system suggested was purely intergovernmental: meetings of heads of state and government; meetings of foreign ministers; and a political commission formed from representatives of governments, without any independent organ responsible for promoting the common interest and giving guarantees to smaller countries. De Gaulle was hostile to all ideas of supranationality, especially in those realms essential for state sovereignty — foreign policy and defence. Thus he would allow no majority voting and no independent commission. He hoped that by leaning on Germany, France could point the policies of the Six (already linked by economic solidarity) in the direction of his own conceptions.

It is clear, then, that there were deep differences, even over the ultimate direction of a common foreign policy and defence. France's partners were very attached to the Atlantic alliance and to NATO, and refused to distance themselves from the United States, while de Gaulle started to do so, diplomatically and even militarily. He created an independent nuclear strike force, and ended up by taking France out of NATO's integrated military structure in March 1966.

In these circumstances, agreement was impossible. Belgium and the Netherlands made their acceptance of this Union of States conditional on the entry of Great Britain into the Community, seeing this as a balance to the Franco-German bloc and a guarantee of adherence to an Atlantic policy. On 17 April 1962 they broke off negotiations over the 'Fouchet plan', named after the French negotiator. General de Gaulle strongly resented this setback, and tried to compensate for it by the Franco-German treaty of 22 January 1963, anticipating co-operation in the fields of foreign policy, defence and cultural matters; but despite regular intergovernmental Franco-German consultations thereafter it was not possible to overcome fundamental differences. In the context of the Six, the foreign ministers, who had got into the habit of meeting since 1959 to discuss international problems, stopping doing so after de Gaulle's first veto of Britain's application for entry on 14 January 1963.

The European Economic Community developed rapidly after the Customs Union and the Common Agricultural Policy were put in place. France behaved positively in this regard but was against the Community's appearing as an actor distinct from the member-states in external matters. She acted on this in the following ways:

- she refused to accord the Community the right to appoint ambassadors to third countries though such countries appointed ambassadors to the Community;
- she required the Council of Ministers to exercise jurisdiction over the commission in its relations with international organizations;
- she opposed the President of the Commission's adopting the protocol of a head of state in relations with third countries;
- she refused to allow the Commission sole conduct of negotiations over agreements of association; and
- she excluded from common commercial policy requests for loans and technical assistance which are important tools in national foreign policy.

The idea of consulting over external policy reappeared after de Gaulle's second veto of Britain's application on 27 November 1967. France's partners, extremely irritated, then decided to use the framework of the Western European Union — established in 1954 to keep watch over the national rearmament of the German Federal Republic — to develop, between the Six and Great Britain, institutionalized co-operation in the area of foreign policy and defence, technology, and finance. De Gaulle opposed this, not wanting to see a political Europe of Seven including Britain, which he considered too 'Atlanticist', at the very time he opposed its entry into the economic Community. He did not agree that the WEU should try to set up compulsory consultation between its members over international political problems. He did not want the WEU to become a political organization under British influence.

The evolution of the French position

After General de Gaulle retired, Georges Pompidou, who was elected President of the Republic on 15 June 1969, understood that France could no longer oppose British entry as this was paralysing the Community. He even saw Britain's membership as an advantage in balancing the growing weight of the Federal Republic of Germany, and in better opposing supranational tendencies. To avoid the danger of diluting the enlarged Community, he wanted to reinforce them by instituting an Economic and Monetary Union. Co-operation in external policy became even more essential to demonstrate the unity of the European Community vis-à-vis the rest of the world; and to harmonize if possible their foreign policies towards the United States, Eastern Europe and the Middle East. France's partners accepted this proposition because Britain would soon be a member of the Communities and because the question of a deep difference between France and its allies over defence policy no longer arose.

The Luxemburg conference of 27 October 1970 specified the

mechanics of European political co-operation in foreign policy. It involved:

ensuring, through information disseminated and by regular consultations a better .nutual understanding of the major problems in international policy; in reinforcing solidarity by harmonizing points of view and, whenever possible and desirable, in common action.

The report of 23 July 1973 went further, and stipulated: 'On questions of foreign policy, each state undertakes not to finally determine its own position without consulting its partners'.

In what body would these consultations take place? When the French government followed the Gaullist line, it insisted on a complete separation from the Community system, staying committed to intergovernmentalism. Therefore political co-operation does not have its own institutions. It operates through meetings of representatives of member-states at all levels (heads of state, ministers of foreign affairs, and senior officials in foreign ministries). This was outlined in the 'Fouchet plan', so similar to the idea of an intergovernmental political secretariat put forward by France after 1971, but failed because of differences of opinion as to its role (France under German pressure wanted to see it political, but the Benelux countries would not have it), and its location (France advocated Paris so as to demonstrate its separation from the Communities, while its partners wanted Brussels for exactly the opposite reason). The Franco-German proposal at the European Council meeting in Milan in June 1985 for an important political union secretariat was rejected from fear that it would overshadow the Commission of the Communities. Finally, the Single European Act of 17 February 1986 which legally established political co-operation, decided to create a modest administrative secretariat to assist the rotating Presidency of the Communities. This would be made up of civil servants from different countries, located in Brussels, so as to be close to Community institutions. In the event the initial French position had to be considerably softened.

This was also the case with the links between political co-operation and Community institutions. From the start, the French government insisted on complete separation. The foreign ministers meet quarterly and official heads monthly in the capital of the country which provides the President, and not at Community headquarters. France has, however, to accept that regular contacts with the Communities must be established. The Luxemburg report of 23 October 1970 anticipated that the Commission would be involved in the business of political co-operation whenever it touched on Community activities, but at the Summit meeting in Paris 19–21 October 1972 the French government insisted that it must be for the governments to decide on commission participation. The meeting in Copenhagen on 23 July 1973 recalled the principle of separation, but equally congratulated itself that continuous dialogue had been institutionalized. In 1975, again, the Chirac government refused to abandon, as the Tindemans report had suggested, the distinction between the centres of decision for political co-operation and those of the Communities. However the creation, on the initiative of President Giscard d'Estaing, of the European Council for the Communities and for political co-operation set rapprochement going between the two systems.

By force of circumstances the Commission, marginalized at the beginning, found itself involved in political co-operation at all levels both ministerial and administrative. The meeting in London on 13 October 1981 took note of this, and the Stuttgart Declaration on European Union of 19 June 1983 confirmed it. Finally, the Single European Act of 18—28 February 1986 institutionalized full and complete involvement in political co-operation, by invoking the necessity for consistency, since it is the Communities which deploy the means of economic action (aid, embargos, etc.) utilized in foreign policy.

The decision mechanisms remain in every way distinct. Like Britain, France has always resisted majority voting in certain areas of external policy (Tindemans report of 1975, Genscher-Colombo proposals of 1981). Besides, political co-operation has not been restrictive. The only requirement of the Single Act is for the 'exchange of information and consultation'. It doesn't include any obligation to arrive at a common position. Each member-state retains the right to decide its own actions or to take positions different from the others. The partners must simply do their best to implement together a European foreign policy, not a common external policy.

Putting political co-operation to work

Political co-operation, as progressively defined, is undoubtedly an interest of French policy. It is an instrument for giving France opportunities to exert her influence, and have her ideas supported by her partners. It could be said that it is a 'multiplier of power'. France has taken a stand in promoting her conception of 'European identity' whereas Britain has remained very much aligned with the United States. But France also experienced difficulties, having partners with very different perspectives and interests. Like Britain, France has the status of a major power (being a permanent member of the Security Council and a member of the nuclear club), a status she does not intend to give up to the advantage of the European entity she wants to develop — a difficult contradiction. In any case, France preserves her freedom of action and can take her own initiatives.

Another problem stems from differences in size among the Twelve, and their divergent interests in the great international questions in which France intends to play a part, with or without Europe. This explains the notion, formerly envisaged by General de Gaulle, of a directory of the major powers, who would take the initiatives, the smaller states being compelled to follow along. Because of the opposition of smaller powers, there is no question of returning to this formula, but for reasons of effectiveness, France has developed, at the margins of political co-operation, bilateral contacts first with Germany (these are essential, and comprise the engine of the Communities) then, less narrowly, with Britain and Italy.

For the past 20 years, the interest of French presidents in political co-operation has known high and low points before being publicly stated. Georges Pompidou, who had wanted an institution for political co-operation, used it from the beginning to promote, among the Six, French ideas about the Near East, which were considered pro-Arab; and about the multilateral discussions at Helsinki, designed to avoid interbloc confrontation. He showed a growing interest in political co-operation as a result of the setback to the project for Economic and Monetary Union, of the Soviet-American rapprochement, and the Kissinger plan to revitalize the Atlantic Alliance. This allowed the Europeans only regional interests, whereas the US had to play the part of leader because of its world interests. In the Arab-Israel war of 1973, Europe had been a 'nonperson', in Michel Jobert's terms, hence the attempt to set up a European entity in foreign policy. At the Copenhagen summit of 14–15 December 1973, France inspired a 'Declaration of European identity', defining general principles and declaring the desire of the Nine to 'see Europe speak with one voice in the major affairs of the world'. This was not to be the case: at the time of the oil crisis and the creation by the United States of the International Energy Agency, France found herself isolated, her partners having ranged themselves alongside the Americans.

Valery Giscard d'Estaing, elected President of the Republic on 19 May 1974, worked towards political co-operation in various ways: through the creation of the European Council; by softening French policies towards the US thus allowing her to achieve rapprochement with her European partners without falling into 'Atlanticism'; and by strengthening Franco-German links with Chancellor Helmut Schmidt, himself mindful of the need to keep his distance from the US. Kissinger wanted the countries of the Community to engage in talks with the US before every important decision they took together and France's partners were inclined to comply with this. President Pompidou, however, had been totally opposed to this preliminary consultation seeing it as a means whereby the Americans would influence European decisions. Giscard d'Estaing adopted a compromise: transatlantic consultations were not obligatory and would only take place if the European Council so decided (meeting at Gymnich 21 April 1974).

France used political co-operation extensively in the implementation of the Helsinki accords on the CSCE, and above all in defining a European position on the problems of the Near East. She persuaded her partners to agree to write into the Declaration of Venice of 13 June 1980 the right of self-determination for the Palestinians, and participation of the Palestine Liberation Organization in the global settlement of the Arab-Israeli conflict. A common position on this was hard to achieve because it differed from that of the United States. This Declaration would come to be considered the apogee of political co-operation, in as much as at the same time the Europeans adopted a different position from that of the US on sanctions against the Soviet Union in 1980, and at the time of the Polish crisis of 1981, while being concerned to preserve detente.

Progress in European cohesion did not stop France from acting on its own and even without consultation in some instances: for example, by recognizing the MPLA in Angola in 1976, and military intervention in Zaire in 1977—78.

Francois Mitterrand, President of the Republic since 10 May 1981, began by distancing himself from political co-operation and equally from the Economic Community. He did not see himself as bound by the Declaration of Venice, he showed himself more friendly to Israel, considered a global settlement to be too ambitious, and advocated a policy of partial accords between the states of the Near East. Political co-operation played no part in the Lebanese crisis, even though several European countries intervened (France, Britain, Italy) alongside the United States.

Subsequently, President Mitterrand, who had initially emphasized domestic French politics, shifted towards reinforcing the Communities and developing political co-operation, especially in negotiations over the CSCE (Madrid conference of 1983). At the same time he gave a new emphasis to the Franco-German partnership. At the time of the upheavals in Eastern Europe and the reunification of Germany, he at first had an impulse for acting on his own, but then drew close to Bonn and favoured the adoption of common positions by the Twelve.

How does one measure the gains and losses for France from political co-operation? It is hard to do this for the foreign policy of any given country: the results vary with the particular problems at any given time, as international life is complex and fluid. Then how do you evaluate the impact of one country's action on the positions taken collectively by a group of states? An obvious problem is the fact that discussions on political co-operation are confidential, and the bargaining needed to over-come divergencies and reach a common conclusion demands discretion. It is not possible to compare the points made by the French government with those adopted under the heading of political co-operation.

It can be said, overall, that France has profited from political co-operation. Many of her ideas made an impact and influenced European attitudes, especially over problems of security and disarmament in Europe, over the Near East, and over relations with the USSR and the Eastern bloc. France's insistence on distinguishing a European identity aroused echoes. While seeking to rally her partners around her ideas,

France has not diminished her freedom of action, and has played her part as a major power.

In the Gulf crisis, the Europe of the Twelve condemned the invasion of Kuwait and placed an economic embargo on Iraq in accordance with the decisions of the UN Security Council, but after that it was virtually out of the picture because of the diverging policies of the member-states and the fact that political co-operation did not touch on military questions. France, like Britain, acted in its capacity as a member of the Security Council, but Paris, unlike London, took a position somewhat different from that of the United States. Only with respect to the post-war situation did the Twelve reach a fundamen.al agreement, with the Declaration of 18 February 1991 defining the measures, at different levels, which would contribute to 'security, stability, and the development of all countries in the region' with the Community's support.

The weakness of Europe showed the need for it to 'exist' in a diplomatic framework, then to bring together the various national viewpoints and adopt common attitudes to external events and situations. Likewise, the setting up of the Economic and Monetary Union should contribute to lifting the taboo over the sovereignty of states in external matters and encourage the 'Communitization' of foreign policy, at least in some areas. France was not ready for this at the time of the Single European Act and was very cautious in foreign affairs, but its attitude has evolved. On 6 December 1990 President Mitterrand and Chancellor Kohl proposed 'a foreign policy and common security extending to all domains' — a new attitude for France to take. The Maastricht Treaty of 7 February 1992 on European union anticipated the defining and establishment by the Twelve of a 'foreign policy and common security' by means of 'systematic co-operation between member countries in the conduct of their policies', and even of 'common actions' in certain areas, the necessity of which being demonstrated by the crisis in the former Yugoslavia.

The problem of defence

There remains the problem of defence, in particular of a military capability to give Europe assured credibility in the field of international relations.

At the start of political co-operation, France did not want it to be competent on questions of defence, taking into account the deep differences in this area between France and her partners. Before long, however, she had to approach them over security in Europe and the CSCE negotiations. The London report of 13 October 1981 emphasised that 'it is the flexible and pragmatic approach to European Political Co-operation which will allow it to tackle political aspects of security'. France, anxious to preserve her freedom of action remained hostile to including all areas of security within the sphere of political co-operation, as the 1975 Tindemans report foresaw, and only accepted the 'political and economic aspects of security' invoked in the Stuttgart Declaration of 1983, defence itself being a side issue.

President Reagan's Strategic Defence Initiative stimulated the French government to promote European co-operation in technology (the EUREKA project outside the ambit of the Community). At the European Council in Milan, the Franco-German project took up again the British formula on the need to tackle 'technical and industrial conditions necessary for security'. In the final analysis, the Single European Act anticipated 'further interweaving of positions on the political and economic aspects of security' (Article 30). Thus the specifically military aspects continued to eschew political co-operation, in as much as some member countries are hostile to their inclusion (Ireland, Denmark, Greece) no less than countries applying for membership (Austria, Sweden).

The result is the attempt by France to reanimate the Western European Union, the only European organization competent in the matter of defence, even though it does not have a military organization at its disposal. The French government was supported by the FRG (at the time of the Franco-German meeting) and by Belgium (its Foreign Minister, M. Tindemans, having already taken this attitude). Britain, not wanting to take any action outside NATO, Italy and the Benelux countries anxious not to weaken the Community structure, were reluctant. The French memorandum of February 1984 was behind the ministerial discussions which succeeded in producing the Declaration of Rome (27 October 1984) which in turn looked towards restructuring WEU to allow it to co-ordinate the views of its members on the specific conditions for security in Europe, and to develop their co-operation over armaments. There is no longer a question of France encouraging her partners to distance themselves from NATO nor of envisaging a European defence outside NATO, but of constructing a 'European pillar' of the Atlantic Alliance. The Chirac government on 27 October 1987 adopted a 'platform on European interests in matters of security', insisting on the need for member-states to assume full responsibility for their conventional and nuclear defence, and maintaining 'coupling' with the United States. At the same time, Franco-German military cooperation developed with the setting up on 22 January 1988 of a Franco-German Council of Defence and the creation of a mixed Franco-German brigade, and, in 1992, of an army Corps.

WEU and political co-operation have thus come closer together. The decisions taken by the WEU now follow consultation among the Twelve. With the entry of Spain and Portugal, the WEU now has nine members, compared to the Community's Twelve. Also, as France wanted to build organic links between the Communities and the WEU, the latter would become part of the Political Union and work out a common security policy. This is what the Mitterrand-Kohl declaration of 6 December 1990 recommended, although Britain and other countries preferred to strengthen the links between the WEU and NATO. The Maastricht Treaty anticipated that the WEU 'would be developed, in that it would comprise the defence of the European Union and act to reinforce the European pillar of the Atlantic Alliance'.

However, the efforts of France to set up a truly European defence policy remain limited by the fact that she is still not part of the integrated military structure of NATO, whereas her partners remain there, and her strategic ideas continue to diverge from those of her allies, especially over the use of nuclear weapons. Yet a degree of rapprochement may be possible as conditions for security in Europe evolve, and NATO adapts to them.

References

Carmoy, Guy de (1970) *The Foreign Policies of France 1944–1968*, University of Chicago Press.

Ross, G., Hoffmann, S. and Malzacher, S. (ed.) (1987) *The Mitterrand experiment: continuity and change in Modern France*, New York, Oxford University Press (Europe and the international Order).

La Serre, F.de, Moreau-Defarges, P. (1983) 'France, a penchant for leadership', in Christopher Hill (ed.) *National Foreign Policies and European Political Cooperation*, London, George Allen and Unwin.

Girardet, R. (ed.) (1988) *La Défense de l'Europe*, Bruxelles, Editions Complexe.

Kaiser, K. and Lellouche, P. (1986) *Le couple franco-allemand et la défense de l'Europe*, Paris, Institut Français des Relations internationales (Travaux et Recherches).

PART III: GOVERNMENT AND LEGAL POLICY

Chapter 14

Sovereignty and supranationalism

Raymond Legrand-Lane

The term 'supranational' is an adjective with a strange fate. It was brought into the limelight by the French government's proposal to set up a European Coal and Steel Community on 9 May 1950; and it was used in the original wording of the Treaty establishing the Community, in a seemingly decisive way, to describe one of the major characteristics the new organization was to have. However, it was omitted intentionally from both the Paris Treaty implementing the ECSC and from the Treaties of Rome, which were the logical upshot and extension of the former. For many years, anything of a supranational nature was considered in political writings to be a mistake to be eradicated or a peril to be combated, in the eyes of most of the member countries. Studies on constitutional law made absolutely no mention of the concept, which apparently belonged more to the vocabulary of ideological quarrels — which have been known to be particularly heated in France — than to any actual legal terminology.

The concept

Obviously, the words 'supranational' and 'supranationalism' have been problematic in the past and will continue to be problematic in the future — as will the concepts they represent, which is cause for even greater concern. We can manage without the words themselves, but, whether we like it or not, the concepts behind them are part of the reality we know of as the European Community. As the Community sphere continues to take shape and develop, its supranational character reaches into more widespread areas, which does not mean that it shall be pervading all areas of Europe, an edifice whose date of completion is yet unknown. In simpler and clearer terms than those of the theoretical considerations, involving the requirements of demand of power in a multinational organization with varied managerial tasks to accomplish, the history of the first decades of the Community is sufficient proof that the course followed from 1950, with the aim of implementing supranational working methods and decision-making procedures, is irreversible. This is not to say that this will take place with no lulls and even halts from time to time in the process.

Let us note, however, that the first time supranationalism was heard of was not with the Schuman Plan, nor even with the voicing of major trends of opinion advocating the building of Europe which developed after World War II. The word 'supranational' was used many years before in describing the League of Nations and the projects for internationalizing specialized sectors to be co-ordinated, either under its banner or in conjunction with it.

It is worthless to try and trace a very elaborate conception of supranationalism back to those unfinished plans and fruitless proposals. They do stand to illustrate, though, that many people were aware, even at that time, that there were common, permanent interests in a number of areas and for all countries which were too difficult to be dealt with through the traditional diplomatic channels or inter-state contacts. Such a conclusion obviously makes us wonder why states agreed to transfer and delegate part of their sovereign rights to organizations independent of governments, as this is what supranationalism actually involves. In Europe, where memories of the Great War have done much to nurture a hardened spirit of nationalism, few politicians are willing to see such concepts develop into realities, and consequently such matters are only taken up in closed circles.

In 1950, the term supranational made a spectacular comeback and started to be used, if not by the public at large, at least at many levels of public opinion. Nothing was done to mask the radical innovation it conveyed. The independence of the High Authority which Robert Schuman proposed, involved a limited, but real, yielding of sovereignty on the part of the states who rallied around the project. One important aspect of the proposal was that it was basically twofold in nature. Beyond the actual content described therein, which alone was to involve the near future, it paved the way for a federalist prospect: the Community had to constitute 'the first real basis for a European federation necessary for the preservation of peace'. Admittedly, the new organization's architects were careful not to draw up a very precise blueprint for a future 'European federation', nor to give any overall guidelines, timetable, or even a rough basis for one. They did, however, establish a link between the concept of supranationalism and that of a federal union of states, though this was to remain unclear.

The French delegation's report, published after the signing of the Paris Treaty, took up on the existence of such a link.[1] Different aspects of the 'supranational concept' were developed in the report and the 'institutional guarantees' that it involved were spelled out, as there was no question of letting the High Authority, an independent body, exercise a limitless, unchecked control. In addition to the basic rules set out in the

Treaty, other institutions, such as the Council of Ministers, the Parliamentary Assembly and the Court of Justice, together with the High Authority, provided a balanced system not unlike the traditional balance of power found in democratic states. It was obvious that this blueprint for European public powers, even with such a limited scope, could be considered to be a 'prototype' of sorts, providing a springboard or reference point for a future federal organization operating over a much wider scope. The conclusion of the report commended such an orientation:

in the interest of the preservation of peace, as was the case with the development of production and the improvement of living conditions Europe, after having come out of the stages of feudal and provincial economy and having entered into the stage of a state economy, must go through the supranational Community. By setting up the supranational institutions providing the guidelines for the future Europe, it is taking its first major step, with no drastic changes, toward that direction.

In terms which are less formal, this supranational and federal orientation had to have been indicated to the governments who were requested to rally behind the Schuman Plan. This plan met with immediate reservations on the part of the British, which later turned into outright opposition. In their minds, supranationalism was in contradiction with their idea (and even more so with their feeling) of national sovereignty which was founded not so much on doctrine or texts as it was conveyed by a consensus of independence and powerful solidarity, maintained for many centuries, over a long-unconquered island history.

In speaking about his contacts following the proposal of 9 May 1950, Robert Schuman developed the arguments behind this position: 'No English government will ever confer on any European organization more authority than that which the Commonwealth bodies have', excluding all traces of supranationalism at the operational level. Why would they be willing to confer powers on an international continental organization which could not, at least at that time, act on as large a scale as the Commonwealth which was the 'apple of their eyes'? Moreover, the guarantees that the provisions of a treaty, drafted under the influence of continental lawyers — who were intent on putting everything in writing — could have given the British, were not reassuring, but sounded like more of a threat for the convinced advocates of the 'unwritten constitution'.[2]

Germany was to enter into the new organization under completely different circumstances. West Germany had been through a lot and was beginning to emerge from the political and legal abyss to which the unconditional surrender of May 1945 had relegated the old Reich. Freely taking part, as founder member, in the European Coal and Steel Community, did not mean sacrificing part of their sovereign rights so much as it meant gradual recovery of their sovereignty, as they would be participating on an equal footing with the other states included in the undertaking.

In addition to these major reasons, there are other causes which are worthy of mention, such as the relatively recent German political reunification, on an historical scale, the culmination of a lengthy experience in confederal organization. On the other hand, sovereignty cannot be traced back to any ancient traditions of territorial unity or centralized power in either Italy or the Benelux countries, as was the case for both Great Britain and France.

Why is it that in French circles, where the problems of sovereignty in view of the prospects of integration were subject to such heated discussions that the term 'supranational' had become greatly discredited, there was no immediate opposition to the first Community project (which could have put a real damper on it)? The arguments put forward seemed to be based on form rather than on content, and public opinion was basically in favour of the Schuman proposal. The main reason for their enthusiasm was that this proposal corresponded to a widespread and sincere European ambition, albeit unclear and noncommittal. After much shallow talk, this ambition was given the opportunity to become a reality, solving, at the same time a difficult and pressing problem, i.e. what to do with traditional German industries. The solution which was being proposed involved a parting of the ways with France's post-World War I policy which had turned out to be disastrous. The unique and promising path that was thus being forged easily met with approval, even though the French public authorities had to waive all or part of their rights for controlling industry, the general public not even thinking for a minute that controlling industry was the state's job.

It can be said that at that time in France, supranationalism was not considered a threat. It was even sailing before the wind, as was the principle of integration by specialized sectors, of which the Coal-Steel Community was the first example. After the 'coal-steel pool' (an expression which was very popular at one time), some key figures and experts suggested setting up other types of pools: a green pool for farming products, a white pool for health products, a transport pool, etc. The economic, technical and social benefits that certain pooling operations could provide were examined giving little thought to the type of European institutions that could handle their management. But was Europe to continue to be built in a number of different economic and technical sectors which were to benefit from the economics of scale, without causing philosophical or legal havoc over the concessions that would have to be made regarding sovereignty?

In the end, the answer to this operation was no. The international economic situation led the French government to make an official proposal for another integration project in an area where the concept of sovereignty and national independence was a problem for everyone concerned. That area had to do with the European Army project, launched in response to pressure from the Allies who, faced with the new perils of the 'Cold War', considered it of utmost importance to remilitarize West Germany post-haste. What were the reasons governing the choice of those who tried to develop and bring to fruition the European Defense Community project, organized according to principles similar to those which were behind the ECSC?

The primary concern was most probably to find a quick answer to a problem which was both real and pressing, as had already been the case with the Schuman plan. They wanted to get around France's reputed absolute aversion to the setting up of a new German army. However, taking advantage of the opportunity, the project's architects hoped to try to speed up the federative process which had made a cautious start with the ECSC, moving from an economic sphere to a sphere which was political above all else. The lengthy debate that took place in France over the ratification of the EDC, and resulted in its final dismissal with the well-known vote on 30 August 1954, gradually started to focus far more on the problem of accepting a supranational power, than on the issue of German rearmament. The proof of this was the speed and ease with which the new agreements authorizing the re-establishment of a German army no longer under Community supervision were signed and ratified by France, after the final rejection of the EDC.

The term 'supranationalism' was still discredited in the opinion of a large part of the French public. It was stripped of its functional meaning by some and was wrongly considered as the expression of a hasty and underhand desire to set up a union of European states in which national independence would be lost, and its material and moral interests sacrificed.

The cautiousness of the Treaty of Rome

Fortunately, this relative discredit affected neither the European concept in its basic orientation, nor even the economic integration which the ECSC had made a reality without undergoing any major difficulties. The intention to broaden this integration to include the whole of the economy, in a project which was examined by the six Foreign ministers of the ECSC member countries meeting in Messina in June 1955, did nothing to rake up any old quarrels. The conference which was held suffered no badgering from the media, but nevertheless marked a turning point for the European *relance*, as the Spaak Committee established the bases for the new communities which the Treaties of Rome put into their final form. The general Common Market and Euratom followed basically the same lines as the ECSC: i.e. they were 'material undertakings implementing a *de facto* solidarity'. Underlying this was the obvious intention of using these structures to build the future united Europe, the exact terms of which were not specified. With the unfortunate EDC escapade in the back of their minds, the drafters of the Spaak Report avoided any expressions with federalist overtones, handling the institutional part of their report in a pragmatic spirit. Paul-Henri Spaak, when addressing the ECSC Common Assembly on the subject of the state of progress of the Treaties of Rome draft, made a point of saying just that:

I asked the experts to approach the problem of the Institutions in a purely objective manner. I did not tell them that they had to try to set up supranational Institutions, I asked them to recommend the Institutions they believed were necessary for the Common Market to function . . . . The lawyers shall thereupon be entrusted with the job of informing us whether the Institutions are supranational or not.[3]

The lawyers, politicians and European militants did not miss the opportunity, if not of giving a yes or no answer to this impossible question, at least of discussing the degree to which the new institutions were supranational in character. As could be expected, the conclusion that was drawn was that the institutions were supranational to a lesser degree than the ECSC. The reaction in most European circles, especially those for whom there was a close link between supranationalism and federal development, was a feeling of disappointment. Was their disappointment warranted? One reason for it was the wrong interpretation of the relevance of the first European Community as an example. The great historical impact of the proposal launching it and its effectiveness as a 'demonstrator' of economic integration, were no reason to believe that the institutional framework set up for its operation had to be followed in every detail in the subsequent stages of building Europe. For one thing, there was no reason to believe that the division of power between the 'integrated' organizations, independent of the states, and those organizations which were responsible for representing these states — which can be considered to be one of the most characteristic signs of the degree to which a body is supranational — would be the same in any Community-type organization. If the founder states of the ECSC did not hesitate in conferring a virtually sovereign independence on the High Authority in its area of jurisdiction, it was because this independence was to be exercised within a material scope with specific limitations and because its activities were subject to the provisions of a law/treaty which had been spelled out in very precise terms.

What the breakdown of attributions between those institutions implemented by the Treaty of Rome revealed, was that there had been a shifting of the supranational toward the national. The new 'site' where the united Europe was being built was considerably bigger than the one that had been opened for integrating coal and steel — and rightfully and successfully so.

In committing themselves to general economic integration, involving the conjunction of so many varied aspects of national life, the states obviously had to make sure the role they played in the Community decision-making or decision-checking process was big enough. This did not mean they had to revert back to the stage of merely managing a new sphere, to be integrated at the intergovernmental level. Under these conditions, supranationalism no longer seemed like a gigantic break-through which involved cutting through the wide wall of traditional sovereignties, but signified, rather, a small hole in a narrow surface. It was still there, though it was less directly operative in the complex decision-making process of the European Economic Community whose scope was becoming larger.

General de Gaulle against supranationalism

No one nurtured any illusions about supranationalism, but not everyone was able to get used to it, as the lengthy confrontation in reaction to the political *relance* projects submitted by General de Gaulle illustrated. On 'getting back to business' in 1958, contrary to what many observers believed, the future President of the Fifth Republic was intent on facilitating the enactment of the Treaties of Rome on the scheduled dates though this was not to say that he no longer suffered from an aversion to institutional systems which he despised. The union which he proposed in 1960 was based on 'regular co-operation between the Western European states . . . in political, economic and cultural areas and in defence matters', whose primary purpose was to constitute a 'regular, organized concert of the governments in charge', assisted by 'specialized organizations' subordinate to the governments. It was obviously out of the question to establish an organic link with 'certain organizations that are more or less extra- or supranational' which 'are not nor are capable of being effective from the political standpoint'.[4] His desire to cut European Communities off from the new organization, perhaps with the intention of placing them under his control at a later date, was part of the reason the de Gaullian proposals were turned down. The author of the proposals did not fully comprehend one of the aspects of supranationalism and tried to eliminate it from the European building process which he was, all the same, intent on pursuing. The 'smaller countries' of the Community did not consider supranationalism to be so much a relinquishing of sovereignty as a device for protecting their own independence within the framework of an international organization; this because it was based on an institutional system laying down a set of established rules to be abided by. Even more important, it gave the less powerful nations a certain advantage in the decision-making process. What they were afraid of were consensus and unanimity rules where the might of the 'big countries', pooling their influence, generally swayed all the other countries in their direction, disregarding the interests of the smaller countries.

Over a two-year period, vainly discussing what was to become the Fouchet Plan, the Benelux country officials proved to be the least willing to agree to what looked like a Franco-German condominium controlling a European edifice, which had gradually been purged from the supranational nature that had characterized it up until that point. For want of the institutional guarantees they preferred to have, the fact that other countries were taking part in the building of Europe meant that there could be a new balance of power less harmful for their interests. This is the reason — paradoxical as it seemed — that they backed Britain's application for membership in the Communities. At first glance, the application for membership was paradoxical on the part of supranationalism's arch-enemies. A third paradox was observed by those who denounced General de Gaulle's opposition to Britain's membership and his intention to build an 'English-style Europe without the English'.

The failure of the Fouchet Plan, being the failure of the first negotiations for Britain's membership, left the institutional status of the Communities unchanged. Even so, the French authorities' battle to come back on the transfer of sovereignties was not over yet. It started up in Community institutions with the 1965 crisis. After their 'vacant seat' period on the Council of Ministers, the French government scored a very important point with the signing of the well-known 'Luxemburg Compromise' with her partners. The major effect of this 'agreement to disagree', as it has been ironically called, was to suspend *sine die* the Council's use of majority voting at the very time it should have become compulsory. Was this the final damper on the infiltration of supranationalism into the Community, of which majority voting was the most obvious sign? Was this to be interpreted as meaning that the time for the kinds of European development where sovereignty had to be relinquished had come to an end?

Had this been the French government's intention, they had only won a Pyrrhic victory. It is true that they had succeeded in having their five partners agree — perhaps not totally reluctantly — to partially devitalize the institutions. Nothing led to a belief, however, that this deactivation had to be permanent or even very long term. The statutory texts remained unchanged and the recommendations to keep a basically low profile that had been imposed on the commission were forgotten quickly enough. As a matter of fact, those recommendations had more to do with the impression many observers had that the crisis over this institution had been handled poorly than with its actual reputation. The coming to a standstill, widely referred to as the Luxemburg Compromise over this right of veto became a real hindrance and put a damper on the decision-making process for a long time, especially as it was taken advantage of far too often. Without minimizing the harmful effects of the veto, especially because it was used far too much, it is undeniable that majority rule on the Council can also be a threat when used wisely by the government representatives, concerned not to jeopardize either system.

In the late 1960s, General de Gaulle's 'anti-supranational' offensive lasted a long time. The Community affected by it did not become inoperative as a result and its usefulness, and even its necessity, were not questioned — it continued to be the only framework in which the European union could develop. The Community's ability to develop was impaired for a time and reduced to a kind of technical maintenance of the existing order in all the member-states including France. Even before General de Gaulle ever left office, there was an awareness that such a situation could not continue and that some solution had to be found to get things moving again over the short or medium term. The European comeback, however, was not to take place until the La Haye summit conference was held in the Fall of 1969, a few months after de Gaulle left office. The correlation between the two events is obvious, even though de Gaullian interdictions sometimes served as handy excuses for masking the lack of European enthusiasm on the part of France's partners, expressed more in terms of verbal criticism than in actual constructive suggestions.

Was the conflict between the advocates of supranationalism and the unyielding supporters of national sovereignty finally over by 1970? This was the case at the government level if we base our observations on the doctrinal aspect of the two concepts, i.e. on what has often been called the 'theological' side. The French officials softened their attitude toward Community institutions; they were not speaking in de Gaullian terms, the rigidity of which de Gaulle alone mastered. In addition to this, within the enlarged Community they soon found partners, such as Great Britain, who had as many reservations as they did regarding the transfer and delegation of sovereignty. This is why the emphasis was placed more especially on intergovernmental co-operation with the Council of Europe implemented in 1974, and on the development of political co-operation.

The uniqueness of the system

Supranationalism, introduced into the European edifice in 1950, has always been a part of its structure. For this reason it is important to determine the place it should occupy and the limits there should be on its scope. The following observations are not an attempt at providing even a partial answer: Europe of the Twelve — an already highly structured organization — is on the verge of undergoing further major developments within the union; while other European countries — some in a state of total upheaval — are being tempted by its development and hoping to become members. All we can hope to do is to provide a few guidelines for thought, rounding off the historical overview, the highlights of which have been given above.

We must first backtrack and look at what was unique about the initial steps that were taken and the process resulting from them. The building of the Community upset the standard categories used by constitutionalists and political scientists in dealing with state unions. Whether federal or confederal in nature, the decision to form a union was always taken at the top and was overall in scope. The declaration of 9 May 1950 did offer the prospect of developing a union of European states on a more or less long-term basis, but suggested the reverse process for setting it up.

It is unfortunate, perhaps, that in setting out the major principles on which the first Community was to be based, the concept of supranationalism, which was intended for immediate use, had always been connected with the 'federal' concept which many Europeans only advocated for the long term. The result of 'the EDC affair' was that far too much emphasis was placed on the confusion over two areas which were not to be considered to be opposite but only distinct from one another. Supranationalism is not the first tier in the building of a European federal state, it is rather the counterpart to the lack of a European federal government having overall competences, in the areas where joint management had become necessary.

This distinction should be kept in mind with the new vistas that are opening up for the Twelve (the Economic and Monetary Union, the Political Union) in which supranationalism, a part of the current Community edifice, could develop in still other areas. It seemed, up to the present, that a line of demarcation had been clearly drawn: supranationalism had been accepted (voluntarily or involuntarily) in the economic areas which had formally been integrated into the Community, but political union was a different problem altogether. Obviously, the frontier thus established had to be somewhat artificial. It gave little indication about the sectors where economic and political activity were interrelated and overlapped with one another. The drafters of the Treaties were careful about how they handled the states' unwillingness to waive their sovereignty prerogatives. The fact that the Single Market is to be implemented in 1993 means that a real Economic and Monetary Union can be put off no longer and the full realization which will take place in several subsequent stages, should broaden the zone of supranationalism.

By broadening 'Europeanization' to include areas which had been heretofore reserved for inter-state co-operation, will the establishment of a political union to be carried out along similar lines have the opposite effect? The meeting of the heads of state and of government – the Council of Europe, in other words – will naturally play an important role in taking the decision which involves primarily the problems of foreign relations in the broadest sense of the term, and security issues. Is such a body not bound to run along the same lines and use the same methods as de Gaulle's project for political union in the 1960s? Obviously no one could imagine that the advocates of the new political union would want to use it as a weapon for combating supranationalism, which is already one of the bases of the Community.

However, some observers believe it is important to stress the fact that there is a decline in supranationalism at all levels of the European edifice while extending its jurisdiction to political matters. We would always be tempted to deal with using methods which fall within the scope of co-operation rather than of integration, even where institutionalism is involved. As they consider this aspect to be a determining factor in shaping Europe's destiny, for them it falls into a confederal perspective rather than a federal one. There is little likelihood that the elements to be used for the future organization of United Europe can be found in the classical constitutional models. The only available points of reference can be found in the development of the Community itself, whose specificity the first President of the EEC Commission, Professor Hallstein, delighted in pointing out a number of years ago: 'The Community is to some degree more than a federation and to some degree more than a confederation'.[5]

A quarter of a century later, the 'provocative paradox' we owe to Walter Hallstein has not been outdated and it could even be said to have been prophetic. It goes without saying it would only make sense to reject the confederal and the federal models if there are other models that could be used in some positive way in their stead. The Community has found one which is both flexible and realistic and combines supranational procedures with the maintaining of sovereign rights, in a context of sharing to be governed by the principle of subsidiarity. Subsidiarity is not a new word, but thus far it has only been used in European circles on a virtually confidential basis. Despite being ponderous from the technical standpoint it came in very handy, as it provided both the explanation and the justification for supranationalism which may never have had such negative connotations if it had been possible to get the message across about its meaning and importance. As there was no formal expression in the wording of the treaties and early texts, it has become necessary to introduce an explicit reference to subsidiarity. This word is not likely to cause such negative reactions or stir up such heated arguments, but it is possible that the general public will not really understand what it means. It is too much to ask the general public to try to probe into the institutional mysteries of the European edifice but every European citizen is entitled to be sufficiently informed of how the Community is organized, how it operates and what its short- and long-term objectives are. A tremendous effort in the areas of information and teaching has to be undertaken, paying close attention to the choice of terms used so as to avoid connotations wrongly conjured up by words such as 'supranational'.

Notes

1. La Communauté Européenne du Charbon et de l'Acier — Rapport de la Délégation française sur le Traité et la Convention signés à Paris le 18 avril 1951 (Imprimerie Nationale).
2. Robert Schuman, (1963) *Pour l'Europe*, Nagel, Paris, p. 115.
3. ECSC Common Assembly General Meeting — *Débats*, March 1956 session.
4. Press Conference of 5 September 1960.
5. In an address at Dusseldorf in July 1965.

Chapter 15

The French legal order and Community law

Patrick Rambaud

Developing community law which was federal in nature has put the legal orders of the member-states to the test, at the same time challenging their ability to adapt to the demands of supranational law which was increasingly becoming a reality.

The French legal order could not be an exception to this rule, especially since some of its specific features appeared to be direct obstacles to the introduction of Community law. Neither the strong kingly tradition it is impregnated with, nor the quasi-dogmatic conception of the law — the expression of national sovereignty — so present in the French legal mentality, had predisposed it for looking at Community administration and the standards it set in any other way than as rivals and even intruders, at least initially.

As realism triumphed in the end, France gradually adapted itself to the consequences of integrating the Community legal order into the national laws of the member countries. This did not always take place in a clear-cut fashion, however, as evidenced by the constitutional provisions governing the introduction of Community law into the French legal order, and the conditions under which it is enforced.

The introduction of Community law into the French legal order

Provisions for the introduction of Community law are set out pursuant to the Title VI of the Constitution of 4 October 1958 (Treaties and International Agreements), confirming the monist solution adopted previously by the Constitution of 27 October 1946. They liken the Community law scheme to that of other types of international rule, denying it its full autonomy which had been proclaimed by the Community Court of Justice.

Constitutional monism governing the relationship between international treaty law and French law, unlike the dualist concepts in force in the United Kingdom, Germany and Italy, is only favourable to the introduction of Community law on the surface. If, on the one hand, it complies with basic characteristics at the outset, on the other, it denies its specificity.

As Monism conferred on international treaties the status of sources of law, directly enforceable within the state legal order, (unlike dualism requiring their prior 'reception' by the municipal legislator), a system guaranteeing compliance with its direct effect and supremacy was obviously advantageous for Community law.

Under Monism, a French judge is empowered to enforce a treaty, provided he considers it to be a source of rights and obligations for individuals, and provided it has been lawfully ratified and published (Article 55 of the Constitution). There is no need for any a posteriori legislative act to 'change' the international rule into a municipal one making it suitable for use by the judge, other than the authorization of the ratification of the treaty concluded by the Executive Branch (Article 53 of the Constitution). Community law shall thus be able to spread its effects into French municipal law unhindered, in the same way as the other international provisions with a similar capacity (e.g. as the European Human Rights Convention).

The international rule thus introduced does not, however, merge with French law. It remains separate by virtue of the supremacy it has over all national legislative or regulatory rules (Article 55 of the Constitution). In the event of contrary provisions, depending on the case, the judge shall either rule out the divergent national rule (repeal of regulatory acts by the action *ultra vires* judge) or else declare it unenforceable (legislative acts). There are firm grounds for the supremacy of Community law, but not any more or less so than for any other international treaty.

As Community law was assimilated *de facto* by the Constitution to international agreements and treaties which were the only ones mentioned therein, the specificity of Community law was not acknowledged as such and its own particular needs were not dealt with. It is subject to an ordinary scheme, taking into account neither the specific terms and conditions sanctioning it nor its sources.

Pursuant to the provisions of Article 55, the treaty was only enforceable in France 'subject to . . . its enforcement by the other party'. Taken literally, this means that its legal strength depends on compliance with the reciprocity condition, which is recognized by the international order, but not by the Community legal order, as the Court has already had occasion to assert unequivocally. The organized system of sanctions has made resorting to defence of this type not only useless but also illegal. Furthermore, no mention is made of derived institutional law (regulations, directives) which is governed by a very different legal scheme, that of treaty law.

The Constitution's obvious disinterest in Community law may seem especially surprising as it was promulgated after the Treaty of Rome entered into force, and even more so as it followed the Paris Treaty. Since it did little more than duplicate the provisions of the previous Constitution making no changes to speak of, the only implicit mention of the Community phenomenon was made in Article 54, the aim of which was to prevent the ratification of treaties whose provisions were considered to be contrary to those of the Constitution (by the Conseil Constitutionnel). French constituents have no intention of relinquishing their sovereignty in favour of the prospects of the European Community. The judge was thus confined within a rigorous framework preventing him from being won over to the position of those who wanted the Community order to be supranational in nature.

All French jurisdictions, without exception, maintained that Article 55 constitutes the only legal basis for the introduction of Community law in France. However, this reference did not keep some of them from echoing the Court of Justice's bold conclusion about the autonomy of such law. However keen they may have been on Community law, French judges will never go so far as to rally wholeheartedly behind the standpoint of the Community judges.

Administrative judges adopted a firmer attitude on the matter than the judiciary judges, which is more than likely due to the nature of the duties they have to perform. Being closer to political authorities than the latter, they are, in effect, the keepers of legality and must see to it that the orthodoxy of the basic principles governing the hierarchy of standards in French law is abided with.

The Conseil d'Etat used Article 55 as a basis for justifying the supremacy of the Treaty of Rome over French law (*Nicolo*, 20 October 1989). From their standpoint, any other basis was unfounded, as was pointed out by Mr Frydman, the government Commissioner, when he challenged the Court of Justice's case law which he considered to be unconstitutional.

The Cour de Cassation, on the other hand, adopted a more moderate tone. Admittedly, the well known *Société des cafés Jacques Vabre* (24 May 1975) judgment established that the basis for the supremacy of the Treaty of Rome was the Constitution, but it did not totally dismiss the views of Mr Touffait, Advocate-General, who suggested merely founding such supremacy on the 'transcendental' nature of Community law, as derived by the Court of Luxemburg. It quotes the Court's terms verbatim when it confirmed this nature (from the *Costa C. ENEL Judgement*: 'by virtue of the specificity, the Community's legal order is directly enforceable in these states and is statutory on their jurisdictions'). In a subsequent judgment, (rendered on 15 December 1975) no reference was made to Article 55, a less solemn chamber having ruled on the case (a civil court and not a mixed chamber as had been the case in the former) and the fact that Article 55 had been left out could well have meant no more than that Article 55 was already considered to be a fait accompli, to be taken for granted.

Whatever the exact scope of the Cour de Cassation's decisions, the fact remains that the French judge, as was the case, in fact, with most of the other national judges (with the noteworthy exception of the Italian judge), did not hold the purely supranational viewpoint that the Luxemburg Court held of the Community legal order. He was not willing to admit that the treaty establishing the Community provided that Community law was a sufficient basis for legality and that no written amendment had to be made to substantiate such legality. In actual fact, this difference did not entail any consequences at the practical level. If Article 55 was indeed the supreme standard or reference for introducing international or Community rule into the municipal order, it was a standard which has been interpreted with enough realism to ensure this rule could be enforced effectively.

Enforcement of Community law

Enforcing Community law was not the judge's exclusive prerogative. The other state authorities were also empowered to so do: i.e. the Parliament and the government adopting the necessary enforcement measures, and the Authorities who implement them. The jurisdictions of all these bodies, albeit to different degrees, were under the influence of Community law.

As keeper of France's legal tradition, which it was necessary to conciliate with the innovations of a legal order stemming from a different tradition, judges had no other alternative than to work out their duties along new lines and to adapt their methods. They were no longer exclusively in the service of the law but became the arbitrators of the respective interests of the municipal legal order and the European (not just Community) legal order — as a matter of fact, the European Human Rights Convention was exercising a greater and greater influence on French law. The judiciary and administrative judges had undertaken the effort of renovation, however daring or quick they may or may not have been. This process is not yet finished even though the major areas have been dealt with these being: Community law, its interpretation, supremacy and previous laws and conditions for enforcement.

As to the interpretation of treaties, the judge's traditional stand had been to declare himself unqualified, provided that the provision to be interpreted is not a mere question of private law, for the Cour de Cassation. The problem would have to involve an interlocutory question the Foreign Minister alone could settle (the Conseil d'Etat had just dropped this stand however, having decided that such matters were included within its scope: *Gisti*, 29 June 1990). Referring the matter to the Minister is only justified if there is a true problem of interpretation involved, or if the wording or scope of the text is unclear. Where there was no problem of clarity, obviously there is no need for interpretation and the judge is empowered to enforce it directly.

The *acte clair* doctrine principle is not contrary in theory to the procedure of bringing matters before the Court of Justice implemented by Article 177 of the Treaty of Rome. The national judge is only to refer a case that has been brought before him to the Court of Justice if real problems of interpretation involving Community law arise; it is pointless to refer a case elsewhere when there is no reasonable doubt as to interpretation (acknowledged by the court). It may be that the scope of this doctrine is not the same as that of Article 177, that the provision considered to be clear by the national judge is not considered to be clear by the Community judge. This situation may arise when the Conseil d'Etat considers a provision that is not really 'clear' to be 'clear' for the sole purpose of keeping the Community judge from interfering in a matter which has not been referred to him (*Shell Berre*, 19 June 1964: on conformity of the 1928 oil law in the light of the Treaty of Rome) or where it is based on one of the articles in the Treaty (from which certain consequences 'clearly result . . .'), to eliminate a court interpretation which seems to be contrary to it (*Cohn Bendit*, 22 December 1978: on the subject of Article 189 of the Treaty of Rome, defining the directive in terms which, according to the Conseil d'Etat, justify its refusal to recognize the direct enforceability of the directives acknowledged as such by the court).

As a general rule, French jurisdictions have been reluctant longer than the jurisdictions of other states to make use of provisions for referring interlocutory matters (as it turned out, this has been a detriment to France's legal influence on Community case law, as neither the judges nor the parties have much occasion to appear before the court, the former because of the way their cases are presented, and the latter because of observations they are capable of making). These reservations no longer exist nor does the reluctance over drawing logical conclusions as to supremacy of Community law.

The supremacy of Community law, the basis for which can be found in the Constitution, as we have seen, was not accepted without difficulty into the French legal order. One of the difficulties it met with was the immunity of legislative acts before the judge, which was only dealt with after a long period of resistance on the part of the Conseil d'Etat.

France's constitutional tradition (forged under the Third Republic) conferred a preferential status on those laws that were passed in Parliament. As the expression of the nation's democratic will, judges consider such a law to have absolute authority. Whether or not it is in complete compliance with the constitutional or international standards which theoretically have supremacy over it, it still has priority as far as judges are concerned. As the supreme standard of reference for judges, it can consequently neither be criticized nor censored by them. In the beginning, this tradition prevailed over Community reasoning. It was behind the

Conseil d'Etat's refusal to rule out a legislative ordinance contravening a prior Community regulation (*Syndicat Général des fabricants de semoule de France* — General Trade Union for French Semolina Manufacturers, 1 March 1968). It was subject to much criticism because of the inherent contradiction which characterized it (why should France be willing to accept the limitations on her sovereignty to maintain the supremacy of her laws before the judge?). Tradition is too much a part of the judge's way of thinking to break with it easily. Nevertheless, this is what happened and there were three stages to this development:

1. The decision of the Conseil Constitutionnel of 15 January 1975 giving the judge the option of checking a law's compatibility with a prior Treaty. Indeed, the Council determines whether or not the check set out in Article 55 is a check of constitutionality. For the Conseil Constitutionnel a law which is contrary to a treaty is not necessarily contrary to the Constitution, thereby rejecting the Conseil d'Etat's reason for refusing to undertake such a check.
2. The judgment rendered by the Cour de Cassation a few months later on the *Café Jacques Vabre* case ruled that one of the customs code provisions was incompatible with the Treaty of Rome. It was the first time in France that a law (i.e. a law passed at a later date) contrary to a treaty was ruled out by a supreme jurisdiction.
3. The aforementioned *Nicolo* judgment in which the Conseil d'Etat finally dropped its former stand (which it had already confirmed on a number of prior occasions), to adopt that of the Conseil Constitutionnel and of the Cour de Cassation. In this case, it only agreed to enforce the law on electing the French representatives to the European parliament on the basis of universal franchise after having checked its compatibility with the Treaty of Rome. The impression that their case law was becoming obsolete and the desire to avoid a conflict with the Conseil Constitutionnel (which, as judge of Parliamentary elections, had itself ruled on the conformity of a law with an international treaty, decision of 21 October 1988) was the reason behind this timely change of mind putting an end to an abnormal situation worthy of criticism, i.e. that of undermining constitutional hierarchy in the name of by-gone tradition. Even if the supremacy of Community rule is at last sanctioned, is it not sanctioned *conditionally*? Does this not depend on the principle of reciprocal enforcement as set out in Article 55?

The principle of reciprocity is a difficult problem for the judge. On the basis of Article 55, he must enforce all its provisions, but in enforcing Community law, he cannot ignore the fact that this condition is prohibited by it. The Cour de Cassation chose to rule out the condition, or rather it recognized that it was met through the legal order set up by the Treaty of Rome, a complete system sparing the French judge the job of checking up on the other parties to make sure Community rules are complied with, as it included an effective range of sanctions in the event of violation (the same line of reasoning led to ruling out this condition for the European Human Rights Convention).

The Conseil d'Etat had made no statement at that point. In the *Nicolo* case, the question had not been put to it yet and they refused to raise any questions voluntarily. It would be logical to adopt the Cour de Cassation's stand, but its intention to consider Community law exclusively in the light of Article 55 and their disinterest in the specificity of such law raised doubts as to what its attitude would be should an incident arise. As to non-Community treaties, they considered that determining how to comply with that condition fell within the Foreign Minister's scope (*Reckhou*, 29 May 1981: on a Franco-Algerian agreement).

The effort of adaptation required of a judge is also required of the public authorities. Both the government and the Parliament have to see to it that minimum harmonization between French law and Community law take place within their respective circles. As the influence of the former on the latter declines and as Community rule has more and more priority over the national legislature's power of assessment (which is the case with the directives which are becoming increasingly detailed), this harmonization becomes even more difficult. In the 'ECSC system', even more than in the 'EEC system', the influence of French law is on a constant decline and this process can only become more widespread as the Community is enlarged and increasingly affected by the influence of *common law*. The Parliament and the Executive Branch will see considerable changes as a result in exercising their competence.

The Parliament was affected the most. As it passed laws for enforcing directives which only left it a small margin for manoeuvre, its role as court of records that the Fifth Republic's constitutional procedure had already overly confined it to become even more pronounced, but, unlike the government, it could not compensate for the limitation on its jurisdiction by taking an effective part in Community decision-making.

The fact that it was the Parliament enforcing Community law inevitably resulted in the restricting of its legislative jurisdiction. It changed its nature by replacing it with a jurisdiction bound to the discretionary power it has in its capacity as representative of the nation through the Community authority, an area conferred on it by the Constitution (Article 34 sets out such areas). This jurisdiction was bound at two levels: on the one hand, the Parliament had to act within a scope determined by Community standards and on the other, it was required to comply with the latter, on pain of decreeing an unenforceable standard (the judge, as we know, refusing to enforce it). The inevitable outcome of the decline of law (which had already lost its sovereignty regarding the Constitution because of the control the Conseil Constitutionnel exercises over it) is the decline of its author. It was no accident if measures were taken denouncing the supranational drifting of the Community legal order developed (such as the bill that was passed by the National Assembly in 1980 making it an obligation for a judge to enforce the law under all circumstances). The real solution to the parliamentary problem does not lie in 'fighting battles in the rearguard', but in involving the parliamentary body in the Community law-making procedure, an involvement which can only take place to a limited extent in the current state of the constitutional texts.

Following the example of other member-states, an effort was undertaken for prior submission of Community projects to the Parliament. Parliamentary delegations for the European Communities were set up (law No. 79-564 of 6 July 1979, amended by law 90.385 of 10 May 1990). The *ad hoc* delegations are the ones to whom the draft directives and regulations falling within the legislature's scope are sent, prior to their examination by the Council. Their powers are limited, though, because they are unable to adopt proposals aiming to govern or control government action (an unavoidable consequence of the strict limitation on parliamentary prerogatives by the Constitution). When it comes down to it, the only role they play is to inform the parliamentary commissions concerned to whom they submit their conclusions.[1]

As an authority commissioned to enforce Community law, the Executive Branch operates at two levels: first it enacts the necessary regulatory measures and then it implements different Community regulations 'on the spot'. It acts first as legislature by enacting the decrees of transposition for the directives within its jurisdiction, (as set out in Article 37 and covering all matters which are not set out in Article 34). In practice, there are more of them than there are laws as, generally speaking, the economic issues the Community deals with are attributed to it by the Constitution. The government is well aware that by the time it comes to the stage of enforcing Community standards, it is too late to preserve, if need be, the basic assets of the national legal order. Only at the drafting stage is it possible to act effectively. On the whole, the points of view of the administrations concerned have been co-ordinated satisfactorily as regards the political and technical solutions to be defended (they are co-ordinated under the interministerial committee for matters of European Economic Co-operation); from the purely legal standpoint, however, as this co-ordination is not so satisfactory according to the Conseil d'Etat (in a paper on Community law and French law), negotiators do not always make sure that the proposals they back are consistent enough with the principles of French law. In this regard, the Conseil d'Etat wants draft Community texts to be submitted to its administrative sections, as is the case with bills or regulations to inform the government as to the legal problems these texts may involve.

The Executive Branch, through the Administration which is an extension of the former, is also responsible for the material implementation of Community laws. In this regard, it acts as no more than an agent executing orders for the Communities, taking the individual decisions which apply, either in granting or denying a given right provided for pursuant to Community regulations. Enforcing Community law involves considerable changes for the Administration which affect not only its duties but its substance.

In the traditional area of administrative activity (keeping public order) the effect of Community law can be seen when a jurisdiction under the authority of a national body is subject to a Community-level jurisdiction. Matters involving the disturbance of law and order, for example, no longer fall within the exclusive scope of the national immigration authorities; decisions they take are examined by Community authorities, subject to their own criteria for judgement. Gradually, such criteria will become part of French administrative law and will end up by emptying French law of its typically national character. As regards economic interventionism, the French authorities now have to function according to the Community's very different line of laissez-faire reasoning, they will have to review their methods on this basis and regulate economic activities rather than making punctilious regulations. Significant changes have been made in this respect in the area of competition. The ordinance of 1 December 1986 did away with the Administration's discretionary check on corporate agreements, replacing it with checking by an independent organization, the Conseil de Concurrence whose decisions are subject to a legality check by the judiciary judge (from the Paris Court of Appeal).

Lastly, the very substance of Administration is affected by the questions raised over the conception of French public service. According to the law (Article 5 of the law of 13 July 1983 on the general status of civil servants), only French nationals may become civil servants, but the civil service will have to open up to nationals of other member-states to comply with the functional interpretation the Court of Justice has given to 'employments in the public service', not included by the Treaty of Rome under the provisions concerning free movement of persons (employment 'involving the exercise of civil service and the attribution of its responsibilities to safeguard the state's public interests', 17 December 1980, *Belgium v. Commission*). Some proposals along these lines were made to the government in 1988 by a working group and resulted in the adoption of the law of 26 July 1991, repealing the requirement that in order to hold certain jobs as civil servants in certain sections, an applicant has to be a French national (set out by decree). A drastic change is to be expected in the French administrative landscape as a result of the enforcement of Community law, but this is only in its beginning stages.

More than 30 years after the entry into force of the Treaty of Rome, the French legal order has undergone a relatively successful and satisfactory mutation: on the whole, it complies with the requirements of Community law. It has given way to the constraints of irreversible development, relinquishing some of its most firmly grounded traditions.

If French law has adapted itself, thereby demonstrating an ability to change which may have been underestimated, this process of adaptation has not been one-sided. French law has also made an invaluable contribution to Community law. The attitude characterizing French judges today, which has been one of wholehearted co-operation with the Community judge, stands as proof that this is not all just a vain hope.

References

Abraham, R. (1990) Droit International, droit communautaire et droit français (International Law, Community Law and French Law), Hachette, Paris.

Buffet-Tchakaloff, M.C. (1985) La France devant la Cour de justice des Communautés européennes, (France before the Communities' Court of Justice) Economica, Paris.

Droit communautaire et droit français (Community Law and French Law) Etude du Conseil d'Etat, Notes et Documentaires No. 4679-81, La Documentation Française, 1982.

Note

1. The revision of the Constitution (25 June 1992) has increased the powers of the Parliament which may now vote resolutions on proposals for Community Acts, transmitted by the Government.

Chapter 16

The impact of the European Community on French politics

Jean-Louis Burban

Every country, seen in its political dimension, is weighed down by a certain number of 'Dreyfus affairs', which are veritable psychodramas on a national scale. Since 1945 we could say that Europe has been for the French, and even more so for its political establishment, a new Dreyfus affair.[1]

Just as Dreyfus affair at the time brutally divided the various political parties, individual families, and public opinion independently of traditional partisan divisions, the almost theological quarrel about Europe which has been kept alive in France since the end of World War II is still splitting not only the left/right political blocs, but also each political group itself.

In 1992, it is not far-fetched to suggest that within the two French political 'blocs' which emerged from the bipartisan constitution of the 5th Republic, Europe might well be the only bone of contention. However, since the early 1980s, and especially since the 30th anniversary of the Treaty of Rome, which the French authorities and the media celebrated in surprising fashion, given that they had hardly paid any attention to the 10th and 20th anniversaries, it is certain that both among the public and within the political parties, Europe has become the object of a much bigger consensus.

Starting in 1985, the 1992 'myth' suddenly reconciled most French political parties with Europe.

But in 1989–90, with the fall of the Berlin wall and the Gulf crisis, the boost these events gave to the construction of the Single Market once again had repercussions on French political parties. As we shall see in conclusion, they found themselves once again echoing the old internal divisions, although not as sharply.

Europe: the new 'Dreyfus affair'

Of course, Europe will have been only one of France's 'Dreyfus Affairs' during the second post-war period. Indochina and Algeria have undoubtedly left more painful scars, since cruel wars were fought over them, but no blood has yet been spilled over Europe. However it has caused much ink to flow and it continues to provoke existential polemics.

At the end of World War II, it was as if France had awakened from a nightmare with two completely contradictory feelings. On one hand was the determination, shared by a large majority, to end European wars once and for all, and therefore to build a European entity, including a political union. On the other hand, however, were those — first and foremost the Gaullists — who wanted to end government instability and overcome the traumatic defeat of the French Army in May 1940. Thus France found itself at once European and nationalistic, and one can say, without exaggeration, that in 1992 this basic split has persisted both within the right and the left.

From 1947 to 1958, under the 4th Republic, the pro-European tendency dominated. The 'third force' governments of the early 4th Republic, made up of Christian Democrats, Social-Democrats and Liberals were all for Europe. This was the epoch of the Founding Fathers, when, after the famous Congress of The Hague in 1948, France championed European political union, which, as we all know, ran up against British scepticism and ended up giving birth merely to the Council of Europe, hardly a truly supranational entity. We also know that these Founding Fathers did not allow themselves to be discouraged: that within a smaller arena, with only six participants, and in a narrower area, confined to certain sectors, they succeeded in creating the embryo of the European Community which has now grown to 12 members.

At the same time, though, under the 4th Republic, which unfortunately was as politically unstable as had been the 3rd Republic, the Gaullist tendency, often with the support of the Communists for reasons other than French sovereignty, grew ever stronger and opposed the idea of a supranational Europe.

As long as the construction of Europe took place within the well-defined economic area of coal and steel, which did not directly affect national sovereignty, the Gaullists and the Communists, though hostile to the project, were unable to stop it. The European Coal and Steel Community, Euratom and the European Economic Community were thus ratified by the French parliament without great difficulty.

However, from the moment when, as was the case with the European Defense Community, the sector to be integrated touched upon the central core of national sovereignty, the Gaullists and the Communists, objectively allied, pursued a relentless fight against the project, which they finally succeeded in stopping in the National Assembly during the night of 30 August 1954. The socialists were divided, as were the radicals and the non-Gaullist right.

The Algerian problem brought the 4th Republic to an end and de Gaulle to power. It should be said that at that time France went from defeat to illusory victory. Humiliations piled up, from Dien Bien Phu to Suez. When de Gaulle returned to power he brought with him the hope that these humiliations would cease, and that the great need for stability would be met.

But still, the European question did not disappear from French political life, in fact the opposite was true. First, de Gaulle implemented the Common Market, which he had opposed, and negotiated the Common Agricultural Policy in return for the Customs Union. Moreover, while the experts of the traditional political parties accused de Gaulle of being lukewarm toward Europe, at least that of the Six, at the same time as he negotiated Algerian independence and distanced himself from NATO, he proposed a project for European States Union. This project, the Fouchet Plan, called for a European Europe, with Paris as its capital. The Plan failed, due to the Benelux preference for the North Atlantic Alliance.

From that point on, relations between France and her partners went downhill. With the 'empty chair' crisis of June 1965, Europe was once again at the heart of French political discussions, since the presidential election by universal suffrage was scheduled for December 1965. De Gaulle had no idea that Europe would be one of the issues. But he could not prevent it from becoming one. A little known senator, Jean Lecanuet, became a third candidate (François Mitterrand being the second) in order to defend the European Community. Of course Europe was not the only reason why, to everyone's surprise, de Gaulle was not re-elected by the wide margin he had hoped for under universal suffrage. Agricultural problems were another, and in fact French agricultural problems dovetailed with those of the construction of Europe.

Under these conditions, de Gaulle, the 'real-politiker', drew certain conclusions, and in return for concessions by her partners, France again took her seat at the Brussels Council. It was then that the political establishment realized that the construction of Europe could never again be excluded from French politics.

Thus, under de Gaulle's successors, notwithstanding the opposition of the Gaullists (who once again had the objective support of the Communists), a slow but irreversible trend towards a greater involvement in Europe began. In 1969 Georges Pompidou accepted the broadening, which he hoped would be accompanied by greater depth. In 1974, Giscard d'Estaing took the initiative of creating the Council of Europe, and accepted that the European Parliament be elected by universal suffrage. In 1979 with Chancellor Schmidt, he launched the European Monetary System.

However, these steps forward were accompanied by considerable resistance from the French nationalists. In 1977, for example, Jacques

Chirac, who was convalescing at the Cochin Hospital, launched an 'appeal' (which has since been known as 'The Cochin Appeal', in reference to the famous appeal of 18 June by General de Gaulle in London), and which constituted a significant stiffening of the RPR (Gaullist) Party with respect to the first election of the European Parliament by universal suffrage. In this appeal Chirac did not hesitate to call those in favour of the election the 'foreign party'. The European question caused the young Prime Minister Jacques Chirac to split with President Giscard d'Estaing in August 1976, the former being a determined partisan of the European elections. Also, the same year, the new Prime Minister, Raymond Barre engaged his government's responsibility (using Article 49.3 of the Constitution), over the ratification of the Brussels Act on the election of the European Parliament by universal suffrage.

Starting in 1981, that is with the election of François Mitterrand as President of the Republic and the arrival in power of the left, the same ideological divisions over Europe could be seen. On one hand the socialist party, itself divided on the question of Europe between its 'right' and 'left' wings, in other words between Pierre Mauroy, inspired by the decidedly pro-European ideas of Guy Mollet, and Jean-Pierre Chevenement, who was very reticent. On the other hand there was the Communist Party, which had always been against the construction of Europe as long as it was not recognized by the Soviet Union. But after some hesitations, President Mitterrand pronounced himself resolutely in favour of France remaining within the EMS in 1983, and following this, he unceasingly worked with Chancellor Kohl to develop the European Community.

Toward a consensus on the Common Market

In the early 1980s, Europe was still divided both on the right and the left. But the European idea, which until then had been limited to a few 'in' people and the political establishment, was suddenly taken up by the public. This vulgarisation of the idea of Europe sometimes seemed like a fashion, which transited through a magic vector, the mythical date of 1992.

While nothing suggested that this date would acquire such prestige in France, it suddenly became the country's 'new frontier'. As Robert Toulemon wrote:

The importance the 31 December 1992 deadline has taken on in the French political debate is a remarkable phenomenon. It was hardly foreseeable that the European Single Act, which was negotiated and ratified in a climate of general indifference, would acquire a kind of fascination among the public, even beyond the politically aware.[2]

In particular, starting in 1987, no political gathering, either political or professional, failed to include the word 'European' and the fatal date of 1992. This was the time when the press, even the mass media, became enthusiastic about building Europe. Every daily newspaper had to have its 'European' supplement, and weeklies were constantly running in-depth analyses. The European elections of 1989 saw the media become Europeanized. Moreover, while a great theological quarrel about Europe had existed among French educators — just as had the debate over Catholic schools — so that since the 1950s Europe had been ignored in the public schools, now public education turned to the construction of Europe: the regional pedagogical documentation centres became Europeanized, and Educational Action Programmes became rampant in junior and senior high schools. It seemed as though the French were taking giant steps to make up for lost time, whereas for the past 30 years — the equivalent of a generation — their youth had received no European education, contrary to the young Germans, Italians, Belgians, Dutch or Luxemburgers.

What happened? Why this sudden attraction for Europe? The deep-seated reason would seem to be the public worries that began with the 1970s crisis, and reached their high point (in terms of unemployment, in any case) in the 1980s. This was the time when the European Community (which did not yet include Spain and Portugal) reached an official total of 18 million unemployed. It was the time when a French minister put a halt to the importation of Japanese videoscopes in Poitiers. It was the time when American/Japanese competition caused European industry to decline sharply, since it was incapable of meeting the new technological challenge, that of the third industrial revolution. Against this crisis backdrop, the public was receptive to the injunction of Jacques Delors, the French president of the Commission of the European Communities: to overcome the crisis and increase growth, a huge domestic market of 320 million inhabitants had to be created. Many books, the first being The European Bet by Michel Albert,[3] inundated the media and the French public. Michel Poniatowsky even daringly entitled his Europe or Death.[4] Consciously or unconsciously this cry soon rallied first an increasing number of economic deciders, then the public. This gave birth to the incredible, unhoped for success of the mythical date 1992, which was perceived as the road to Europe's economic salvation.

Under these conditions, the parties which had traditionally been hostile or sceptical regarding the European project, changed their minds. When it came to the RPR and its leader Jacques Chirac, the about face was spectacular. As presidential candidate in May 1988, Jacques Chirac actually made Europe, or at least the Single Market, one of his rallying cries.

Only the Communist Party resisted the overall atmosphere, even though one could make out a slight modification in its attitude toward Europe — or rather, in its anti-Europeanism. In any case, it only represented 7.7 per cent of the vote in the European elections of 1989, whereas 10 years earlier, it had 20.5 per cent.

It is true that, meanwhile, the far right had awakened and its nationalistic message had in a way picked up where that of the RPR had left off as it became more European, as well as taking many voters from the weakened Communist Party. In the European elections of 1984, the Front National surged forward with 11 per cent of the votes, then took 12 per cent in 1989.

Within this context of a European consensus, the French parliament could calmly take up the ratification of the European Single Act in 1987. The Prime Minister was Jacques Chirac, since the right had won the 1986 legislative elections. Of course, there were still some diehard Gaullists behind Michel Debré, and of course the Communists damned the Single Act, but it was ratified by a comfortable majority. In practice, the Single Act turned out to be highly profitable for the building of Europe, mainly by restoring the institutional mechanisms which had been sketched out in the original treaties of Paris and Rome: the majority vote in the Council, for example, and greater power for the European Parliament which at last was granted some legislative power.

The European Union in the French domestic debate

There was, indeed, a growing consensus among the parties and the public concerning Europe. However, toward the end of the 1980s and in the early 1990s, the issue was not only the common market or the great internal market; and meanwhile, as a result of international events (the fall of the Berlin wall, the Gulf crisis, etc.) the Europeans were no longer content with merely an internal market to look forward to. They were also thinking about more basic questions: the problem of monetary and political union.

With respect to monetary union, we can say that it was President Delors and his Commission who made it a matter of personal concern, running up against British reticence. Notwithstanding this reticence, the Intergovernmental Conference on European Economic and Monetary Union opened, eventually culminating in the summit of Maastricht. As for political union, which was dealt it at the Second Intergovernmental Conference, it was the European Parliament that wanted it, and finally got its way. Quite logically, it presented four important reports on the future European Constitution, including Emilio Colombo's report *The Constitutional Bases of European Union*.[5]

The Treaty of Maastricht of 7 February 1992, provided for the creation of Economic and Monetary Union and made the Community competent to deal with foreign affairs and security. From that point on, as in 1953—54, national sovereignty was at the heart of the matter. That is probably why, just as they had before, though happily on a lower register, at the moment of truth, the French political parties reconstituted the same divisions, which once again split both right and left.

On the right, then, in 1990 the Social Democratic Centre (the CDS and the Christian Democrats), adopted a truly federalist European platform in their Saint-Malo Convention, while the rest of the Union for French Democracy (the Giscardian UDF and the radicals) were partisans of a 12-nation European Union, within the framework of the existing Community. On the other hand, the RPR, modifying its doctrine, once again had doubts, and in its National Council of December 1990, repudiated the 12-national community in favour of 'Greater Europe', which would be open not only to the members of the European Free Exchange Association, but even to the newly independent countries of Eastern Europe, in other words, in favour of a Europe 'from the Atlantic to the Urals', as General de Gaulle was wont to say.[6]

On the left, the Communist Party has still not laid down its arms with respect to the European Community, and also affirms that Europe should extend from the Atlantic to the Urals. The Socialist Party itself is still divided on certain issues. The French socialist deputies to the National Assembly that took part in the Parliamentary Conference in Rome involving the 22 parliaments of the Community, disassociated themselves from the majority of their French colleagues by abstaining on the final declaration on European Union.[7]

It was over the ratification of the Maastricht Treaty, however, signed in 1992, that the French political establishment really split, in a similar way to the split over the European Defense Community. On the left, as on the right, the same causes seemed to produce the same effects; and the split is widening within each party.

On the right, the RPR revolted and split in three: Charles Pasqua, in the Senate, and Philippe Seguin,[8] at the National Assembly, sounded a lot like the Michel Debre of the 1950s, when in the name of national sovereignty and French grandeur, they denounced the Treaty of Maastricht; while the deputy Patrick Devidjian staunchly declared himself in favour of it, and the head of the party, Jacques Chirac, hesitated, then left each party member to vote his conscience, announcing he would vote in favour of the Treaty.

On the left, aside from the Communist Party which called for a firm 'no', Jean-Pierre Chevenement distanced himself from the Socialist Party, the majority of which was in favour of the Treaty. He too denounced Maastricht in terms which sounded as though they came from another age, seeing in it nothing less than yet another episode in the almost thousand-year struggle between France and the Holy German Empire!

Only the centre, although less structured, was more cohesive in its support for the Treaty.

When the Constitutional Council decided that the Constitution had to be amended before the Maastricht Treaty could be ratified, fire broke out in both houses. While other countries were preoccupied with the question of defence, or the role of the Parliament, or other aspects of the treaty that focused on various points of hesitation, in France it was the problem of European citizenship, in other words the possibility for citizens from other Community countries to vote in local elections, that set off the *furor*. It should be mentioned that the French Senate is drawn from municipal councillors, thus the Senators are particularly sensitive to this aspect of the Treaty.

Since, meanwhile, to everyone's surprise, the Treaty was rejected by the Danes, President Mitterrand announced that there would also be a referendum in France. On 20 September 1992, the Treaty of European Union was approved by only a 51.04 per cent 'Yes' vote, with 48.95 voting 'No' and 30.31 per cent abstaining. But some people's 'No' vote was more against the Socialist Government than against the Treaty.

From this point on, the European question became a public one, and once again the building of Europe has divided the political parties, the cities and the countryside, the elite and the man on the street, young and old. Once again, a great national debate has been opened.

Notes

1. A judicial and political scandal which deeply divided French public opinion between 1894 and 1906.
2. Magazine *Pouvoirs*, No. 48, 1989, 'Le mythe de 92'.
3. Albert, M. (1984) *Le Pari Européen*, Paris, Le Seuil.
4. Poniatowsky, M. (1984) *L'Europe ou la mort*, Paris, Flammarion.
5. Colombo, E. (1990) Doc. Az./301 European Parliament.
6. Rassemblement pour le République *Manifeste pour l'Union des Etats d'Europe*.
7. But the President of the socialist group in the European Parliament, the French representative Jean-Pierre Cot, voted for the Final Declaration. Aside from the reservations on the paragraph concerning the Joint Agricultural Policy, which was the reason given by the other socialists to explain their abstention, it seems to have been also due to the specific situation of the French representatives, confronted with the twin loss of power both in the European institutions, in particular the Council of Ministers, and of the French regions.
8. Seguin, P. (1992) *Discours sur la France*, Paris, Grasset.

References

Bussy, M-E. de (1975) 'Les partis politiques et les Communautés Européennes sous la Ve République', in Rideau (Joël) *et al.*, *La France et les Communautés Européennes*, op. cit. pp. 101—61.
Gerbet, P. (1975) 'Les partis politiques et les Communautés Européennes sous la IVe Republique', in Rideau (Joël) *et al.*, *La France et les Communautés Européennes*, Paris, Librairie Générale de Droit et de Jurisprudence, pp. 77—99.

Lemaire-Prosche, G. (1990) *Le Parti Socialiste et l'Europe*, Paris, Editions Universitaires.

Manin, P. (1966) *Le Rassemblement du Peuple Français (RPF) et les problèmes européens*, Préface de C.A. Colliard, Paris, Presses Universitaires de France.

Pinto-Lyra, R. (1978) *La gauche en France et la construction européenne*, Préface de François Borella, Paris, Librairie Générale de Droit et de Jurisprudence.

Saint-Ouen, F. (1990) *Les partis politiques et l'Europe, une approche comparative*, Paris, Presses Universitaires de France.

PART IV: SOCIAL AND CULTURAL POLICIES

Chapter 17

The impact of the Community on industrial relations in France

Jacques Rojot

In beginning this study, it must first be pointed out that industrial relations in the EEC are very much divided along national lines and that there are extremely strong differences between countries. For instance, the level of bargaining varies from plant to national inter-industrial, with all the possible intermediate variations. The representation of employees at the workplace varies from elected to appointed, union-only or work council. The structures of employers associations and labour unions are also very different: they can be unified or divided; craft based or industry based; and can have different jurisdictional lines and ideological standpoints.

It can be added that there is very little automatic incentive towards unification of industrial relations. Historically, the rise of the national union occurred because it could provide local unions with a service they needed and could not avail themselves of alone — namely a better control on the labour market in an expanding product market. Employers Associations followed. It is extremely questionable whether the international union can benefit from the same circumstances as moving from a national to an international centre of decision-making raises delicate and crucial issues of distribution of power. Ultimately, a labour movement rests upon working-class solidarity and there are strong grounds to doubt that this exists at an international level, at least to the extent that it would go beyond paying mere lip service to the causes and carrying out token actions of support. There are also more mundane issues, obvious and simple but difficult to resolve — such as differences in national cultures and languages — which must be taken into account.

Finally, the elements of European industrial relations are tentatively built and thus relatively weak so moves towards interaction at that level are not really significant. The EURO-TUC is mainly a lobbying group near the EEC rather than an emerging decision-making centre and some European unions, such as the French CGT and the Portuguese unions, are not part of it; few International Secretariats, the EMF for instance, have equivalent institutions at the European sectoral level; and the employers organizations, the UNICE admittedly more than the CEEP, are wary of tackling industrial relations issues at the European level. No significant progress has been made towards European collective bargaining since the idea was launched in the 1970s. The few multinational enterprises which hold mutual information meetings with the unions from the different European countries where they operate (BSN-GD and Thompson, for instance) do so at the initiative and sufferance of their top management and the OECD guidelines and the ILO declaration of principle remain voluntary and without any enforcement mechanism. The Vredeling proposal never became a directive and the fifth directive and the statute of a Euro company, on the planning board for so long, remain at the status of projects. Finally, the social dialogue between the social partners remains shy of any hint of collective bargaining.

There are, therefore, to date, neither any real European industrial relations, nor even a significant movement towards them. Industrial relations, at least until the very recent past, have remained pretty much a national matter. It is thus not surprising that, from the employers as well as from the union side, little attention has been paid to the influence of the EEC on industrial relations.

This state of affairs is, in fact, hardly surprising. As its name amply demonstrates, the European Economic Community was originally conceived with almost purely economic aims. The social purposes, although not totally ignored and despite being mentioned as a goal for harmonization in the original section 118, except for some very specific provisions, had to take a remote back seat.

Of course, over time the Commission and Council of Ministers found that ingrained in the treaty was the basis for directives which would influence specific aspects of industrial relations. However, their objects are covered in other areas of this volume than industrial relations and their target was definite points, not the result of a general or influential nature.

In that light should be quoted the directives of 1975 on massive dismissals, of 1977 on mergers and acquisitions, of 1980 on the insolvency of employers, and those between 1975 and 1986 on equal treatment at the workplace between men and women. It should be noted, however, that French labour law often granted workers a protection equal or better than that implicit in the directives. However labour law has been modified on some specific points in some cases, for instance, in the case of the insolvency of an employer. Also, some other directives and even regulations taken in virtue of specific provisions of the treaty in sectoral areas have had a marked impact, notably in agriculture and trucking. Finally, if a labour case pending in front of the French courts were to involve the interpretation of the treaty, the French supreme court had decided that the case was to be held in abeyance until it was given by the Court of Justice of the Communities.

This situation started to change only very recently. The elements engineering this change were to be found in several significant areas, though of varying importance, at the level of the EEC decision-making bodies. The events to be singled out as benchmarks of change are notably the Commission's white paper with its 300 proposals endorsed by the Council of Ministers; the decision of the December 1985 European Council in Luxemburg to move towards the creation of an internal unified European space without any internal barriers; and the most significant modification of the Treaty of Rome by the Unified European Act of February 1986.

The move towards a European Community without internal barriers — whether of a tax, physical or technical nature — to the circulation of capital, people, services and goods is of course in itself bound to have an impact on industrial relations in general terms. However, more specifically, the pursuit of a 'European Social Space', initiated by the Delors Presidency of the Commission and recently debated within the EC will have a much more direct influence on French Industrial Relations, if it is carried out effectively.

Its first element has been the European Social Charter, which was itself the object of much debate before it was accepted. As an end result of this debate, the Charter itself is only a solemn promise, devoid of substantive content and of the means to enforce its lofty aims. However, it is a declaration of the principle that the search for competitiveness and economic growth cannot be pursued without social progress.

Its second element is the Action Program drawn up by the Commission in order to implement parts of the Charter at Community level. The action programme concerns parts of the Charter only, in deference to the principle of subsidiarity which establishes that the Community should act only when the objectives that it aims to reach can be achieved more effectively at its own level, than at the level of the member-states (or lower). The Community, therefore, considers that responsibility for the implementation of certain of the social rights mentioned in the Charter rests with the member-states, or their constituent parts, and the social partners. It should be noted at this point that the Commission has actively encouraged the establishment of a dialogue (at Community level) between the social partners, and that some results have been achieved on this point, as the results of the Val Duchesse meetings testify. However, in the areas where it thinks that action at Community level is necessary, either because there is no other possible avenue, or because a Community-level framework is necessary to help implement decentralized action at country level, the action programme lists the activities to be initiated by the Commission in order to implement the relevant rights enumerated in the Charter. It covers initiatives in the following areas: the Labour market; employment and remuneration; improvement of working and living conditions; freedom of movement of workers; social protection; freedom of association and collective bargaining;

information consultation and participation of employees; equal treatment for men and women; vocational training; health protection and safety at the workplace, and the protection of children and adolescents, the elderly and the disabled. Proposals from the Commission will be distributed over three years.

The action programme, in its general introduction, does not explicitly define the legal instruments that will be employed in order to embody these proposals. It only indicates that it will take account of the fact, in selecting those instruments, that its proposals should be implemented under the forms of laws or collective agreements, leaving room for the involvement of the social partners.

For at least part of its initiatives, it appears that the Commission's strategy in order to implement the programme will rely on directives on the basis of sections 100 and 118a, involving a close co-operation with the European Parliament and only a qualified majority vote in the Council. This is, for instance, demonstrated by the recent directive on atypical work. From the legal standpoint it is hotly debated among European labour lawyers whether such a strategy is in fact possible. Therefore it is not, at the present time, certain that the action programme will become a reality. In other words, between a non-existent past and an uncertain future what is the present impact of the Community on French industrial relations?

Traditionally, French industrial relations are characterized by several prominent features. A basic characteristic is the predominance of the role of statutory law. Many matters which in other systems would be the subject of collective agreements are, in France, covered by statutes imposing a minimum set of conditions.

A second characteristic, within this framework, is the importance of four legal doctrines in outlining the essential features of the system. The first is the predominance of the individual contract of employment, between the individual employer and the individual employee, over collective agreements in the government of the employment relationship. A dismissal or a resignation, for instance, are to be understood in terms of the termination of an individual contract of employment. This contract need not be in the form of a written document specifying terms and conditions; rather its existence is assumed as soon as an employment relationship materializes and is deemed to have an implicit legal content made up of statutory labour law, administrative regulations, shop rules, custom and applicable collective agreements for their duration, if any. Of course, the parties may add explicitly to that implicit content, as long as it improves the lot of the employee or if it is specifically allowed by statute in other cases.

Second, is the right to manage the business which rests solely with the employer. There are, of course, qualifications to this power to manage. The employer must act within the law, which sometimes narrowly restricts what is permissible, for example, in the case for dismissal.

However, the employer remains sole judge of what is good for his business and is free to act as he wishes. There is no system of co-determination. Works Councils have only advisory powers and the courts have systematically denied themselves the power to affect the validity of the employer's managerial decisions. Consequently, as long as he remains within the framework of legality, in terms of complying with existing laws and regulations, the employer is granted the power to issue orders to his employees and to establish the shop rules. The employment contract is legally characterized as a link of subordination.

Third, is the right to strike, which is constitutionally protected. It is submitted to certain statutory and judicial regulations, but cannot be disowned having been granted by the constitution. Therefore, there is no such thing as a peace obligation. Collective agreements could at best contain provisions restricting the power of the union to call a strike, for instance, by implementing a compulsory delay of notice, but they could not suppress the action. This restriction would apply only to the union and could not deprive any given group of employees of their right to strike, as this right is their own, not the union's. The notion of wildcat strikes is therefore irrelevant given that a strike can generally be called legally at any time, for any reason and by any number of people. The fourth doctrine is the right to organize, which is legally protected, as is also its counterpart, the right not to join a union. All discrimination, both positive as well as negative which is based on union activities is unlawful. This means that there is no such thing as a bargaining unit or exclusive jurisdiction. As soon as a collective agreement is signed by an employer and any given representative union, it applies to all his employees, top management included.

Within this broad legal framework, the model of an industrial relations system is one of industrial unionism. However, unions are divided along ideological lines. Five union centres exist with different persuasions: Marxist, Socialist, Social Democrat, Christian-Catholic and a corporatist centre the affiliation to which is reserved for managerial and supervisory and technical staff. All these centres gather local unions, organized along both geographical and industry lines, and have the right to appoint in company and in plant delegations. A major employers association is organized along the same lines, having developed in reaction to the union's appearance.

Has this model been deeply affected recently? On the surface and regarding its day to day functioning the answer has to be negative. However, a more in depth analysis reveals a two-sided impact, though an unbalanced one.

In terms of the first impact, first and most noticeable to experts recall-ing some of the facts mentioned earlier: the directives in the labour field have had an impact upon French labour law, which had to be modified in some instances to comply with them. Second, some of the regulations, notably in trucking, have had an indirect impact on industrial relations matters. Third, when a legal point requires interpretation of the Treaty, French courts defer to the European Court of Justice. It should be added that probably of more importance is the definition of its competence by the European Court of Justice itself. Instead of limiting itself to a 'strict constructionist' attitude, that is, of insuring compliance with the law in the interpretation and application of the Treaty, it has considered itself competent to decide if measures taken by the administration or courts in the member-states were or not compatible with fundamental rights, recognized and protected in the member-states and also enshrined in international treaties signed by them. Such a decision, of course is bound to have a direct impact on industrial relations, given that the Court can be seized by an individual and that the fundamental rights include social rights such as social justice, equality and the like. Finally, the social dialogue, at a global level such as at Val-Duchesse and possibly in some cases at multi-national enterprises level, is bound to have, eventually, some influence on attitudes, and probably a more factual impact at sectoral level.

The second impact is of a different nature, it is indirect. For a few years, the potential consequences of social Europe have been pondered by the actors of the French industrial relations system, and to a lesser extent already taken in account in the expectations and strategies of some of them. Whereas until the mid-1980s the industrial relations aspect of European organization was blissfully ignored, nowadays labour leaders and employers take officially public positions on the subject.

At the main employers association level, although it fully supports the UNICE doctrine of subsidiarity (and as such pleads for as little as possible community legislation) and is opposed to any kind of community-wide collective bargaining, there is a recognition that social Europe is in the making and that employers should be a party in its creation. To some extent it is considered already to be a reality. There has been a marked evolution during the past two years and it is recognized that the topics evoked in the social dialogue and/or debated within the Commission may become 'topic of consultation', between the social partners in France (*Le Figaro*, 26 January 1989). At the level of individual employers, the awareness of the internal market does not seem limited to economic aspects. A survey of October 1989 (*Les Echos*, 23 October 1989) shows that French employers rank the European social harmonization equally in importance with the creation of a European central bank and a European currency (67 per cent very important), although behind the harmonization of fiscal rules (87 per cent very important) and of technical norms (83 per cent). Already, large individual companies integrate the European perspective into their social strategies. In a few cases they do this by setting up various means of consultation with employee representatives Europe-wide, more often it is achieved in the elaboration of policies regarding managers mobility, revision of the structure of labour costs, social consequences of investments and disinvestments.

From the labour side, the leaders of two of the main labour centres in 1988 had successively called attention to the risks of a unified Europe with a 'social desert'. With the exception of the centre with a Marxist ideology, opposed to the dangers of a Europe becoming 'a jungle of the capital', the four other union centres support the European single market. They are aware of the necessity of their action at national level and of a unified action at community level, in order that improvements in conditions of work and life be guaranteed, social dumping be avoided and employees be party to corporate decisions regulating their fate.

In practical terms, however, few factual initiatives have been taken. This leads to a conclusion which confirms the earlier statement, that the main impact on French industrial relations of the EEC is in its beginnings and more at the level of expectations than action.

Finally, the uncertainty surrounding the Maastricht Treaty's impact and the controversy around its potential effect on European industrial relations, made it impossible to evaluate the future of this area.

Chapter 18

Equality between men and women in the workplace

Annie Sabourin-Ragnaud

The preambles to the French constitutions of 1946 and 1958 guarantee equality between men and women: 'the law guarantees that women shall have rights equal to those of men in all respects'. One of the most important demands of women today concerns equality in the workplace where, despite all the progress made in recent years, women still encounter much discrimination. Three tendencies characterize the situation of women in France. First, women are employed in ever-increasing numbers. In 1975, for example, 72 per cent of men were employed and 41 per cent of women. In contrast, in 1985 only 66.5 per cent of men worked, while the percentage of working women had increased to 45 per cent. In absolute terms, 10.5 million women and 13 million men were working in France in 1986. Women thus account in large part for the increase in the French labour force since 1975. Between 1975 and 1982, the labour force increased by 1.7 million people, of which 1.5 million were women.

The second characteristic of women in France today is that they are more affected by problems of unemployment. Sixty per cent of those people seeking jobs are women. The rate of unemployment is 12 per cent among women and only 8 per cent for men. In one single year, the number of young men enrolled at the Jobs Centres (ANPE) decreased by 13.2 per cent, whereas that of young women fell by only 7.1 per cent. In contrast, enrolment for women between the ages of 25 and 49 increased by 7.5 per cent during the same period. The third tendency seen in the French workplace is that more women work than ever before, and they have longer careers than ever before. Women are more likely today to go back to work after the birth of a child. Their careers are thus longer and longer.[1]

The lack of equality between men and women at work is striking. Despite the dramatic increase in the number of women opting for careers, women on the whole work in jobs requiring fewer qualifications, that are not stable and that are often underpaid. For example, the majority of people employed under fixed term contracts are women, and a larger percentage of women (12.6 per cent) work for the minimum wage (SMIG) than men (5.1 per cent). Similarly, women are less represented among the ranks of highly qualified, and thus well-paid, jobs.

European law and International law may help ameliorate the working conditions of women in France. In fact, France has already ratified two international conventions:

1. Convention no. 111 of the International Labour Organisation (Organisation Internationale du Travail) (ILO) of 25 June 1958, concerning discrimination in the workplace (ratified by France on 15 April 1981); and
2. The United Nations Convention of 18 December 1979, for the elimination of all forms of discrimination against women (ratified by France on 1 July 1983).

Similarly, the European Community (EC) has played a key role in promoting equality between men and women. Since 1975, it has adopted five directives concerning women and work. France has also adopted a number of measures promoting the principle of equality, the most important of which is the 'Roudy law' of 13 July 1983. This law mandates equality under the law and promotes equal opportunity. While practice does not always follow the prescriptions of the law, it would appear that women are beginning to enjoy more opportunities than previously.

Discrimination

In the application of certain European directives, the French legislature has adopted a number of dispositions meant to combat discrimination against women in the workplace. Two European directives are particularly important: that of 9 February 1975, on equal pay, and that of 9 February 1976 on equality in the workplace (working conditions, hiring practices, training, promotions). Of all these job-related issues, two are vital for women: hiring practices and equal pay.

Hiring practices

Women have difficulty getting hired because of tradition and because of their relative lack of training and skills. The activities of the EC concerning training and job counselling are helping women to overcome the last two handicaps. However, tradition still works against women in the workplace. First of all, the criteria of many jobs are gender-related and, in addition, there is still a certain 'paternalist' mentality limiting women's access to certain professions. There is also separate recruiting for men and women in certain domains, as is the case, for example, for civil servants in France. The Community Court of Justice in Luxemburg has already rendered a number of judgments against France because of this practice.

Job announcements with a bias regarding gender are forbidden by the Directive of 1976 and by the Roudy statute, incorporated in the French Labour Code as Articles 123 et seq. Article 3 of the former states that: 'Equality implies the absence of all discrimination based on gender during hiring, including the decision as to the qualifications necessary for the job'. The French Labour Code states: 'No one may refer to or have someone else refer to gender or marital status in a job offer'. This article is significant because it is aimed not only at employers but also at those who publish and circulate job announcements.

These provisions none the less conflict with an employer's right to set the job qualifications for the hiring he does. In practice, a company can always cite a woman's lesser qualifications as the reason for its preferring a male candidate. Sex-based discrimination is indeed difficult to prove in the absence of the company's admission that it refused to hire a woman because of her gender. This law is therefore rarely applied.

One criminal case in point involves an institute for the training of special educators.[2] The institute published an announcement looking for a free-lance psychologist. A young woman applied for the job, and her candidacy was reviewed. The institute ultimately told the woman that it had chosen another candidate and notes: 'we have selected a man who has the same qualifications as you'. The woman filed a complaint charging gender-based discrimination. The court held that 'the language of the letter was awkward but insufficient for a showing of wilful discrimination based on gender'.

The penalty for gender-based discrimination is specified in Article 152—1 of the French Labour Code: 'Every infraction of Article 123—1 shall be punished by a prison sentence between two months and one year, or a fine of between 2,000 and 20,000 French francs, or both'.

The Roudy law expanded the concept of unfair discrimination. Until 1975, for example, Article 416 of the Penal Code qualified as unfair discrimination that which is based on ethnic origins, customs, marital situation, nationality, race and religion. A statute dated 11 July 1975 added sex-based discrimination to the list. The penalties for Article 416 of the Penal Code are the same as those for Article 152—1 of the Labour Code. The Roudy law of 1983 emphasized the potential broadness of the 1975 law. In 1975, Article 416 of the Penal Code encompassed only the refusal to hire, and dismissals. Since the Roudy law, Article 123—1 has been interpreted to forbid other practices involving sexual discrimination, 'especially questions of transfers, refusals to renew a contract, remuneration, job qualifications. . . .' This list is not restrictive because it uses the adverb 'especially'.

An evolution in favour of the protection of women is thus discerned. However, Article 123—1 contains an important limitation. Non-discrimination is the rule 'except as otherwise stated in other sections of this code and except when gender is a determining factor for the exercise of the job or professional activity'. A special ruling (*décret*) prepared by the Conseil d'Etat lists the jobs or professional activities for which gender is a 'determining factor'. Article R 123–1 of the Labour Code (as added by the Ruling of 25 May 1984) enumerates these jobs: artists asked to play a male role or a female role, and models. These are the statutory exceptions to the principle of non-discrimination between men and women in the workplace.

The Roudy law significantly modified the text of Article 416 of the Penal Code. In its form of 1975, this text stated that a company could discriminate if it could prove that it had a 'legitimate reason'. It was up to the court to decide what was a 'legitimate reason' (*motif légitime*). But the text allowed the employer to try to give a reason other than gender discrimination for his refusal to hire, or his dismissal of a woman. For example, a court in the city of Blois (le Tribunal Correctionnel) held in 1976 that an employer seeking to hire a teacher could require that the candidate be a man, because the job would necessitate frequent travel and the ability to maintain discipline during class. In contrast, the High Criminal Court (la Cour de Cassation criminelle) on 25 May 1983, rejected a job offer specifying male candidates only which cited as justification the difficulty of the work involved (carrying loads of 30–40 kilograms).[3] In any event, the Roudy statute eliminated a 'legitimate reason' as a basis for refusing to hire or for dismissing a woman. Gender-based discrimination is therefore easier to prove and thus to prevent.

Another obstacle women encounter when looking for work are 'paternalist' measures 'for the protection of women'. Perhaps justified at the beginning of this century, these measures are certainly obsolete in the light of the progress of technology since then. Article 3 of the directive of 1976 specifies that 'the authorities must revise those legislative, executive and administrative measures which are contrary to the principle of equal treatment and for which the justification of protecting women is no longer valid'.

In France, the legislature has intervened most actively in the area of safety and hygiene on the job. Accordingly, Article L 234 and R 234-5 *et seq.* establish the loads which men and women are capable of carrying, as well as the activities which women may not carry out: the manipulation of dangerous substances such as mercury, cilium, and so forth (see also the Ruling (*décret*) dated 5 August 1975). The most controversial protective measure today is that which forbids women from working at night. This ban was formulated in Convention 89 of the International Labour Organization, ratified by France in 1953. Article 213–1 of the Labour Code states that no work shall be done at night in an 'industrial workplace', and the statute of 1941 extends this principle to public offices, the professions and so forth. However, the statute of 2 January

1979 lifted this ban in several cases (women working in managerial positions, women working on cleaning teams, etc.).

The Statute dated 19 July 1987, on the organization of the workday (Article 213—1 of the new Labour Code), contains certain provisions meant to protect the 'social' function of women. As a result, it is only 'when issues of national importance are involved that women may work at night'. This possibility must, however, be stated in a special collective agreement concerning the sector and in a special agreement at the level of the company concerned.

The Statute of 19 June 1987 also eliminates certain restrictions on the employment of women: that women not work more than 10 hours a day; that they not do successive workshifts; and that women not work in workshops and on construction sites on legal holidays.

All in all, the law has moved rather slowly on the front of women's rights in the workplace. This is particularly worrying in the context of the current reappraisal of ILO's Convention no. 89. Certain countries still support this convention, i.e., Belgium, Italy and Portugal. Others, having previously ratified the convention, now denounce it, i.e. France, the Netherlands, Luxemburg and Ireland. Finally, countries such as the United States, Great Britain and Germany have refused to ratify this convention. In this context, the Community Court of Justice in Luxemburg condemned France in the *Stoeckel* case of 25 July 1991 for failure to apply the directive of 9 February 1976. With the agreement of the female personnel, Mr Stoeckel had women working on the conditioning of cassettes at night. The Court pointed out that equal treatment means the same working conditions for men and women. The member-states must revise those measures 'for which the original justification of protecting women is no longer valid'.

Companies have none the less reached agreements with the unions on working at night, particularly in the metallurgical industry. Fifty-five such agreements were signed in 1988, 50 in 1989. Bull signed an agreement in 1990 authorizing nocturnal work by women when necessitated by production demands. Because of these realities in the workplace, international authorities have begun to modify their position. In June 1990, the International Labour Organization — with the benediction of all the unions present, except the communist one (CGT) — accepted the possibility of women's working at night, on condition that there be a special agreement within the industry concerned and appropriate compensation. In the absence of a clear European policy, French legislation has tried to strike the appropriate balance on this question. Similarly, the Labour Minister has recently proposed legislation on this subject. The proposed legislation stipulates that any introduction or extension of work at night must be subject to a special agreement (*convention ou accord d'entreprise*) within the company or be authorised by the competent labour inspector. Such special agreements must specify the additional compensation given those employees who work at night. Certain unions oppose this legislation (CGT and CFTC), while others are not opposed in principle (CFDT and CGC).

The existence of parallel recruitment for men and women in certain fields also leads to inequality and discrimination. This has long been the case for civil servants in France. Recently, the EC Commission and the Community Court in Luxemburg ruled that French legislation had to be amended in accordance with the Directive of 1976. The statute of 10 July 1975 created the recruitment system for civil servants and was intended to remove all obstacles to the implementation of the UN Convention of 1953, concerning women's political rights. The latter was ratified by France in 1957 and published in 1975: 'Women shall have the right to hold public office and to work in the government/bureaucracy'. However, Article 7 contained an exception to this principle of non-discrimination, when 'the nature of position or the working conditions involved so justified'. On 25 April 1981, the Commission held that Article 7 conflicted with Article 2 of the directive of 14 February 1976, which forbids all restrictions on access to government employment, 'except when gender is a determining factor with respect to the nature or the circumstances surrounding such employment'.

In response to the findings of the Commission, the French legislators modified the statute of 1975 by passing the statute of 7 May 1982, which accepted the possibility of separate recruitment by sex when gender is a determining factor for the exercise of a particular office. The ruling of 15 October 1985 lists the cases for which separate recruitment is possible for men and women: the police, the educators (*attachés d'éducation*) working for the Legion of Honour, the educators in the prison system (*administration pénitentiaire*), customs officials, physical education teachers and primary school teachers. In response to an order issued by the Commission on 12 August 1983, France removed primary school teachers from the list (ruling of 2 February 1987), as well as physical education teachers (ruling of 30 April 1988).

None the less, the Community Court of Justice ruled against France on 30 June 1988: 'by maintaining a system of separate recruitment by gender for certain personnel in the prison system, as well as for the national police, the French Republic has not respected the obligations of the treaty'.[4] The ruling of 6 August 1985 eliminated separate recruitment for customs officials. As a result, only the educators for the Legion of Honour and certain personnel for the prison system are still recruited separately by sex. One can therefore say that France at last follows the directive, and one should emphasize the effectiveness and tenacity of the Commission in achieving this result.

In a separate affair, France was condemned on 25 October 1988 by the Community Court of Justice, again for failure to apply the Directive of 1976.[5] The Commission claimed that France, by not taking the necessary measures within the deadlines set forth by the directive of 1976, had not met its obligations under the treaty. Article L 123–2 of the Labour Code does stipulate that no clause giving preference to an employee because of his/her gender shall be put into a collective bargaining agreement (convention collective). But Article 19 of this same statute creates an exception for special rights given to women by virtue of custom, individual employment contracts and collective agreements in force on the date of this law's promulgation. The Commission argued that this exception would leave people free to negotiate and did not provide for a remedy if collective negotiation led to unsatisfactory results.

Another issue of importance is discrimination concerning remuneration. One study made by the Centre d'Etude des Revenus et des Coûts (CERC) demonstrates that the average salary of women is 30 per cent below that of men. The study identifies certain factors which explain the gap: the number of women in general work in areas which are not as well paid as those in which men work; women holding jobs which in general require fewer qualifications than those held by men; women on average having less seniority; women working more often in areas where low salaries are the norm; and sometimes employers simply discriminating against women by paying them lower salaries. 'Equal pay for equal work' is a demand which has been sought for years. Convention no. 100 of ILO, adopted in 1951; Article 119 of the Treaty of Rome; and a European directive of 10 February 1975 all recognize the need to satisfy this demand.

The principle of equal pay is in the French Constitution and the statute of 22 December 1972. In addition, the Roudy statute reinforces this principle by establishing specific guarantees and sanctions. It states that 'each employer shall pay the same remuneration to men and women for the same job or for a job of equal value'. Similar language is seen in the relevant sections of Article 119 of the Treaty of Rome and Convention 100 of ILO. The principal of equal pay raises three broad issues:

- what is 'equal work';
- what is 'equal pay' and
- how does one prove that any differences are due to sexual discrimination?

Equal work

The statute of 1972 speaks of the same 'job' or of 'work of the same value' without defining what these concepts mean. The legislature evidently wanted to leave employers some flexibility when evaluating jobs in their companies. The courts would then have the power to review such evaluations. However, two recent cases (*arrêts*) demonstrate the courts' hesitancy to second guess employers.

The first decision concerns 52 saleswomen at a department store

(Galerie Lafayette) in Montpellier who demanded the same salary as that of the salesmen in the same job category. The court reversed the decision of the lower court, stating that it should have looked to see whether 'within each job category, some jobs none the less receive a higher salary for reasons unrelated to gender, such as the particular difficulties involved'. In other words, the lower court was asked to try to find a reason other than discrimination for unequal pay, despite the admission that the jobs were identical.[6]

The second case (the 'Essilor case') involves a company with two factories. Women worked in one factory; men in the other. The work appeared to be the same, but the women's salaries were lower than the men's salaries. The court stated that there is no 'gender-based discrimination' if it can be shown that there would be the same difference in salaries if men worked in both factories.[7] Another example involves a court which stated that there is sex-based discrimination when bonuses for attendance are given to men but not to women (Cass. Crim. 22 June 1977, Marcoux).

The Roudy statute clarified some of these issues:

Two jobs are considered to have an equal value when they require of the employee comparable knowledge, as evidenced by a title, a diploma or practical experience, and comparable abilities resulting from experience, responsibilities and physical or emotional stress.

The text emphasizes that the definition of 'equal value' requires looking at all the facts and circumstances. For example, a job causing considerable emotional stress might be equal to one demanding physical strength. This is an important notion for women. The Roudy statute solves the problem posed by the Essilor case, when a company has several working sites: when comparing people having the same job or jobs of equal value, 'differences in remuneration between two working sites in the same company shall not be based on gender'.

This, in fact, overturns the result of the Essilor case. Employers must ensure that men and women receive the same remuneration for jobs of equal value. Article 140–2 section 2 defines remuneration as 'the base salary plus all the advantages and benefits paid to an employee'. Moreover, 'job categories, the criteria for placing people within such categories and the methods of calculating remuneration must be identical for male and female employees'.

Despite these rules, one still finds discrimination against women with respect to salaries. Salaries are the result of three factors: the qualifications of the jobholder; the general description of the category within which the job falls, which is usually contained in the collective bargaining agreement; and the specific definition of the job as the application of particular abilities to particular tasks. It is the employer who identifies and analyses the specific tasks required of an employee in a particular job so it is here that the employer can discriminate against women. An employer can define jobs usually filled by women in certain ways, and those filled by men in other ways.

The law can remedy this problem when the same jobs are held by both men and women. The situation is more difficult when there is not such 'mixing'. In a noted case, for example, the female 'typists' of a magazine demanded the same pay as the male 'correctors'. They argued that the two jobs were similar in practice, but management contended that the two jobs were defined differently: 'typing' for women; and 'editing' for men. Training for the women 'typists' was also less intensive. In practice, the employer hired women to be 'typists' and men to be 'correcters', but because the company did not define the two jobs in terms of gender, the law on equal pay appeared not to apply.[8]

However, the Roudy law introduced another innovation. In cases between women and their employers, Article 140—8 places upon the employer the burden proving discrimination was not the reason for unequal pay. Before this law, the employee had the burden of proving that gender-based discrimination was the cause of unequal pay.

Equal opportunity

The Roudy statute also contains certain provisions meant to encourage equal opportunities for women. For example, the law requires each employer to present an annual report to an internal employees' committee (*comité d'entreprise*) which compares the relative situations of men and women concerning hiring, training, qualifications, job specifications and remuneration. This report is meant to encourage negotiations to eliminate inequalities. A study done in 1987 concluded, however, that such reports do not currently lead to concrete propositions for change. It may be that the complexity of the law in question discourages such employees' committees from making proposals; but another explanation may be that, in the current socio-economic and cultural context, inequality appears normal. In any event, the Roudy statute does provide for the possibility of compensatory measures 'temporary in nature, and intended to promote equality between men and women'. Unfortunately, the text does not explain what is meant by such measures, often called 'affirmative discrimination (*discriminations positives*)', which can involve recruitment, training, organization in the workplace, and working conditions. In addition, the legislature stated that collective bargaining agreements must include a clause concerning such 'catch-up' measures.

This law also allows companies to set up programmes promoting equality in the workplace. Article 123—4 states: 'in order to promote equality between men and women in the workplace, the affirmative measures cited in Article 123—3 can be adopted through a plan negotiated within the company'. The law stipulates that the state can give some financial aid to companies, provided that such measures concern training, promotions or the organization of the workplace, and that they be 'measures intended to serve as examples of the need to achieve equality on the job'. The employer must enter into a contract with the state to receive this aid, which can amount to 50 per cent of the cost of the training, 50 per cent of the other costs of implementing the plan and 30 per cent of the salaries paid during the training period.

It would appear for the moment that few companies adopt this sort of plan, at least publicly (around 22 or 23 as of October 1989).[9] Most of the companies that did adopt such plans simply dressed up their annual training plan (already required by law) as a plan for the promotion of equality in the workplace. It is in fact difficult to identify in these plans measures aimed specifically at problems of equality. These plans are rather designed to improve workers' productivity in general, not to improve working conditions for women. In short, companies have appeared reticent to adopt such plans, and the unions have been slow to act on such issues. In this context, the Minister of Labour therefore decided to offer contracts aimed at companies with fewer than 200 employees, to be awarded on a case-by-case basis. This programme was launched on an experimental basis in six regions and appears to have had some success.

The Roudy law also expands the right of unions to start civil actions on behalf of employees. The power of unions to start actions on behalf of others was originally limited in scope. Since 1981, however, the legislature has broadened this power to include actions involving the employment of foreigners (Article 341−6) and of temporary workers (Article 124); actions involving employers' associations (Article 127−6); and, since 1983, actions involving equality in the workplace. Article 123−6 states: 'unions represented in a company may file an action on behalf of an employee resulting from Articles 123−1 and 140−2'. The union must inform the employee of the proceedings and allow him 15 days to raise an objection. If he does not, it is presumed that he approves of the suit. In addition, the employee does not have to be a member of the union bringing the action, and he may intervene in the proceedings at any time. It should be noted that associations for the protection of women's rights do not yet have a power similar to that described above for unions.[10] And yet, an analogous power has been given to associations for the struggle against racism, and to consumers' associations.

The Roudy statute also prevents an employer from dismissing an employee who has brought such an action against the company. The source of this law is in the directive of 1976, Article 7: 'the Member-States must take all necessary measures to protect workers against dismissals taken in reaction to a complaint or a lawsuit intended to enforce the principle of equality in the workplace'. And Article 123−5 of the Labour Code states that:

A dismissal is null and void when it involves an employee who has brought a civil action against the employer on the basis of a breach of the principle of equality between men and women, and when it is shown that the dismissal has no foundation in fact but is rather in response to such civil action pending against the employer.

Three conditions are thus necessary for the court to declare a dismissal void:

1. the dismissal must occur after the filing of the complaint;
2. there must not be some other justification for the dismissal; and
3. the dismissal must in fact be intended to punish the employee for initiating the civil suit.

The statute is difficult to apply, because of the difficulty of establishing the link between the dismissal and the lawsuit. None the less, this provision should have a dissuasive effect. In practice, a judge can apply the provision once he is convinced that the employee's legal proceedings led to the dismissal. The judge could infer this connection upon finding no legitimate motive for the dismissal.

Moreover, this provision is the only one which allows a dismissed employee the 'right to be reintegrated' (Article 123—5). The employee can demand that he be given his job back, or he can opt to receive damages equal to at least six months' salary.

Sanctions and monitoring procedures

Infractions with respect to gender-based discrimination have a criminal aspect (*domaine correctionnel*). However, violations of the principle of equal pay are generally punished by fines (*sanctions contraventionnelles*) (Article R 154 of the Labour Code). Because of the punitive aspect of cases concerning equality in the workplace, the court has to detail the reasons for its decision. The statute of 1983 provides for the same penalty as that in Article 416 of the Penal Code: 'a fine between 200 and 20,000 French francs and a prison sentence between one month and one year'. The court can order that the judgment be posted in certain places and published in the newspapers of its choice (Article 152 of the Labour Code). In any event, sanctions for violations of the principle of non-discrimination can be suspended. This innovation reflects the objective of this legislation (Article 152—1 of the Labour Code), which is to correct an injustice, not to punish. This possibility also applies to violations of the principle of equal pay.

These articles fill in certain gaps in the Labour Code. Before the statute of 1983, there was no criminal penalty for an abusive transfer or for a failure to promote resulting from sexual discrimination. Now a woman can bring such a violation to the attention of the authorities.

The Roudy legislation also provides for monitoring procedures to promote equality. Article 123—7 of the Labour Code requires employers to post the text concerning equality. In addition, this legislation reinforces the role of the Labour Inspectors, who can report any violations of the rules concerning equality in the workplace. They also have the power to demand evidence of how remuneration is calculated in the company. Finally, the legislature decided to create a special court, the Conseil Supérieur de l'Egalité Professionelle, to promote the debate on equality in the workplace. Its role is to help define and apply the rules on equality. One of its purposes will be to promote compensatory measures and write periodic reports on what has been accomplished.

The legal arsenal in France has been considerably strengthened by the Roudy statute of 1983. It goes beyond some abstract notion of equality and establishes procedures useful in the fight against discriminatory practices. Accordingly, this statute broadens the applicability of the principle of discrimination to include all aspects of working life, and it establishes rigorous criminal sanctions. It eliminates the possibilities employers once had to dismiss women and places the burden of proof on the employer concerning equal pay. With respect to equal opportunity, the law affects all people in the workplace. It may be true that the periodic reports required by this legislation have not yet had the desired effect, but the law gives broader powers to unions, prohibits punitive dismissals and criminalizes certain sanctions. Moreover, the Community Court of Justice is committed to implementing the European directives on equality. In conclusion, one can hope that these efforts at the national and European levels will help to improve the working conditions of women. The massive entry of women in the workforce is irreversible, and such laws are necessary to end persistent discrimination against them.

Notes

1. 'Les Petites Affiches' 15 December 1989: '*Liberté, égalité, féminité*', G. Koubi, C. Neirinck.
2. Cass Crim, 17 January 1984. D. 1984 IR p. 230.
3. Bull no. 154 D. 1983, 575.
4. CJCE, 30 June 1988, *EEC Commission v. France case 318/86*. Recueil français de Droit Administratif 1988, p. 976.
5. CJCE aff. 312/86 *Commission v. France*.
6. Cass. Soc., 24 November 1976 Buel no. 69, p. 503.
7. Cass. *Soc. Essilor c/Mme Scheffer and Mme Nozière*, 9 June 1982, Bull. nos 380 and 381, p. 282.
8. Margaret Marvani, '*Mais qui a peur du travail des femmes*', *l'Histoire du clavier enchaîné*, Ed. Syros, 1985.
9. '*Les plans d'égalité professionnelle*'. Appraisal done by CNRS and published in la Documentation Française (1988) and Le Monde of 19 October 1989.
10. It was one proposition of the Baudouin report (1975).

Chapter 19

Consumer policy in France

Max Peyrard

A market economy presupposes, in theory, a balance of powers between the consumer and the producer. In reality, it is obvious that the imperfection of markets requires readjustment measures in favour of consumers: such is the objective of the consumer protection policy.

This part of economic and social policy covers, in fact, a relatively broad and complex area which concerns particularly:

- information on goods, necessary to allow the consumer to have a free choice;
- price policy, which must be the result of an adequate supply;
- safety of products, goods and services, and the liability of the supplier in case of damage caused by a defective product;
- the regulating of unfair trade practices;
- consumer credit which avoids discrimination;
- unfair and misleading advertising;
- consumer representation when economic policy is being drafted;
- the capability of public authorities to control the application of protective measures; and
- possibility for the injured consumer or his representative to take a case to court.

The objectives of the French consumer protection policy, as well as those of the Community policy, have been drawn up in the light of these ideals. Considering the diversity and scale of problems to be resolved, however, a lot is still to be done even if considerable progress has been made over the last 15 years.

In this chapter the characteristics of French policy will be examined, followed by Community policy, to try and measure their reciprocal influence.

The French consumer protection policy

French consumer protection policy has been considerably strengthened by a law of 18 January 1992, which deals mainly with consumer information, repression of abuses of consumer weakness, establishing joint representation, comparative advertising and various provisions, among which a project for a 'Consumer's Code'.

French legislation on consumer policy at the present moment can be grouped under six headings which will deal in turn with consumers' representation, information and protection; the implementation of this protection; and with recent developments on advertising and the 'Consumer's Code' project.

The consumers' representation

Consumers' representation is assured by consumers' associations. They provide to the public results of comparative tests, studies and investigations made on some products and services and inform consumers on their rights through legal advice.

An association can get official approval when it fulfils three conditions:

- to be registered under the law of 1901 (regulating associations);
- to have among its objectives protection of consumers; and
- to be 'representative', i.e. to exist for more than one year, to publicly and effectively see to the consumers' protection and to have a significant number of members (10,000 for a 'national' organization).

The approval is given for five years and can be renewed by ministerial decision for national organizations, and by decision of the 'prefet' for the local ones.

Consumers' associations are federated at regional level in 'regional technical centres' (*Centres techniques régionaux de la consommation* — CTRC) which are essentially co-ordination bodies and approved associations may initiate three kinds of legal proceedings:

- a civil action to make up for damages that have been caused to the consumer or to the common interest of consumers (if there is at the same time a penal offence and a common injury) or in order to put an end to unlawful practices;
- a direct action in order to get the withdrawal of improper clauses in standard contracts proposed to consumers. The notion of improper clauses is not specified in the law but a Community directive is being prepared which will include a list of such clauses;
- an action in 'joint' representation (law of 18 January 1992, art. 8) which allows them to act, on the behalf of victimized consumers, for

a penal as well as civil action, under certain conditions. It is a collective action, inspired by the 'Class action' existing in USA and
Québec legislations and at the stage of proposal in the Community,
reserved to approved associations, which may act only on behalf of
'clearly identified' consumers.

Moreover, the two biggest consumers' associations approved at a
national level are also involved in state institutions. These are:

- the National Consumers Council (Conseil National de la Consommation — CNC), which expresses its opinion on bills, private bills
  and regulations drafts which have an effect on consumers and local
  consumer committees (Comités départementaux de la Consommation) which give their opinions on matters concerning consumers,
  competition and price supervision;
- the National Consumers' Institute (Institut National de la Consommation — INC), founded by the law of 22 December 1966, has
  become, since the decree of 4 May 1990, a public agency, of an
  industrial and commercial character. It has a threefold mission as a
  testing centre for comparative tests, a centre for study and training,
  and a centre for resources and information. It publishes a monthly
  magazine of information for consumers (called *50 millions de consom-
  mateurs*) including a monthly updated report on comparative tests, a
  weekly publication for consumers' organizations (*INC Hebdo*), gives
  weekly 15 minute TV programmes and offers a videotext system
  (Minitel *3615 INC*).

  Its board of directors is composed of 18 people: 10 representatives
  of consumers and users; five experts in the field of consumer policy,
  appointed by the State secretariat for Consumers' Affairs; and three
  representatives elected by the INC's staff.

From the political point of view, responsibility for consumer policy at
government level lies with the State Secretariat for Consumers' Affairs
which is integrated, generally, with the Ministry of Economic and Financial Affairs, or, sometimes, in the Ministry of Commerce or the Ministry
for Women's Rights.

From the administrative point of view, the Ministry of Economic and
Financial Affairs has set up a Directorate-General for Competition,
Consumer Affairs and Fraud Prevention (Direction Générale de la
Concurrence, de la Consommation et de la repression des fraudes —
DGCCRF) with, at local level, a Departement (County) Bureau. The task
of these state and local administrative services is to promote competition
and strengthen the information to and position of consumers.

Consumer associations consider there is still a lot to be done as regards
publicity about loans. An enquiry in 1991, covering 400 advertisements,
reveals that the nature, purpose and duration of the schemes offered

conform with legal requirements generally, but that this is not the case when it comes to identifying the lender and the total cost of the loan, especially as far as permanent loans are concerned.

As regards excessively damaging clauses, the regulations governing them, withdrawn from the law of 18 January 1992, are the concern of a special law which will be eventually passed in co-ordination with the proposals of a Community directive. This project, which foresees a widening of the area of competence for the Commission on excessively damaging clauses, accepts the setting up of a legal framework which will enable a judge to identify a harmful tendency in a contract, without the need a priori for a text defining this type of clause. Also it would extend the notion of harmful clauses to services contracts.

The consumers' information

The Presidential Order of 1986 states the principle of prior information for the consumer, not only on price of goods and services, like the order of 1945, but also on possible restrictions of the contractual liability and on particular terms of sale (maintenance contracts, guarantees and after-sale service contracts, matrimonial brokerage contracts). This order is complemented by the law of 1989 which organizes the communication of standard contracts.

The law of 1992 (art. 2 and 3) specifies the three particular obligations of a professional salesman towards the consumer:

- to give information on the essential characteristics of goods or services before the conclusion of the sale;
- to indicate the time period of availability of spare parts;
- to indicate the maximum time period for delivering goods for fulfilling obligations.

Added to this, the professionals in distance sales (by mail, phone, radio, TV or computer) have to indicate with precision the name and address of their business, a postal box number no longer being sufficient.

As far as the credit industry is concerned, all the details useful to the borrower (and to his/her guarantor) to assess elements of cost and reimbursement, must appear in the contract so that he/she can easily compare them to his/her income. Since the law of 1992, it is forbidden to advertise for 'free of charge credit' away from the saleman's business premises, if the loan granted is over the amount of FRF 140,000 (ECU 20,000). For property credit, adverts must indicate the length and cost of the deal, the existence of a cooling-off period of 10 days and the obligation to the salesman to reimburse sums of money paid by the consumer in cases where the latter withdraws within the time laid down.

The cooling-off period for the return of goods, or for the withdrawal of the contract, is currently in use for any operation concerning an important commitment of the consumer (purchasing of a property, of a car, matrimonial brokerage contract) or in cases where sale methods differ from those used in traditional commercial outlets (such as mail order, doorstep sale, or distance sales).

Consumers' protection measures

Some practices or activities which present a particular risk for the consumer are either forbidden or regulated, by way of protecting the consumer. This ban concerns not only sales with bonus, but also the offer of free bonus consisting of goods other than those of the main transaction. Also forbidden are 'pyramid sales', whether on goods or services, and credit offers superior to the value of the product which has been bought.

Refusing to sell is also banned, except in the real-estate business, or in the case of a contract concluded in consideration of the buyer's character, or if a legitimate motive of refusal exists (ban on sale, abnormal aspect of the sale, non-availability of the product). Moreover, batch sale or set quotas are banned, except if it is in the consumer's interests or if it is possible to buy separately elements from a batch.

Regulations concern primarily operations of TV-selling or TV-buying. Consumers' associations had hoped to see them forbidden but this would only have resulted in encouraging their development outside French borders. This is the reason for just instituting the seven days cooling-off period after receipt of the product which has been ordered, during which it may be returned. Also illegal are advertisements for lotteries which oblige participants to send money and also their drafting is subject to precise rules. Finally, periods of 'clearance sales' are carefully controlled, as well as the consumer's information on those operations and even the use of the term 'clearance sales'.

The law of January 1992 (art. 1) has extended the repression of abuses of consumer weakness, the point being to avoid an ignorant consumer having his/her consent forced out of him/her in an emergency case (as, for instance, for a repair on a motorway), or in a situation of strong pressure outside traditional commercial outlets (such as trade exhibitions, promotional meetings or journeys). It is, on the whole, a prolonging of the provisions on doorstep sales (see above).

It is interesting to note that since 1 July 1992, banks and other financial institutions (among them, the Post Office), offer a 'minimal banking service', after the signing of a 'charter' with the consumers' organizations. In order to avoid the exclusion of lower-income groups, every consumer will have the possibility of opening an account, to proceed to mail order or telephone payments and to have at his/her own disposal cheque facilities and a banking identification document, and, eventually, to obtain a credit card and a cheque-book.

In the field of security, the law of 21 July 1983 has established blanket provisions to protect the consumer's security at the time of utilization of goods or services. It imposes preventive measures to prevent accident (in conformity with the security standards already in force under pain of ban or regulation by decree) and, in case of danger, authorizes the direct intervention of the Consumers' Committee for Security at the appeal of any individual or legal entity, including the videotext system Minitel *3614 Securitam*. This Committee may also itself impose restraint *ex officio* and, in case of emergency, may deliver information to the public or intervene with the producer (for instance, it has prevented a baker from concealing a pin in a Twelfth-Night cake disguised as a bean!) or to alert the distribution channels, including those outside France. It disposes of powers of investigation which cannot be objected to either on the grounds of professional secrecy or trade secrecy and it may open hearings. It expresses opinions, published in the *Official Gazette*, on the enforcement of regulations and measures to be passed (161 opinions in seven years) and publishes an annual report, a weekly bulletin and practical notices, and also manages a resources service available on Minitel (videotext system).

The implementation of the consumer's protection

The implementation of the consumer's protection is assured by the intervention of control inspectors and has been strengthened still more by making it easier for a consumer to take a case to court or to the Ombudsman. Terms of sale, as well as terms of credit, can be controlled by officers of the Ministry of Financial Affairs' Directorate-General for Competition, Consumer Affairs and Fraud Prevention. They can also ascertain and sue for offences concerning banned or regulated activities (lottery, pyramid sales, forced sale, matrimonial brokerage contract) and those concerning sales of loose goods and counterfeiting. An annual report is issued by the Directorate-General. These agents also have power of consignment not only of dangerous products but also to products which do not conform to security regulations.

The consumer can also apply to the local Bureau for Competition, Consumer Affairs and Fraud Prevention by telephoning the 'green' number 05 12 05 12, (free of charge) or by writing to a 'Box Number 5,000' in his county, whereby his letter will be forwarded to the right quarters.

By way of example, the inspection at the end of 1991 of 350 funeral undertakers under private or state management, has shown that 40 per cent of them were in infraction, either by the absence of price labelling, or due to inadequate documentation, etc. In the same way, the inspection in 1991 of 1,000 car renting agencies made apparent numerous breaches of the regulation, particularly in the areas of terms of contracts and misleading advertising.

Taking a case to court has recently been made easier for consumers. Since the law of 5 January 1983, the consumers' associations may act more effectively because the civil action from approved associations enables them to ask for damages for prejudice against all consumers and for the suppression of illicit actions or of illicit clauses in contracts. They can also pursue those goals by joining the action of an individual consumer, thanks to the joint action of the law of 1992. In the same way, associations for the protection of investments in real estate or in financial products can sue in court to defend the investors' collective interest: so, following the request of an individual member, the National Federation of Investment Clubs (Fédération Nationale des Clubs d'Investissement — FNCI), approved as representative since November 1991, has, in February 1992, brought an action against a public corporation about which the Securities and Investment Commission of the French Stock Exchange (Commission des Opérations de Bourse — COB) has sent on the file to the court for 'communication to the public of false or misleading informations on its financial statements'.

Minor disputes, taken to a magistrates' court, can have the choice between two procedures better adapted to their settlement: a simple statement enables them to be referred to the court (if the dispute involves a sum of money below FRF 13,000 — ECU 200) and the judge can render an 'enforcing injunction' against a professional so that he has to fulfil his obligation (if under FRF 30,000 — ECU 4,500), if he has signed a contract to do so.

Since 1990, the consumers most deeply indebted benefit from a measure whereby a local committee analyses each case and can set out a scheme of amicable arrangement, by getting the agreement of the debtor and of the main creditors, or, by way of default, of a procedure establishing a redress by the civil court.

There is also the possibility of calling on a conciliator, appointed by the President of the Court of Appeal, whose decisions are not compulsory, except if the parties in dispute have signed to agree with the official ascertainment.

Concerning the 'over-indebtedness of households', application of the law of 1989 always creates some difficulties in its assessments. The Cour de Cassation has judged that an indebted person has not to prove his sincerity because it is taken for granted, and that the judges' decisions are final in determining measures to be taken in order to assure the civil redress of the debtor. Such measures are: rescheduling the reimbursement; limiting the reimbursement to only the remaining capital owed; and eventually, even, a total cancellation of the debt, if this measure is the only one compatible with the debtor's resources.

However, in case of a 'debt contracted for the needs of or in pursuance of professional activity', (for instance, a lease taken out for a company that an individual manages or has shares in), he/she cannot profit by the law, which is applicable only for debt contracted for a lease given to a third person, including a member of his family. This law continues to raise protests from banks and shopkeepers who notice that, if it has reduced the number of misleading advertisements (particularly the ones offering 'credit free of charge'), it is also open to abuse from people who borrow from several credit companies, and then use the provisions of the law to refuse to repay the loans.

The right to distrain the Ombudsman has been conferred on consumers' associations by the law of 6 February 1992 (related to local administration). They have to follow the usual procedure of transmission of the complaint by the way of a member of the parliament (representative or senator).

Recent developments concerning the control of advertising

The law limiting very heavy advertising on tobacco and alcohol was voted in in December 1990 after some heated debates. The text allows for banning all advertising on tobacco from 1 January 1993. The enabling decree of 30 May 1992 specifies the terms for bringing it into operation, particularly in 'public places', including workplaces and restaurants, where it will be forbidden to smoke.

As far as alcohol is concerned, from 1 January 1993, advertising will be confined to adult newspapers and will have to be informative and accompanied by a health message. It is only in the areas where wine and spirits are produced that advertisements in the form of signs and posters, as well as small public notices and items inside specialized shops, will be authorized. It will be forbidden to sell alcohol in petrol stations between 10 p.m. and 6 a.m.

Comparative advertising is also another very controversial part of the law of 18 January 1992 (art. 10), though it is inspired of the British system which sets strict deontological rules, and is approved by more than 70 per cent of the public opinion (according to public opinion polls). In order to avoid denigration, the text allows for the comparison to be 'objective, carried out over significant and verifiable characteristics of the products being compared', and, as the Cour de Cassation has ruled, since 1986, on the price of comparable goods. The advertiser will have to prove that his message is true, and the advertisement has to be transmitted to the targeted competitor within a time at least equal to the one needed to cancel an advertisement in the media used. In the case of misleading comparative advertising, the court may order the annulment of the said advertisement, and the media may be sentenced, as an accomplice, to bear the cost of publication of the judgment and, eventually, of one or several rectifying advertisements. Penal sanctions are provided for in cases of misleading advertisement or counterfeiting of a trade mark.

Towards a 'Consumers' Code'

Article 12 of the law of 18 January 1992, provides for a 'Consumers' Code', which would bring together all the texts of laws and regulations concerning relationships between professionals and consumers and which could be the starting point for other new texts.

A project on such a 'Code' was studied and presented in February 1990: it proposed new institutions and new rules, having mentioned the definition of a consumer as 'a person who gets or uses goods or services for his personal use'.

Among the proposed institutions, one can notice the collective agreements for consumers (on which the legislative ratification would make them compulsory even for the non-signatories); the creation of a Guarantee Fund (with the purpose of indemnifying victims in cases where the responsible person is insolvent); a Fund for consumers' help (which would advance money needed to take an action to court and would be financed by professionals' illicit profits); and the creation of a joint action (which was introduced by the law of January 1992).

As far as new rules are concerned, the main propositions concern the ban on advertising which could lead to dangerous consequences, the admission of comparative advertising (by the law of 1992), the creation of a new offence when there is damage caused to the health or to the life of a group of people, the penal responsibility of legal entities (the Penal Code being in process of modification), and the authority given to the judge to raise *ex officio* means of protecting the consumer (introduced in the law of 1992 for misleading comparative advertising).

For its part, the State Secretariat for Consumers' Affairs, while continuing to act on the main points — the unfair terms in contracts, the over indebtment and the internal security — plans to put in work conciliators to solve small consumers' disputes (400,000 complaints registered every year) that the courts are too congested to deal with efficiently. Moreover, allegations on the nature of new foodstuffs, products described as 'light' (calorie reduced), slimming or for extra strength, are to be scrutinized.

The Community policy for the protection of consumers

The Treaty of Rome aims to facilitate the free movement of individuals, goods, services and capital, by means of economic policies which will be crowned by the Single Market in 1993.

The protection of the consumers' interests only appears expressly in Article 39—1e, devoted to agricultural policy and in Article 85—3, concerning competition policy. However, in the Treaty preamble, signatory parties 'set their efforts towards a main objective of constant improvement of the living and working conditions for their peoples'.

It is on this basis that a common policy for consumers' protection has slowly developed, which has consequently relied on an autonomous legal reference in the Article 100—3, of the Single Act of 1987, until the coming into force of the Article 129—A of the Maastricht Treaty.

The stages of European policy for consumers' protection

In 1962, a 'liaison committee' was created, consisting of representatives of trade unions and consumers' associations, but one had to wait until 1972 to see a summit of heads of state and governments of the member-states ready to launch the consumers' policy. This leads to the creation of a specialized bureau, within the Directorate-General for Competition policy, and the implementation of the Consumers' Consultative Committee, where the main organizations for the protection of consumers were represented.

Finally, in 1975, the Council of Ministers adopted an initial programme for the information and protection of the consumers, focusing on five fundamental rights: the right to protection of security and health, the right of redress in case of damage suffered, the right to protection of economic interests, the right to representation and, the right to information and education.

A second programme, adopted in 1981, confirms orientations of its predecessor and insists on the necessity to take into account consumers' interests in the various Community policies. From this view-point, directives or any other legal acts are based on various articles of the Treaty. In this way, Article 100, on the free movement of goods, is at the root of the Directive 79—112 on the labelling and the presentation of foodstuff to the final consumer and of the Directive 84—450 on the prohibition of misleading advertising. The Article 235, relative to areas not covered by the Treaty, is at the root of Directive 79—581 on indication of price of foodstuffs, and of the Directive 84—133 on the system of rapid information on dangers arising from the use of consumer products.

It is only with Article 100—A of the Single Act, in force since 1 July 1987, that the policy for consumers' protection has taken for basis 'a high level of protection for the consumer' and has at its disposal a legal autonomous reference which has since been used.

In 1989, with the perspective of the Single Market in 1993, the Commission of the European Community published a three-year action plan for 1990—92, with the aim of completing its action in favour of consumers' protection in four important fields: representation, information, security of products and transactions.

Health and security protection of the consumers

With the '*Cassis de Dijon*' judgment in 1979, the European Court of Justice has decided that any product legally produced and traded in one member country must, in principle, be admitted to the markets of other countries which are members of the common market, except if there are imperative demands of protection for the consumer and for public health.

This mutual recognition of national laws resulted in the situation that, since 1984 every new national project of regulation or of standard must be notified in the advance to the Commission which will inform other member countries and can elaborate a European standard if necessary. Moreover, Community Directives can restrict themselves to set essential requirements for health and security, national standards meeting these characteristics which from now on are approved at European level, thus enabling the free movements of the goods concerned.

This is the reason why many 'product-based' Directives have been adopted regarding various products such as cosmetics, textiles, pharmaceutical products and industrial products (cars, tractors and toys).

The protection of consumers' economic and juridical interests

Several directives have been adopted regarding misleading advertising, doorstep sales, manufacturer's liability in case of damage because of a defective product, consumer credit (2nd directive of 22 February 1990 on the 'annual total effective cost to the consumer'), set-price travel tickets (directive of 1990), the recommendation of the commission of the Community on payments transactions (credit cards), the resolution of Council of Ministers on the access of consumers to courts, to information and to education.

The three-year action plan of consumer policy (1990–92)

In this action plan, the commission emphasizes the improvement of consumers' representation and information, as well as the security of products and transactions. As regards consumers' representation, studies are being made to set up a global legal instrument to assure a better access by consumers to the courts; and as far as information is concerned, after having harmonized the requirements for financial services, the Commission prepared a project concerning advertising broadcast on both radio and television, and wants to eliminate obstacles which are still opposed to comparative advertising and misleading advertising (proposal for a directive, modified on 11 July 1991) and to ban advertising for alcohol and tobacco (proposal of directive, modified on 21 May 1992).

The security of consumers has been the subject of two texts. The first on general product safety led to a Community Regulation of 15 October 1991 which constrains member-states that are without relevant provisions, to bring into working order within two years legislative, statutory and administrative stipulations, as well as the indispensable control institutions: so these new provisions will suppress the distortions in competition that French businesses are susceptible to by the application of the French law of 21 July 1983 which laid down the same stipulations.

The directive of 25 July 1985 on defective product liability will be supplemented (proposal for a directive on 21 July 1991) to include civil liability of service supplier.

The Community Regulation on the conferring of an ecology label takes explicitly into account security requirements (OJEC 18 January 1992).

In the field of transactions, the proposal for a directive was modified on 24 March 1992: it concerns unfair clauses in sale contracts and, particularly, a blacklist of terms regarded as abusive which will be considered null and void.

For distance sales, a proposal for a directive was brought into action by the commission on 10 June 1992 (OJEC on 23 June). It includes common stipulations applicable to all techniques of communication in the field of contracts negotiated at a distance (by way of TV, videotext, computer, fax machine, etc.) and a recommendation inciting professionals of this industry to produce a 'code of fair behaviour'.

Lastly, a proposal of regulations for foodstuffs produced from biotechnology has been prepared by the Commission: but a scientific investigation will have to be done before they can be put on the market.

The Treaty of Maastricht

In Article 3 s, the Treaty of Maastricht, it is stated that '. . . action of the Community includes . . . a contribution to the improvement of consumers' protection'. A new article, 129–A, is entirely devoted to the consumers' protection which thus benefits from a reference text, which is specific and unambiguous, authorizing the Community to realise 'a high level of consumers' protection . . . by specific actions . . . which cannot prevent a member-state from maintaining or setting up more strict measures of protection' (see in Annex 2 the text of this article).

One may foresee that consumers' protection at Community level will be made easier by these stipulations and strengthened by the influence of certain member-states, particularly the northern ones, of which the number is likely to be increased by the admission of new members.

The influence of French and Community policies upon each other

The development of protection policies for consumers has been globally beneficial. One may consider, briefly, that the influence of the Community regulations has essentially shown itself in a liberal way, in order to favour the functioning of a free market economy: the increase in competition is beneficial to consumers as prices go down because of a wider opening of the French market to foreign competitive products, particularly the ones from Community member countries, such as refrigerators or airplane tickets. In many cases, for consumer goods, quality has been improved at the same time.

One may also conclude that the common policy has largely contributed to emancipating the French consumer: the paternalistic role of the French administration has been reduced to the benefit of the consumer, him/herself, having become more adult, or to the benefit of representative associations. He/she can now express or defend him/herself in a more autonomous way, including those occasions when it is necessary to be protected from the State's bureaucratic control.

With a parallel development of the two policies, the consumer has gained more power in public life and the transposal of Community legislation into French law has been achieved without difficulty: very often French legislation was elaborated and put into operation before, or in the same period as, that of the Community.

The heated debates in the European Parliament at the beginning of 1992, about the ban on advertising for tobacco, have shown that the French law of 1991 ('loi Evin') has had an influence on the discussion, including particularly the prohibition of avoiding the provisions by using the same trade mark for cigarettes and for fashion clothes.

On the other hand, the French manufacturer loses a part of his 'monopoly power' as an exclusive supplier to his fellow citizen, both on the basis of market share and on the basis of prices, eventually even on quality when the competition is keen.

He can no longer count on the state's support, traditionally interventionist (colbertist), to use the argument of the consumers' protection policy as an excuse for protectionism: even a State monopoly cannot stop people using European goods imported from other member-states, that has had, as a result, to persuade French manufacturers to make strong efforts on the price and quality of their own products.

To conclude, consumers' associations will have to develop and organize themselves in a more efficient way in order to fulfil at the same time their national and European roles. In addition to the links established by the main national associations in the area of official institutions, one may now see the development of direct ties between local associations on two sides of a frontier, facilitating the resolution of transfrontier litigations, because the possibility of benefiting from competition by using a foreign supplier is limited when consumers do not know the regulations and trade customs of this neighbouring foreign country.

Annex 1: main laws and regulations on consumers' protection in France

1. More recent texts:
— law on consumer protection (18 January 1992 — OG 21 January)
— law of 6 February 1992 (relating to local administration) conferring to consumers' associations the right to distrain the Ombudsman
— law limiting advertising for tobacco and alcohol ('Loi Evin' — 10 January 1991 — OG 12 January)
— decree taken to apply the law against bad effects of tobacco (29 May 1992 — OG 30 May)

2. On the consumers' information

• on prices
— Presidential Orders of 30 June 1945 and of December 1st 1986 on prices and competition
— decision of 7 September 1977 on price information
— decision of 10 November 1982 on information on price per unit for some prepacked products
— decision of 3 December 1987 on the legibility of information, prior information for particular terms of sale (delivery charge, putting into operation), proof of the information when an audiovisual technique is used

• on contractual clauses
— art. 28 of the Presidential Order of 1986 on contractual clauses (follow up of the product)
— decision of 22 December 1987 on warranty and after-sale service for domestic electrical goods
— law of 23 June 1989, art. 6 on obligations for matrimonial agencies
— law of 23 June 1989, art. 3 on handing over of a standard contract to every individual or legal entity permitting to fight preventively against unfair terms

• on credit
— law of 10 January 1978 on consumers' information and protection for credit operations
— law of 13 July 1979 on consumers' information and protection for real-estate credit
— law of 23 June 1989 and 31 December 1989 completing these two laws

— ethical code elaborated by professionals of trade and advertising on advertising for consumer credit (1990)
- on cooling-off period, return and withdrawal rights
— law of 6 January 1988 on return period of 7 days following the delivery, in all operations of distance sales (TV-sales, phone sales)
— laws of 23 June 1989 on harmonization of the period of 7 days and extension of the withdrawal period for buying goods and services particularly for real-estate and matrimonial matters

3. *On measures for consumers' protection*

- on forbidden practice or activities
— Presidential Order of 1986, art. 29, on sales with bonus
— law of 5 November 1953 on pyramidal sales of goods, extended to services by the law of 23 June 1989, art. 4
— laws of 23 June 1989, art. 2 and 31 December 1989, art. 2, on terms of payment exceeding the value of the product which has been bought
— Presidential Order of 1986, art. 30, on refusal of sale, sale in batches or fixed quantities

- on regulated practices and activities
— law of 23 June 1989, art. 1, on TV-sales and TV-buying
— law of 23 June 1989, art. 5, on advertising lotteries
— decree of 6 November 1962 completed by decree and decision of 22 September 1989 on clearance sales

- on consumer security
— law of 21 July 1983 (OG 22 July)

4. *On consumers' representation*
— law of 22 December 1966 establishing the National Consumers' Institute (Institut national de la Consommation — INC) became since the decree of 4 May 1990 a public agency (with industrial and commercial character)

5. *The implementation of consumer's protection*

- on the powers of the officers of the DGCCRP in charge of inspection
— Presidential Order of 1 December 1986 and law of 23 June 1989 on terms, conditions, lotteries, pyramidal sales, and consignment
— law of 31 December 1989 on display of loose goods and counterfeiting

- on possibility to consumers to go to Court
— laws of 27 December 1983 and 5 January 1988 on consumers' associations right to be associated in a civil action and act in Court under conditions

- law of January 1988 on the protection of investors' interests in stocks and shares
- decree of 4 March 1988 on procedures for minor offences

• reinsertion of the consumer in economic life
- law of 31 December 1989 on the settlement of difficulties tied to excessive debt of individuals and families (amicable settlement with creditors and civil judicial redress)

Annex 2: Article 129 a of the Treaty of Maastricht

1. The Community shall contribute to the attainment of a high level of consumer protection through:
   (a) measures adopted pursuant to Article 100a in the context of the completion of the internal market;
   (b) specific action which supports and supplements the policy pursued by the Member States to protect the health, safety and economic interests of consumers and to provide adequate information to consumers.
2. The Council, acting in accordance with the procedure referred to in Article 189b and after consulting the Economic and Social Committee, shall adopt the specific action referred to in paragraph 1(b).
3. Action adopted pursuant to paragraph 2 shall not prevent any Member State from maintaining or introducing more stringent protective measures. Such measures must be compatible with this Treaty. The Commission shall be notified of them.

Bibliography

Babusiaux, C. (1990) 'Le droit de la consommation, reflet de l'évolution économique et technique', *Revue française d'administration publique*, October–December.

Commission of the European Community (1990) *Three year action plan of consumer policy in the EEC (1990–1992)*, 3 May.

Desforges-Buche, M-C. (1990) 'Evolution du droit de la consommation', *Revue de la concurrence et de la consommation*.

Economic and Social Committee of the EEC (1992) *Report on the consumer and the internal market*, April.

Institut National de la Consommation (INC), weekly review *INC Hebdo*.

Van Der Miert, K. (1990) 'L'Europe de la consommation', *Revue française d'administration publique*, October–December.

Van Der Miert, K. (1991) 'Objectives of the European Community for consumer protection', (Speech at the Economic and Social Committee of the EEC, 6 September and introductory message at a Seminar in Hannover on Consumer Information, 9 September).

Chapter 20

Mass-media policy

Danielle Bahu-Leyser

Unlike areas such as agriculture, energy or transportation, mass-media has only been extensively considered for the past 30 years. One reason for this is that governments, including Western European governments, have always considered legislation and regulations governing media to be dependent on them. Additionally, media operates and is relevant only in the specific context of the countries concerned; which prevents it from being easily suited for export.

However, with the emergence of multinational mass media groups such as the Compagnie Luxembourgeoise de Télédiffusion (CLT), the Berlusconi and Hachette groups, private radio and television channels appeared that ended state monopolies in countries such as France. This, coupled with the introduction of cable and satellite television, produced changes in the early 1980s. This explains why member-states reconsidered their policies and community institutions reviewed the organization of media within Europe. This action was followed by resolutions of the European Parliament and directives issued by the Commission of European Communities.

In parallel with establishing this legislative framework, the national governments and professionals of EC member-states took tangible action. In the majority of cases, measures were supported by the Brussels Commission. It could be argued that interest shown by European institutions in specifying and implementing a common media policy within the 12 member-states was the result of outside pressure. It may have been a reaction to American and Japanese domination, in contrast to positive action in the audio-visual sector.

Currently, a common European audio-visual organization is still embryonic and may be subject to great changes. Therefore, it is still premature to measure the spin-off from audio-visual action on the French media environment. It may be necessary to review stages leading towards an authentic European Television area. The purpose of the resolution of the European Parliament in Strasburg in October 1985, was to set up such an area. It now seems appropriate to consider the foreseeable effects of joint action on the audio-visual sector in France.

As in many cases of European co-operation, France and Germany were responsible for providing the impetus for a European Audio-visual Organization. As early as 1973, state representatives signed an agreement for constructing four identical satellites for direct beaming of television programmes. This complied with the standard D2-Mac/Paquet (transmitting and receiving TV pictures). This recently developed standard was the result of co-operation between the French company Thomson and Philips of Holland. The programme concerned TDF 1/TDF 2 for France and TV-Sat 1/TV-Sat 2 for Germany.

Technical and political problems resulted in a delay in the implementation of the agreement. Finally, it was decided that TV-Sat 1 would only be operational in 1987, TDF 1 in October 1988, TV-Sat 2 in August 1989 and TDF 2 in August 1990.[1] One reason for this delay was an external event namely the decision taken by the International Union of Telecommunications (IUT) at the Geneva Conference in June 1977. The number of direct television channels was then limited to five per country i.e., for powerful frequency channels.

In the same year, Post and Telecommunications Authorities of 26 European countries decided to join forces for constructing and operating telecommunications and data transmission satellites. The European Organization of Satellites (Eutelsat) was thus born. Eutelsat entrusted a consortium, led by the French company Matra and British Aerospace, with the task of implementing a first programme comprising four ECS satellites (Eutelsat 1). These were scheduled to be launched between 1983 and 1988. In 1986, Eutelsat decided to initiate the second generation of ECS (Eutelsat 2) satellites. These were constructed by a consortium led by two French groups (Aérospatiale and Alcatel-Espace). The first satellite in the Eutelsat 2 series was successfully put into orbit on 30 August 1990 by the Ariane launcher.

In parallel, France-Télécom, the largest shareholder with 11 per cent shares in the European Organization of Satellites, constructed and launched its own telecommunications satellite (Télécom 1) in April 1984. Télécom 1 was backed by Télécom 2 in 1991. It is planned to launch Télécom 3 soon. Meanwhile, the Germans developed their Kopernicus project which resulted in putting a first satellite into orbit in 1987.

In practical terms, these satellites, originally designed and manufactured for transmitting audible, written and digital data, were very soon used for radio and television transmissions. The main reasons for this decision were based on availability. In fact, this type of satellite can be used earlier than those used to direct television programmes. However, their low levels of transmission require large parabolic aerials measuring between one and four metres in diameter. These are relayed at ground level by cable networks.

To end the confusion following failure of negotiations with France in assigning one TDF channel to the Compagnie Luxembourgeoise de Télédiffusion, Luxemburg decided to equip itself with its own satellite system. This was christened Astra and was constructed by the American industrial group General Electric. These medium-power satellites could be picked up by individual parabolic aerials. However, they do not comply with the rules established by the Geneva conference of 1977. The first satellite, launched in 1988, contained 16 channels as did the second, launched at the beginning of March 1991.

This was a blow for the forecast profitability of direct television satellites and led the French and German governments to consider subsequent action for the TDF/TV-Sat programme. This was especially the case in Germany where audio-visual policy decisions are taken directly at Lander level. Some Lander did not hide their preference for a strictly national solution to the problem.

The crisis between Paris and Bonn deepened to the point of endangering action taken by 'the Twelve' and the Commission of European Communities. Top of the list was the Eureka 95 programme, implemented to counter the danger of a Japanese monopoly of High Definition Television.

Eureka 95: European high-definition television

During the spring 1986 plenary session of the conference organized by International Broadcasting Consultative Committee (IBCC — an organization attached to the UN) held in Dubrovnik, ex-Yugoslavia, the 12 EEC member-states, supported by other Western European countries, decided to counter the Japanese attempt to gain international recognition for its high-definition television standard Muse.[2] The 19 states comprising the European High Technology Research Organization (Eureka) held a meeting in London at the end of June at which it was agreed to form an audio-visual section.

This project is 95th on the list of Eureka programmes (hence Eureka 95) and comprises two phases. The purpose of the first phase was to specify a joint standard for High Definition Television. The second phase concerned establishing a common programme for related recording and display equipment accessible to the general public. Six EC countries took part in this programme. These were Germany, Belgium, France, Italy, the Netherlands and the United Kingdom. This team was joined by Finland, Sweden and Switzerland. The initial budget for the Eureka 95 programme was set at 200 million ECU (approximately 1.5 billion French francs). An additional budget was provided by the dynamic Franco-Dutch tandem, Thomson-Philips. This was the driving force and the main source of finance for the project.

However, the high stakes fully justified this investment and Roger Fauroux, the French Minister for Industry at that time, estimated that there was a market of 60 billion French francs up to the year 2000 and approximately 250 billion francs for 2005.[3]

The D2-Mac/Paquet standard – transition to HDTV

Current Hertzian television broadcasting, transmittal and diffusion systems irrespective of whether they comply with American NTSC, German PAL or French SECAM standards, are capable of processing three components in television simultaneously. These are the picture, colour and sound. There is always a danger of interference between components in all these systems and poor reception can result, e.g. interference between picture and sound.

Such defects are corrected to obtain quality worthy of cinema standards by processing the three components simultaneously. Technically, this involves high quality picture and sound coupled with greater available space on the sound band. Programmes in several languages can thus be broadcast simultaneously. However, current audio-visual facilities and equipment cannot operate to 'High Definition' standards and must be entirely replaced. In contrast to the Japanese, Europeans have opted for a step-by-step approach. They consider it preferable to ensure a certain degree of compatibility with equipment currently available on the market.

This is why the standard D2-Mac/Paquet[4] was established. It is a transition between the Pal, Secam and HDTV standards. Thus, traditional equipment, fitted with a simple decoder, can now receive programmes transmitted by D2-Mac/Paquet. This situation is similar to that of black and white sets in the mid-1960s. These were able to receive the first programmes transmitted in colour. Subsequently, a television complying with the D2-Mac/Paquet standard will be able to receive HDTV broadcasts.

The French and German direct television satellite programme provides for an initial application of this intermediate standard. It is monitored by the European Space Agency (ESA). This organization has also selected this standard for the Olympus satellite project. Belgium, Denmark, Spain, Italy, the Netherlands, the United Kingdom, Austria and Canada are also participating in this project. It is probable that this favourable environment will incite other EC members to opt firmly for the D2-Mac/Paquet system. In November, 1986, the Brussels Commission published a directive in which the standard was granted Community standard status. Official recognition of the recommendation issued several months previously by the European Broadcasting Union (EBU) was thus obtained.

A complete set of television equipment complying with the D2-Mac/Paquet standard was successfully demonstrated at the international audio-visual equipment fair in Brighton during September, 1988. This was part of the Eureka 95 programme and illustrated the progress Europeans had made in mastering innovative audio-visual technology in the course of two years.

However, there were delays in the TDF/TV-Sat programme caused mainly by incidents with the Ariane launcher. The Paris Government was also reticent about pursuing the TDF programme. This seemed to dampen the enthusiasm of France's German partners and voices were raised in favour of a national standard PAL +. This would have been an improved version of the PAL standard. The Franco-German summit of September 1989 had to be awaited before misunderstandings were resolved. Both sides reaffirmed their undertakings on the D2-Mac/Paquet standard. Could the 12 EEC member-states still respond to the Japanese threat by presenting a united front at the meeting of the International Broadcasting Consultative Committee held in May 1990? The 12 member-states and partners decided to implement the second phase of the Eureka 95 programme and a credit of 500 million ECU (3.5 billion French francs) was assigned for this purpose.

Vision 1250, industrial launching of HDTV

Vision 1250 is tangible evidence that the 12 EEC member-states are determined to respond to the Japanese challenge in the high definition TV field. However, Eureka 95 was still basically a research and development programme on a Western European scale.

Therefore, to provide greater impetus to the industrial stage, EC member countries signed a document creating a European Group of Economic Interest (EGEI). It was decided to name this group Vision 1250[5] and it officially came into existence on 11 July 1990. It comprised industrial organizations, broadcasters, producers and creators. French organizations involved were the Thomson Industrial Group, French Television and Radio organizations such as the Office Français de Radio et de Télévision (OFRT), the Société Française de Production (SFP) and France-Télécom, the unique EGEI operator.

Legally, Vision 1250 took over from the French GEI, International HD that was set up in 1988 by French public authorities, SFP and Philips-France. From its beginning, International HD took a European stance and in recognition received a credit of 15 million ECU (slightly less than FRF 100 million) from the EC. Like its predecessor, the purpose of Vision 1250 was to promote production of high-definition television programmes within the European Economic Community. This took concrete form with the loaning of essential equipment such as cameras and video recorders, to producers and broadcasters. Related consultancy, technical assistance and demonstrations organized on a national scale were included in its scope.

However, the French finally surrendered to their partners wishes, especially the British and Germans who were reluctant to accept French supremacy within the EGIE. In consequence, the head office of Vision 1250 was based in Brussels and not Paris as France-Télécom would have preferred for continuity and efficiency reasons.

Media 92: measures taken to encourage a common European broadcasting policy

Although the importance of technology within the audio-visual sector cannot be denied, it should never be forgotten that it is merely a medium for producing and broadcasting artistic work in the cinema and on television. Therefore, it is pointless to counter the Japanese in the fields of high-definition television equipment related to chips and 16/9 flat screens, if only American series and Japanese cartoons are broadcast.

In 1988, the United States supplied Europe with 700 million dollars (approximately 4 billion francs) worth of television programmes. In addition, Japanese cartoons accounted for 60 per cent of the 11,000 hours broadcast throughout the EC. This should be compared with the mere 350 hours of Community-based cartoons!

On account of this, in 1986 the Brussels Commission took a number of concrete measures to encourage the development of the audio-visual production industry. This was known as 'Media' and in 1988 it became the Community programme Media 92. Concurrently, the Ministers of Culture of the 12 EC states decided in November 1986 to designate 1988 as 'European Cinema and Television Year'. Its purpose was to make every member country aware of what was produced within the Community.

Originally, a modest budget of 13.5 million ECU (approximately FRF 95 million) was assigned to this programme. From 1991 to 1995, a budget of 250 million ECU (FRF 1.75 billion) comprising loans or advances in anticipation of takings, was allocated. Currently, the project includes about a dozen mechanisms. These concern the fields of audio-visual creation and cover production, broadcasting and financing.

From 1986 to 1989, European Institutions such as the European Council, the Council of Ministers and the Brussels Commission can be proud of accomplishments in organizing a European Audio-visual Area. These institutions have specified and obtained recognition within the 12 EC countries for a joint standard concerning design and manufacture of high definition television equipment, i.e. the standard D2-Mac/Paquet. They have set up a programme to encourage creation, production, broadcasting and financing of national works or co-productions of EC states.

The legal and regulatory system will now have to replace this audio-visual system with an authentic common audio-visual policy. The Commission is moving in this direction. In 1989, it succeeded in making the 12 member-states accept the directive entitled 'Television without Borders'.

'Television without borders' Directive

On the basis of the 'Green Paper' published by the Brussels Commission in June 1984, under the title 'Television Without Borders', the European Parliament adopted in October of the following year, a resolution in which support for encouraging European productions was demanded (Media 92 plan). The paper specified the contents of a Community directive on broadcast advertisements and set down the main lines of a second directive concerning author rights.

Armed with such support, the Commission submitted a first project for a directive to the EEC Council of Ministers. The scope of the text was as follows:

- the country of origin of programmes. This included minimum quotas for the various works issued within the Community;
- advertisements. A maximum daily number of advertisements calculated with respect to the entire length of broadcasts on radio or televised television;
- protection of children and young people; and
- author rights.

Differences of interest between the various EEC partners and other countries (the United States have a protectionist policy in this field and do not subscribe to European Institutions limiting broadcasts of American series via the internal quotas of the 12 states), did not facilitate discussions on the project for a directive. A modified version was, therefore, submitted to the Council of Ministers in March, 1989. It now contained no further references to author rights. These will be covered by a separate directive.

Two different schools of thought are in competition for establishing a second version of the Community directive. The first, to which France resolutely belongs, is arguing for voluntary measures to increase and defend internal production. The group defends the principle of broadcasting quotas. The second group defends liberal ideas; it is spearheaded by Germany and Britain and wishes to maintain free enterprise.

Following extremely tough bargaining, worthy of the earliest 'agricultural marathons', the 12 member-states finally reached an agreement on a text on 13 April 1989. This involved removing the requirement for a 60 per cent quota for works originating from Europe. This would be replaced by a qualitative formula and be less stringent for broadcasters. This agreement was submitted to the European Parliament for approval but this organization required that the 60 per cent quota should be re-established. The document had to wait six months before finally being adopted on 3 October 1989. This event was greeted with enthusiasm by European audio-visual authorities and the Eureka audio-visual programme[6] was initiated.

However, quotas for 60 per cent of European works have yet to be re-established. In fact, the contents of the second project for the Community directive 'Television without Borders' was subsequently contained in the Convention 'Trans-Frontier Television' issued by the Council of Europe. As previously, the initial project for broadcasting quotas of European programmes was further eroded. This convention was signed on 5 May 1989 by 10 countries, four of which were EC member-states, i.e. Spain, Luxemburg, the Netherlands and the United Kingdom.[7] Therefore, it was now difficult for states which like France defend the quota system, to take a firm stand and endanger the first attempt by the Community to provide regulations in the audio-visual field.

Finally, the only concession granted by the Liberal camp was the clause known as 'No retreat'. This stipulates that under no circumstances the proportion of European works broadcast within every member-state should be less than the average number of such programmes during 1988.

Effects of common audio-visual policy on France

Given the slight retreat that has taken place today, the effects of the common audio-visual policy on France from industrial, cultural and strategic viewpoints should now be considered.

Industrial effects

The industrial stakes of high definition television consist of replacing a total of approximately 750 to 800 million televisions throughout the world with small cinema-type units with high picture and sound quality. Existing video recorders will either be replaced or available for a first purchase; all picture, sound production and broadcasting equipment such as cameras, studios, transmitters and parabolic aerials will be renewed.

This explains the total of FRF 250 billion suggested by Mr Roger Fauroux in estimating the world market for audio-visual equipment up to 2005. Furthermore, European television manufacturers are currently supplying 80 per cent of equipment within the Community and 30 per cent of such equipment throughout the world. It is natural that they wish to preserve these market parts and improve them where possible.

In response to this challenge, France is one of the Community's trump cards in its struggle with the Japanese. With the Thomson group, French industry is in the forefront of the European arena. Thomson in co-operation with the Dutch group Philips, launched the European standard D2-Mac/Paquet and this tandem is now spearheading 'General Public' European electronics. For example, whilst current televisions contain approximately 30 per cent of electronic components, D2-Mac/Paquet televisions will contain 70 per cent and HDTV 90 per cent.

On the other front of European and Japanese rivalry, namely that of flat screens, France has three out of the four European champions in the race. These are the Thomson group, the organization Planécran, created by the Sagem company and the Centre National d'Etudes en Télécommunications (CNET), the Laboratoire d'Électronique, Technologique et d'Instrumentation (LETI, belonging to the CEA group). Here again, the stakes are high as apart from high definition television, the flat screen market also embraces the computer equipment sector.

Cultural effects

As European producers only produce a small number of fiction programmes for television, expectations are also promising with a market of approximately 250 billion francs up to the year 2000. French audio-visual professionals will be able, provided they use the means offered by MEDIA 92 correctly, to find openings in the Great European Market of 1992. This is especially true since French production in this field is backed by the two direct televisions satellites TDF1 and TDF2, an international French-language system 'TV 5 Europe' set up in co-operation with Belgium, Canada and Switzerland plus a televised channel structure with a markedly European stance known as 'The Sept'. In October 1990, reunified Germany became associated with this channel and ARTE was subsequently founded in Spring 1992.

However, will French authors, producers and broadcasters be able to seize the opportunity presented to them? Will the French language claim its right to exist in an audio–visual sector that is increasingly submerged by the English language?

It is legitimate to review this situation and fear for the worst. It is common knowledge that TF1 has been broadcasting a daily series known as 'Riviera' since the first half of 1991. This soap opera, similar to Santa Barbara is managed by a subsidiary of the American group 'Interpublic'. Although the first 260 episodes of this series were produced by the SFP with a majority of French actors, in compliance with the provisions of the Conseil Supérieur de l'Audiovisuel (CSA), and obtained the status of a French Language production, English was the working language! To justify this choice, management of the French Channel 1 explained that it was a Pan-European production in which English, Spanish and Italian actors took part. To back their arguments, it was demonstrated that this policy enabled all episodes to be subsequently sold to German, British, Spanish and Italian channels. This was a doubtful argument as apart from Britain, the episodes will be dubbed in all respective languages including French.[8]

Strategic effects

The strategic effects on France of the common audio-visual policy and, in particular, that of the high-definition television option will be dependent on industrial and cultural considerations.

In industry, a strong 'General Public' electronics sector will provide support for the 'Industrial' electronics sector and others such as the Aeronautics, Arms, Space, Computers and Nuclear Industries. In parallel, technology and know-how used for flat screens in high-definition television should logically have some spin-off on everything concerned with industrial display systems, such as radar, simulators and test screens etc.

Investments made by France in defence of European HDTV are counter-balanced by French efforts for maintaining economic and military independence.

The French language is currently third in the league-table of languages spoken in the world, behind English and Spanish. This contributes considerably to French influence abroad and France's vocation as a 'great power'. Such a policy could also be attractive to non-aligned countries. Television seems to be an effective means of maintaining or re-reinforcing the presence of the French language within Europe and elsewhere, provided audio-visual professionals agree to comply with certain criteria.

Conclusion: why is France investing in the European audio-visual field?

Since the beginning of the 1980s, several events led the 12 EC member-states to become conscious of the fact that their destinies with respect to the audio-visual field were linked.

The on-rush of deregulation that took place in all Western European countries resulted in the emergence of private television channels. Use of satellites signifies that national broadcasts overlap into other countries. Finally, the Japanese are now ready to take world control of innovative audio-visual technology.

Conceived as a defence against the Japanese in 1986, the European audio-visual policy is now a reality that revolves around the three central themes of technology, culture and legislation.

France was initially as reticent as its partners in letting the EC intrude into the audio-visual field. This was especially true since such action was not governed by the Treaty of Rome. However, France subsequently played a positive role in specifying action the Brussels Commission was competent to take or drawing up the Common European audio-visual policy.

Examples of such action abound and illustrate the authentic undertakings made by France in consolidating European policy. Therefore, from their design stage, the TDF1 and TDF2 satellites comply with the European standard D2-Mac/Paquet. Similarly, to gain German support for this standard, the French government accepted that the governmental channel 'Antenne 2' broadcast German programmes via the TDF1 and TDF2 satellites. Furthermore, the state-owned Thomson group is in the forefront of European TVHD industry with respect to both the electronic component and flat screen technologies. In 1989, the French Government also became less firm in its policy in favour of minimum quotas for broadcasting European programmes. This policy was softened to permit adoption and ratification of the Community directive 'Television without Borders'. Finally, International HD was purely and simply terminated in 1990 and replaced by its European equivalent Vision 1250.

In return, it is true that the French are relying on counter measures from their European partners. Industrial and Cultural spin-off should be equivalent to concessions made by the French. Nine million francs were assigned by the French Government to Thomson for providing it with the means of meeting the goals set for the second phase of the Eureka 95 programme.

European governments are now ready to embark upon an initial review of action taken, especially the measures taken by Germany. The Germans have, in fact, finally adhered to the D2-Mac/Paquet standard and are the first state to have joined ARTE, the initial European culture-oriented channel.

Overall, the French Government has great expectations for openings created by Thomson know-how in the field of audio-visual equipment. Such spin-off should have favourable effects on other high-tech sectors such as the computer industry. Thus, France is hoping that HDTV will be an efficient medium for French cultural influence throughout the world. This could be possible, provided producers and management responsible for French broadcasts do not merely accept the easy 'English-Language' solution for simple budgetary considerations.

The most spectacular action taken by France in favour of 'Audiovisual Europe' was the decision by Mr Paul Quilès, at that time the French Minister of Post, Communications and Space, to drop the French national satellite programme for direct television satellites in favour of the Europesat European Programme. This programme is led by the organization Eutelsat.

Certainly, this decision was not taken for purely altruistic reasons. Successive breakdowns that occurred in the TDF1 and TDF2 satellites plus aggravating disputes between the two French satellite channels Euromusic and the 'Sept' clearly demonstrated the limits of a simply national programme. There is a risk that the European satellite programme for television broadcasts will require less public expenditure.

Nevertheless, the resolutely European stance of France clearly demonstrates that it will never drop its wish to create a common audio-visual policy.

In such conditions, it is easy to understand the disappointment of the French authorities when the European Commission decided, on 19 February 1993, to stop all development on D2-Mac/Paquet standard and to join with the American standard. This decision results from British obstruction, German hesitations and pressure of broadcasting companies, among which the French TV chain *Canal Plus* has taken a leading position.

A part of the European 20 year-long audio-visual adventure finishes then. It is too early to evaluate the consequences of the EC decision on the French audio-visual field, but we can already consider that, by withdrawing its audio-visual technology, the European Community has just missed an opportunity in the quest for its cultural identity.

Notes

1. Its solar panels were not deployed and TV-Sat 1 was never able to operate. As for TDF1 and TDF2, their usefulness was limited by failures of electronic tubes.
2. MUSE is the acronym for Multiple Subnyquist Sampling Encoding.
3. Figures given in a declaration made at the Summer University at Carcans-Maubisson (France) in August 1990 on 'New World Screens'.
4. D2 identifies the type of process selected for transmitting sound and pictures. Mac is the abbreviation for 'Multiplex analogiques par composants'. Paquet indicates the transmission mode of signals (definitions provided by France-Télécom in *Fréquences*, no. 24 dated June 1989).
5. 1250 relates to the number of lines in a high definition television picture which contains twice the number of current PAL or SECAM pictures.
6. Launched in October 1989 and initiated by France, Eureka audio-visual is the television programme section of Eureka 95. Based on the same logistical and financial principles as that of the Community programme MEDIA 92, Eureka audio-visual is open to all European countries including the CIS (ex-USSR) and ex-Eastern Bloc countries.
7. France only signed this convention in February 1991.
8. 'American-style soap opera', see *Le Monde*, 10 January 1991.

References

I — Books

Bahu-Leyser, D., Chavenon, H. and Durand, J. (1990) *Audiences des Médias — Guide France-Europe* (Media Audiences — France-Europe Guide), Eyrolles, Paris.

Decaux, A. (1989) *La politique télévisuelle extérieure de la France* (French Foreign Television Policy), La Documentation Française, Paris.

Lange, A. and Renaud, J.L. (1989) *The future of the European audio-visual industry*, The European Institute for the Medias, Manchester.

II — Files and Reports

Conseil supérieur de l'audiovisuel (CSA) (1990) *Rapport annuel, 30 Janvier - 31 Decembre, 1989* (Annual Report 1989), Imprimerie Nationale, Paris.

Eurostaf Dafsa (1987) *L'audiovisuel en Europe - Enjeux, acteurs et stratégies* (Audiovisual Industry in Europe — Stakes, players and strategies), Paris.

Young and Rubican-France, Nov, (1989) *Convergences et Divergences culturelles en Europe Occidentale* (Cultural Convergences and Divergences in Western Europe), report of the Young and Rubican Colloquium — TF1, Paris.

III — Articles

Gérard, L. (1990) TVHD — S'unir ou périr (HDTV Unite or Perish), *Industries et Techniques*, 6 April.

Humblot, C. (1988) La Difficile avancée du feuilleton européen (Difficult progress of the European Series), *Le Monde Radio-TV*, 12—13 June.

Lemaitre, P. (1992) L'obstruction britannique retarde l'adoption d'un plan communautaire sur la TVHD (British obstruction delays the passage to a common plan on the HDTV), *Le Monde*, 21 November.

Morgan de Rivery, E. and Morgan de Rivery-Guillaud, A.H. (1989) Satellites allowing for direct reception by the user: technological progress calls for changes in the applicable law and for a European plan of action, *Droit de l'informatique et des Télécoms*, no. 89/3.

Mousseau, J. (1989) Une télévision européenne est-elle possible? (Is a European television possible?) *Communication et Language*, no. 79; La politique audiovisuelle de la Communauté Européenne (The audiovisual policy of the European Community), *Communication et Language*, no. 81.

Samuel, P. (1990) Haute Définition: un engagement irréversible (High Definition: an irreversible undertaking) *Pourquoi?* no. 256, August and September.

Wingalon, J.L. (1988) Horizon 1992: La Sept en Orbite (The Seventh channel in orbit), *Le Monde Radio-TV*, April 24—25.

Index

Note: Page numbers in **bold** type refer to **figures** and page numbers in *italic* type refer to *tables*.